S0-AHC-100

The American
Foreign Legion

An Association of the U.S. Army Book

The American Foreign Legion

Black Soldiers of the 93d in World War I

Frank E. Roberts

Naval Institute Press
Annapolis, Maryland

Naval Institute Press
291 Wood Road
Annapolis, MD 21402

© 2004 by Frank E. Roberts
All rights reserved. No part of this book may be
reproduced or utilized in any form or by any means,
electronic or mechanical, including photocopying and
recording, or by any information storage and retrieval
system, without permission in writing from the publisher.

Library of Congress Cataloging-in-Publication Data
Roberts, Frank E., 1933–
The American Foreign Legion : Black soldiers of the 93d
in World War I / Frank E. Roberts.
p. cm.
Includes bibliographical references and index.
ISBN 1-59114-734-4 (alk. paper)
1. United States. Army. Division, 93rd—History.
2. United States. Army—African American troops.
3. World War, 1914–1918—Participation, African
American. 4. World War, 1914–1918—Regimental
histories—United States. 5. World War, 1914–1918—
Campaigns—France. I. Title.
D570.393rd .R63 2004
940.4'1244'08996073—dc22
2003027264

Printed in the United States of America
on acid-free paper ♾
11 10 09 08 07 06 05 04   9 8 7 6 5 4 3 2
First printing

Contents

Foreword

Army regulations authorize a soldier to wear the shoulder patch of the last unit with which he or she served in combat, though custom has always dictated that the soldier choose which unit patch to be worn if combat service had been in more than one unit. Because I served in three different wartime combat divisions, I chose to wear the Blue French helmet on a black circle for my retirement. As such, I was the last soldier in U.S. Army history on active duty to have worn the patch of the 93d Division.

I shared some of the original members' experience. The 93d was a black division in a white army, a unit composed of citizens who wanted to serve, but to whom society had failed to grant either the legal equality or the basic human acceptance that it did its European heritage citizens.

In World War I, the division was broken into separate regiments and attached to the French Army, an army with black colonial troops. There, it found a way to excel, and to prove the bravery and the dedication of its men against a common enemy. The French recognized one of its regiments with the first unit award of the Croix de Guerre to an American unit. From the ranks of its four regiments, which were forced to fight separately while attached to French units, more than 3,500 men fell in battle, and 591 of them sleep in fields in France with their white comrades, the only equality that the U.S. Army then granted them.

By war's end, no one doubted their heroism. The Blue Helmet soldiers earned forty-two Distinguished Service Crosses, and the French awarded four of their Medaille Militaire, their highest award, and 325 individual awards of the Croix de Guerre for battlefield heroism to soldiers wearing the Blue Helmet patch. The famous 369th Infantry, which had earned the first unit citation from the French, also fought in the line for 191 days of combat, longer than any other American regiment.

In April 1991 President George Bush posthumously awarded the Medal of Honor to Cpl. Freddie Stowers, of C Company, 371st Infantry Regiment, 93d Division for heroism in 1918, a soldier who had died advancing while leading his men after he had been wounded several times. Stowers embodied the spirit of the 93d, and America finally remembered one of its loyal sons.

In World War II, the division again found itself unwanted, and was split up and confined to rear area work details and "mopping up" of bypassed Japanese in the northern Solomon Islands and the Bismarck Archipelago in the southwest Pacific theater. Ninety-third men raided Japanese strongholds, and many fought in gallant but unheralded small unit actions. While our casualties were many times fewer than suffered in World War I, the 93d's men added one Distinguished Service Cross, five Silver Stars, and nearly seven hundred Bronze Star medals to the division's battle honors. We were true to the example of duty set by those who had gone before. We had kept the soldier's faith.

Black soldiers have served honorably and heroically in every war since colonial days. They did not fight to win equality, they fought because they were Americans. There is no greater brotherhood or sisterhood than that of the battlefield. The soldier who advances under fire and yells "cover my move" relies on a trust greater than anyone can explain. No longer is that trust reliant on a race or gender test, only the willingness to serve. The 93d helped prove that patriotism, heroism, and brotherhood have no color, creed, or litmus test beyond what is in the human heart. I am proud to be an American soldier, and I was proud to be the last man to wear the 93d's patch for all those who had gone before me.

Lt. Gen. Julius W. Becton Jr. (USA, Ret.)

Former 2d Lieutenant, 369th Infantry Regiment, 93d Division, 1945

Acknowledgments

M y heartfelt thanks and gratitude go to the following people for their generous assistance, guidance, and contributions in the writing of this book:

Zenobio and Genevieve Acosta of Brussels, Belgium, for photographing and providing valuable information about the monument of the 371st Infantry Regiment at Bussy Fermé, near Ardéuil-Montfauxelles, France, and the monument of the 372d Infantry Regiment near Monthois, France.

Maurice Noizet, mayor of Ardéuil-Montfauxelles, France, for photographs of the monument of the 371st Infantry Regiment at Bussy Fermé and information on military operations near Ardéuil-Montfauxelles.

Ghislaine Bovee, Rockwall, Texas, for her assistance in interpreting French text, writing letters, and speaking with various persons and officials in France to gather information for the book.

Kathy Melston, director of the Rockwall County Library, and her entire staff for all of their work in locating and obtaining the hard-to-find books, documents, and reference materials used in this book.

Lt. Col. Roger Cirillo, Director of Operational and Strategic Studies, Association of the U.S. Army, for his efforts in bringing this book to publication.

Lt. Col. Julian M. Olejniczak, vice president for publications and editor in chief of *Assembly* magazine, Association of Graduates, U.S. Military Academy, for materials and for encouragement in writing this book.

Col. William H. Kern, U.S. Army Reserve, for materials on the 371st Infantry Regiment and ideas and encouragement in writing this book.

John T. Greenwood, chief of the Office of Medical History, U.S. Army Medical Command, for providing valuable suggestions in the writing of this book.

Melinda Conner, my copy editor, for her excellent work in editing the manuscript and bringing the book to its final form.

Thanks to the following for their individual contributions: Maj. James B. McCabe, Illinois National Guard; Capt. Randol L. Rogers, Ohio National Guard; and all of the historians of the various regiments, battalions, and companies of the surviving National Guard units of the 93d Division.

Most helpful in locating hard-to-find materials were staff members of the National Archives; the U.S. Army Command and General Staff College; the U.S. Army Military History Center at Carlisle Barracks, Pennsylvania; the curator of the 372d Infantry Museum; and the Dallas Public Library, Dallas, Texas.

And finally, special thanks to my wife, Jane, for her constant encouragement, enduring patience, and valuable assistance in bringing this project to completion.

The American
Foreign Legion

INTRODUCTION

A Foreign Legion Is Born

Just over one kilometer south of the township of Ardéuil-Montfauxelles in the Champagne region of France, a monument in the shape of a short obelisk rests on the gentle slope of a low hill called Bellevue Signal Ridge. The monument, of rough-hewn white granite, is about two meters square at the base and was just over three meters high before a German artillery shell blew away part of the upper pyramid in June 1940. Engraved on each of the four sides of the obelisk are the names of officers and men of the 371st Infantry Regiment of the French 157th Division killed in action nearby during a major Allied offensive lasting from 28 September to 6 October 1918. Anyone curious enough to make the long hike up a narrow path leading across an open field to the isolated monument would find that those names engraved in the hard stone are not French, but rather American, and they all belong to a single U.S. Army regiment.[1]

How did these men come to be serving under the command of a foreign army? When the United States entered the war in Europe in 1917, Secretary of War Newton D. Baker issued specific instructions to Gen. John Pershing, commander of the Allied Expeditionary Forces (AEF), that all American units would serve under the direct command of AEF headquarters. The existence of that isolated monument would seem to suggest that Pershing had contradicted the secretary's policy. In fact, Pershing used an obscure clause in the formal policy statement to dispose of four regiments of American infantry troops that neither he nor his corps or division commanders wanted. Pershing decided that the 371st Infantry and its sister regiments—the 369th, 370th, and 372d—which made up the 93d Division and were composed of black enlisted men and black and white officers, were undesirable and not essential to the AEF and quietly ceded them to the French Army.[2]

Pershing was not the first general to dispose of an unwanted military formation. Ironically, one of the more flagrant episodes was instigated by the French government in 1835 when some four thousand French Army officers and men, all political outcasts by virtue of having opposed the regime in power, were ceded to Spain to fight in a civil war and were then forgotten.

After four years of hard and courageous campaigning with poor equipment and arms, little logistical support, and no pay, the few hundred survivors were summarily dismissed by the victorious Spanish government. These officers and men then marched across the interior of Spain, begging food on the way, and reported to a French border garrison post where they applied to be of further service to their government. As a reward for their unusual loyalty, the officers were reduced, some to the ranks, and lost all seniority. Many, including a future field marshal, Lt. Achille Baziane, were shipped to Africa to fight another war and once again were forgotten.[3]

That was the story of the first French foreign legion. This is the story of four American infantry regiments—three National Guard and one conscript—that made up the 93d Division, and of their officers and men, who shipped out to France with high hopes and ideals, incomplete training, and insufficient equipment and were cast out to serve with a foreign army.[4] Their French commanders came to respect them for their fighting spirit and heaped praise and decorations on them for their courage and steadiness under fire; the French people came to admire them and called them "partridges" and *magnifique* for their cockiness and élan; the Germans came to fear them and called them "black devils" and "blood-thirsty black men" for their ferocity and fighting skill.[5] This is the story of the extraordinary accomplishments of the 369th, 370th, 371st, and 372d Infantry Regiments of the 93d Division, U.S. Army—the Légion Étrangere Americaine—and the courage and heroism of the officers and men of that division, both black and white.[6]

CHAPTER I

The 93d Division's First Regiment

These colored soldiers belonging to these combat units [93d Division] demonstrated that, if properly trained, equipped, and led, they will equal the best soldiers in any army in the world for bravery and fighting qualities.

> Hon. Hamilton Fish, U.S. Congress,
> former captain of the 369th Infantry

The story begins with the initial formation of the 369th, 370th, 371st, and 372d Infantry Regiments, the nucleus of the 93d Division while it existed in World War I. Each regiment's history will be told in turn: its experiences while serving in the French Army in World War I, its return to U.S. Army control, and finally its return home to the United States and subsequent disposition.

The 369th Infantry, the first of the numbered regiments of the 93d Division, was originally the 15th New York Infantry Regiment, National Guard. Organized in 1916, it was the newest of the three National Guard regiments of the 93d Division. It was also the first to move to France and the first exposed to action, and it served the longest in the front lines.

The 15th New York Infantry Regiment Is Born

The Honorable Charles S. Whitman, elected governor of the state of New York in 1916, was a longtime admirer of the four black regiments of the Regular Army and had followed in detail their activities during the Mexican Punitive Expedition of 1916. As war clouds gathered in Europe, he realized that the United States could soon become involved in the conflict and that the bulk of the organized forces available to fight such a war would have to come from the National Guard units of the various states.[1]

Whitman, an able attorney, was aware of an obscure New York State law that authorized the formation and training of black National Guard units.

Shortly after taking office, he proposed to William Hayward, a close friend and one of his political appointees, that he form and command a regiment of infantry composed of black men in the enlisted ranks and for the most part in the officer billets as well.[2] Hayward accepted the challenge. On 2 June 1916 Governor Whitman signed into law a bill authorizing the 15th New York Infantry Regiment, National Guard. On 16 June 1916 Whitman ordered the regiment to be formed with Hayward as its colonel and first member. As Hayward would later suggest, that proved to be the easy part.[3]

Hayward was a lawyer by training and trade, and an assertive, hard-driving overachiever of high moral courage by nature. He had proved competent enough in his law career to become a judge at a very young age in his native state of Nebraska. As the son of U.S. Senator Monroe L. Hayward he had developed a solid understanding of the workings of politics at the local, state, and federal levels. He also proved to have a well-founded belief in the Roman concept of the citizen-soldier when at a young age he joined the 2d Nebraska Volunteer Infantry Regiment and served as a captain in the Spanish-American War. On his return from active service, Hayward joined the Nebraska National Guard; he became a colonel in his late thirties, commanding the 2d Nebraska Regiment of Infantry. In 1910 Hayward moved his private law practice to New York City, and in 1913 he accepted a position in the public sector as assistant to then District Attorney Charles S. Whitman; the two men became close associates. In 1914 Hayward managed Whitman's successful campaign for election to the office of governor of the state of New York and in 1916 served in the same role to ensure Whitman's reelection. Shortly after Whitman was sworn in as governor for his first term, Hayward was rewarded for his services by being appointed public service commissioner for New York City.[4]

As his first official act as commanding officer of the 15th New York Infantry, Hayward called on the mayor of New York City, the Honorable John Purroy Mitchel, and requested assistance in finding appropriate buildings in suitable locations to serve as armories. With Mitchel's backing and the quick and able assistance of Lawrence V. Meehan, superintendent of the Armory Board, the first two of several buildings around New York City were leased to house the regiment.[5]

The 15th New York Infantry's first armory building was a rundown dance hall in one section of an ancient structure on the corner of 132d Street and 7th Avenue in the Harlem section of New York City. The dance hall had a large open room and an adjoining smaller room, which were designated to serve as the main armory assembly hall; a basement, included in the lease, provided sufficient security for a supply room. On the adjoining corner on 131st Street, in the same structure, what had been a cigar store would serve as the regiment's headquarters and administrative offices.[6]

With the first facilities in place, Hayward began a recruiting campaign to man his newly commissioned regiment. Recruiting posters were printed and taped up in the windows of the dance hall and cigar store, and quick results came in the enlistment of Private Bunting as the second member of the regiment. That modest addition got the recruiting drive under way, and by October 1916, with the able assistance of five of Hayward's very first officers—Capts. Napoleon B. Marshall and Charles W. Fillmore, and Lts. Demus L. Reid, George C. Lacey, and James R. Europe—the regiment found itself numbering more than one thousand officers and men.[7]

Of those first officers, all black men, Captain Marshall was typical of the type Hayward sought for the 15th New York Infantry. After graduating from Harvard Law School, Marshall, who had made a name for himself at Harvard as an athlete, set up a law practice in Harlem. When a German submarine torpedoed the British liner *Lusitania* on 7 May 1915, with losses including 128 Americans, Marshall immediately wrote a letter to President Woodrow Wilson offering his services in recruiting a volunteer all-black regiment of infantry for U.S. Army service.[8]

As a newly appointed officer of the 15th New York Infantry, Marshall's assignment according to the regiment's Table of Organization and Equipment was commanding a machine-gun company, with special duty as acting regimental provost marshal. During his first few weeks in the regiment, however, Marshall was pressed into temporary duty as a recruiting officer. He spent many hours standing on street corners in Harlem soliciting candidates to bring the regiment and his machine-gun company to full strength.[9]

With the recruiting drive progressing well in the hands of capable officers, Hayward turned to the next challenge, finding the uniforms, rifles, equipment, and supplies necessary to furnish and support an infantry regiment. No requisitioned equipment of any kind had yet been received from the New York National Guard, and it became apparent to Hayward that supplying a black unit was not a high priority for the officer in charge of the quartermaster depot. Hayward once again relied on his knowledge of how to work the political system. Through the good offices of his main supporter, Governor Whitman, and with official pressure applied by Gen. Louis Stotebury, the adjutant general of the New York National Guard, the regiment soon began to receive shipments of critically needed equipment and materials.[10]

The most difficult items to find—and the most necessary for training an infantry regiment—were Springfield rifles, the standard issue weapon of the U.S. infantry soldier. Hayward's repeated requests to the U.S. Army Ordnance Department had gone unheeded, so he began to search for other means of solving the problem. Clandestine inquiries to certain allies within the U.S. Army Quartermaster Department informed Hayward that between five hundred and one thousand new Springfield rifles were being held in ordnance depot storage for issue by the federal government to civilian shooting clubs under the Civilian Marksmanship Program.[11] Hayward swung into immediate and somewhat imaginative action. As he later recounted:

> I started the darndest set of rifle or civilian shooting clubs you ever heard of. . . . [T]he presidents and secretaries of all these different shooting clubs all lived in the same place, namely the office of the Public Service Commission in the municipal building in New York. . . . [N]obody did discover it until we had all the rifles that were available for shooting clubs.[12]

Lieutenant Europe, one of the first officers to enlist, was in civilian life a highly skilled and talented musician, bandleader, and composer who was very popular in the New York City area. When Hayward discovered Europe's impressive background in music, he recognized the opportunity for a little showmanship that might gain public recognition for his unit within Harlem's black community. A military marching band would surely enhance the regiment's recruiting efforts as well as provide an easily attainable morale booster for the regiment's personnel.[13]

Hayward called Europe to his office and asked him to take over leadership of the regimental band in addition to his job as a platoon leader in the machine-gun company. Hayward told Europe that if he took the assignment he would be expected to assemble a first-class group of musicians and promised him any reasonable help needed to accomplish the job. Europe accepted the offer and went to work recruiting musicians in Harlem and around the New York City area to man a regulation army band of twenty-eight members.[14]

When Europe had recruited enough musicians, he invited Hayward to hear their first efforts. Hayward's opinion of the band's initial performance was positive, if not overly complimentary:

> In the beginning the band was pretty bad, but it made a noise, and at the time we had twenty-eight bandsmen it made twenty-eight noises all at the same time, mostly not in tune or in rhythm, but the band, such as it was, plus the uniforms, such as they were, plus the rifles, without bayonets, of course, because civilian rifle clubs had no use for bayonets, all contributed to our parades through Harlem, and the parades all contributed to recruitment.[15]

Lieutenant Europe was not satisfied with the band either. He reminded Hayward of his initial instructions to assemble a first-class band and suggested that a satisfactory marching band required at least forty-four musicians, and that sixty would be ideal. Europe also explained that he had contacted several well-known and highly talented local musicians who had expressed a willingness to enlist in the regiment as riflemen and play in the band as extra duty. The problem was that most were married and had children to support, and abandoning their well-paid jobs for an army private's pay would create severe financial hardship for their families.[16]

Hayward again dipped into his political well. He went to visit Daniel C. King, a friend of his known as "Tin Can" King due to his successful can manufacturing business, to persuade King to write letters of introduction to twenty or thirty wealthy friends. Once the letters had reached these individuals, Hayward planned to ask them for contributions to expand the 15th New York Infantry's regimental band.[17] King asked how much money Hayward expected to get from his wealthy friends. Hayward replied that he hoped to get as much as ten thousand dollars. King thought for a moment and then replied that it was too much trouble to write thirty letters; he reached into his desk drawer, pulled out his checkbook, and wrote a surprised Hayward a check for the full amount.[18]

With King's generous contribution, Europe was able to recruit bandsmen from as far away as Puerto Rico; he even got Frank de Broit, considered the greatest cornet player of the time and something of a prima donna, to join up. Hayward's fund raising and Europe's recruiting soon gave the men in the regiment a source of great pride. The band would later reap great rewards for the regiment and the entire U.S. Army in the field of public relations when it was sent on special tours and command performances in France.[19]

Another little-known contributor to the welfare of the regiment came through the good offices of Capt. Arthur Little, who had come to the unit from the supernumerary list of National Guard captains and had been placed in command of a company.[20] Because the 15th New York Infantry was so recently formed, it had not yet built up an adequate nonappropriated unit fund. These funds, acquired from sources other than government revenues, were used to buy such morale-building luxuries as magazine subscriptions, books, phonographs and records, and sports equipment for the entertainment and recreation of the men.[21] Little spoke with a friend who was known to have some influence with the multimillionaire John D. Rockefeller Jr., explaining the need for contributions to the regimental nonappropriated fund. Soon thereafter a check in the amount of five hundred dollars signed by John D. Rockefeller Jr. arrived at the armory to the attention of Little, accompanied by a note stipulating that the donation be kept confidential. A few weeks later, Little reported to Rockefeller that his contribution had scored positive results on the morale of the regiment. Another check in the same amount arrived shortly afterward from Mr. Rockefeller, again with a note requesting confidentiality.[22]

By February 1917 the regiment had more than twelve hundred enlisted men but was still critically short of officers. That same month the U.S. Army notified Governor Whitman and the adjutant general's office that in order to be recognized for federal service, the regiment would need to have fifty-one regimental officers on orders of assignment. All of the qualified officers on the New York National Guard supernumerary list had already been absorbed into other established and recognized National Guard units preparing for mobilization, leaving Hayward up the proverbial creek with no official source of officers to draw on to satisfy the federal recognition requirement. Hayward was not above proselytizing to get his regiment a complete complement of officers. He went to work to persuade several friends who were assigned to other National Guard regiments and battalions in the New York City area to request transfer to the 15th New York Infantry. Eventually the colonel's powers of persuasion got him his fifty-one officers.[23]

On 8 April 1917, two days after Congress declared war on Germany, regular officers of the U.S. Army arrived to inspect the regiment for its readiness to be federalized. Two weeks later the War Department announced that the 15th New York Infantry, National Guard, was a viable unit and could be mobilized for federal service. The regiment was ordered to come to its war strength of two thousand officers and men; Hayward, having anticipated the directive, had the regiment up to strength five days later.[24]

As soon as the regiment was on notice to be federalized, equipment and materials began to flow into company supply rooms. Even with the increased rate of supply shipments, most of the men were still either without uniforms or only partially outfitted. Nevertheless, the regiment departed early on Sunday morning, 13 May 1917, for the New York State Military Reservation near Peekskill for eighteen days of intensive drill and rifle practice.[25]

The various battalions and detachments of the regiment were to travel first by foot to the elevated railroad, then to Grand Central Station, and finally by the New York Central Railroad to the New York State Military Reservation. There had been no space or time to hold battalion- or regiment-sized formations, much less to drill, so the march from the armories in the Bronx and Harlem to the trains turned out to be little better than organized chaos. As the officers and sergeants of the regiment struggled to get their units into some semblance of military march order, proud family members, friends, and well-wishers lined the route, cheering on the tyro soldiers of the newest regiment in the New York National Guard.[26]

The demographics of the 15th New York Infantry as it departed for its first real training stint left no doubt that it was a product of New York City. The four companies of the 1st Battalion came from Manhattan, the four companies of the 2d Battalion came from Brooklyn, and the 3d Battalion's companies had men from both Manhattan and the Bronx.[27]

After two weeks of intensive drill and training at the New York State Military Reservation, the 15th New York Infantry broke camp early on Memorial

Day, 30 May 1917. The officers and men retraced their steps to New York City, arriving in time to participate in a military parade of New York National Guard units scheduled to proceed up Riverside Drive at 9:00 AM that same morning. The eighteen days of concentrated soldiering had hardened the regiment, given it organization, and instilled in its men the snap of experienced soldiers. Every member was dressed in regulation uniform with blanket roll slung from left shoulder to right hip and rifle precisely aligned at right shoulder arms. Compared with the other New York National Guard regiments marching with many untrained recruits in civilian clothing, the 15th New York Infantry appeared to be well on its way to becoming a professional military organization.[28] Captain Little later said of the affair: "It was our Decoration Day parade of 1917 and the generous reception given us by the citizens of New York on that day that enabled our men to visualize in some degree the greater parade to come."[29]

But two weeks of training and a parade were one thing; total preparation for war was something else. On Sunday morning, 15 July, Hayward received orders that the regiment was to be assembled that very day to begin the process of being mustered into the U.S. Army.[30] The swearing-in ceremonies and paperwork necessary for transfer into federal service were completed that same day, and the next morning the regiment moved to Camp Whitman near Poughkeepsie, New York. In this new post, built and operated by the Regular Army, the officers and men of the regiment would continue in earnest the military training begun at Peekskill.[31]

The unit's training, conducted by Regular Army personnel, concentrated on field combat tactics and platoon and company maneuvers. Formal schooling focused on Moss's *Privates' Manual* for the enlisted men, while the corporals and sergeants studied and practiced the *Non-commissioned Officers' Manual* and *Company Training in the Attack, and the Defense, Including the Field Orders for Enlisted Men.* In addition to their normal duties, all officers of the regiment received staff and command training. All of the training was designed to accelerate the transformation of a previously undisciplined mob of partially trained civilians into a combat-ready unit.[32]

Although the officers and men of the regiment made good progress in their training, the regiment soon received disappointing orders. After completing only thirty days at Camp Whitman, the regiment was directed to take up various construction and guard duties in and around New York City. Regimental Headquarters, Headquarters Company, and the supply company returned to the cigar store and dance hall armory building in Harlem. The 2d Battalion, under the command of Maj. Munston Morris, moved to Camp Upton, near Yaphank, Long Island. The 3d Battalion and the regimental band, under the command of Maj. Edward Dixon, went to Camp Dix, near Wrightstown, New

Jersey, to assist in construction of new camps in the area. Marshall's machine-gun company went to Ellis Island to guard German internees. The 1st Battalion, under the command of Maj. Lorillard Spencer, was divided into independent companies and detachments and sent to guard German internees, naval ammunition dumps, the navy yard at Brooklyn, various industrial plants, and tunnels and bridges along the railroad lines running out of New York City.[33] Hayward and the other officers of the regiment could not know that this move by the U.S. Army to slight their training and utilize the regiment in noncombat roles was an omen of grave proportions.[34]

To guard the railroads, the 1st Battalion was broken up into small detachments commanded by sergeants and corporals and dispersed throughout the countryside to what were considered to be danger points along the tracks. The men stationed at these remote sites soon made friends with local townspeople, who, seeing the men's primitive living conditions, responded by providing furniture and other household items for their tents along with frequent gifts of pies, cakes, and other special items to add to the comfort of the men.[35]

Incidents both fortunate and unfortunate occurred during this period of railroad guard duty. Fatalities caused by such things as sentinels being struck by passing trains or drowning during off-duty swims occurred at the rate of about one a week. Violence in the form of knife and gunshot wounds, although less frequent, added to the stress of remote guard duty. In one bizarre incident a civilian was shot and killed when he fired a pistol at a sentinel after being challenged. On a positive note, a German agent who had successfully eluded the Secret Service was captured and turned in by an alert guard post.[36]

For the service provided by the regiment from 15 August to 8 October, Hayward received the compliments of the Assistant Chief of Staff, Headquarters, Eastern Department, U.S. Army. During that period the officers and men of the 15th New York Infantry had performed their duties in an outstanding manner and had the unusual record of having suffered no loss or destruction of any property under their care. Moreover, no formal complaints of any kind had been filed concerning any type of disorder occurring between the members of the unit and the civilian populace.[37]

During this period Hayward learned that the 27th Infantry Division, made up primarily of New York National Guard units, was to make its farewell parade down Fifth Avenue in New York City before departing for Spartanburg, South Carolina, to train for overseas duty. Hayward, who had received no orders to join the division—as those in authority had previously implied would be the case—or to march in its parade, sent a request that the 15th New York Infantry be allowed to march with the division. He was turned down with the barely plausible excuse that the regiment could not be released from its detached duty.[38]

Hayward then learned that at a later date the 69th New York Infantry was to parade down Fifth Avenue as it was leaving to become a part of the 42d (Rainbow) Division, a composite of units from twenty-six states and the District of Columbia. When he requested that the regiment be allowed to march with the 69th New York Infantry Regiment and also be assigned as a regiment of the 42d Division, he was again rebuffed. Little later recalled that Hayward was told: "Black is not one of the colors of the rainbow."[39]

Hayward felt extreme personal disappointment and bitterness when his regiment was excluded from these parades. He must also have begun to feel some concern that the men he had recruited with the promise of service to their country as combat soldiers might become permanent guards and construction workers, either at home in the United States or in Europe.[40] In his usual manner, Hayward leaped into action. First, he made a solemn promise to his officers that the regiment would go to France as combat soldiers. Second, he assured them that they *would* have a parade down Fifth Avenue—if not now, then when they returned from France. Furthermore, he said, the 15th New York Infantry would be the only regiment in that parade. One can only wonder if he knew how prophetic both his suspicions and his promise to his officers would prove to be.[41]

Hayward then turned his attention to getting the regiment off construction and guard duty and back into combat training. He started another campaign of constructive agitation of the army's upper command structure, something at which he was becoming quite adept. "From that time on," Little recalled,

> the Colonel never rested in his efforts to get the regiment started along the route for war training and France. He attacked the railroads for not guarding their own tunnels and bridges. He ridiculed the Navy for not being able to guard its own munitions at Iona Island, and its own ships at Erie Basin. He agitated a protest against the great National Army cantonments, Upton and Dix, being filled with newly drafted soldiers under brand new officers of the three months' Plattsburg training, depending upon our men for the maintenance of order and safety in their camps while the soldiers of junior service were being pushed ahead of our men in the preparation for coveted service overseas.[42]

Once again, Hayward's persistence paid off. Orders arrived at regimental headquarters during the first week in October for the regiment to prepare for movement to Camp Wadsworth, near Spartanburg, South Carolina.[43] In one of several ironic twists of fate, the 15th New York Infantry would continue its combat training at Camp Wadsworth with the same 27th Division that had excluded it from the New York City parade.[44]

CHAPTER 2

The 15th's Trials
at Spartanburg

They were soldiers who wore their uniforms with a smartened pride:
who were jaunty and alert and prompt in their movements; and who
expressed as some did vocally in my hearing and all did by their attitude,
a sincere heartfelt inclination to get a whack at the foe with the shortest
possible delay.

> Reporter Irvin S. Cobb, on the 369th
> and 371st Infantry Regiments

The army's decision to send the 15th New York Infantry to train in a southern state in a camp near a fair-sized city would cause severe problems
for Colonel Hayward and his men. On 31 August 1917 the *New York Times*
published an ominous article about the city of Spartanburg's response to the
posting.

> Following the receipt of a report that the Government intended to alter
> its original plan and include the Fifteenth Infantry, colored, in the troops
> to be trained at the camp here, the City of Spartanburg officially pro-
> tested to the War Department against the sending of these troops, on the
> ground that trouble might result if the Fifteenth refused to accept the
> limited liberties accorded to the city's colored population. Mayor J. F.
> Floyd, in his protest, called attention to the recent outbreak of negro
> troops at Houston, Texas.[1]

The article went on to quote Floyd: "With their northern ideas about race
equality, they will probably expect to be treated like white men. I can say right
here that they will not be treated as anything except negroes. We will treat
them exactly as we treat our resident negroes."[2]

"The recent outbreak at Houston" referred to a mutiny by a few members
of a company of the 3d Battalion of the 24th Infantry, a Regular Army regiment of black enlisted men and white officers stationed at Camp Logan near
Houston, Texas. The battalion had recently been sent there from Columbus,

New Mexico, after serving for many years in isolated posts in the western states. At Camp Logan they had their first real experience with the Jim Crow laws of the South.[3] On 23 August 1917, about a month after the regiment arrived at Houston, a soldier of the 3d Battalion tried to stop a Houston policeman from beating a black woman. For his efforts the soldier was pistol-whipped and arrested for drunkenness. Later that day, a member of the battalion's military police detachment sent to inquire about the arrested soldier was also pistol-whipped in the police station, and when he tried to flee was caught, pistol-whipped again, and arrested. Word spread quickly through Camp Logan that the military policeman had been killed while in custody at the Houston police station.[4]

In response to that rumor, a few men of one company of the 3d Battalion picked up their arms and went into the city to find and release the soldiers being held or to recover their bodies. A brief, uneven, and deadly firefight ensued between the trained soldiers and an ad hoc group of armed civilians backed by the Houston police. Twelve civilians, five police officers, two black soldiers, and one army officer died in the fight. The officer, Capt. J. W. Mattes, was killed while trying to bring the soldiers under control. The news of this event sent a chill through the South and fueled opposition to the stationing of any black soldiers there other than units raised in southern states. In response to the event, the War Department returned the battalion to New Mexico in late August 1917.[5]

Over the objections of the people of Spartanburg, the 15th New York Infantry—less the 1st Battalion, which continued on guard duty despite Hayward's efforts to extricate it—shipped out by several train sections and arrived at Camp Wadsworth on 10 and 11 October 1917.[6] On their arrival the men found that their cantonment area was an abandoned field surrounded by a pine forest only partially cleared of brush and small trees. As Captain Little described it: "We had a beautiful site for a winter camp—partly on a picked cotton field and partly in a pine grove."[7]

The regiment had two or three days to settle in before beginning training, so the officers laid out a temporary camp in spots where the men could erect their dog tents and build makeshift shelters. The heavy clearing and drainage work had already been done by the Regular Army, so work teams set about felling smaller trees, digging more drainage ditches, and converting the designated area into a functional army camp.[8] Tools, tents, horses, mules, and construction materials were for the most part available from the post engineers, and some of the men had brought along their own hand tools. Where critical shortages existed, the men resorted to the time-honored military method of "scrounging," a euphemism for obtaining the item needed from another unit or from the nearest supply depot through unorthodox means—in other words, stealing. One private burdened with a skewed sense of honesty, asked if he could find the tools needed to complete a project, answered in a manner that would make the crustiest sergeant wince: "Yes sir . . . I can find 'em. I got a hammer already. And it's my own. I know it's my own 'cause I stole it."[9]

Regardless of the conditions in which they found themselves, the men were glad to be officially in training, and enthusiasm ran strong in the regiment. Little described them as working like a "pack of beavers." Soon a marsh became firm ground, a well-constructed bridge crossed a stream, rail fences were erected, a road was hard-surfaced, and other structures to support camp life began to appear. In the spirit of using any material available, an old barn near the camp area was disassembled and the salvaged lumber was used to repair and reconstruct a dilapidated stable to house the regiment's horses.[10]

Camp life began to fall into a routine as the men took up a regular schedule of training that matched that of the 27th Division. The entire regiment had a lot of catching up to do. They were three to six weeks behind in their combat training due to the construction and guard duty assignments they had been given in New York. As a means of instilling pride and increasing the men's morale, formal guard mounts were promptly instituted and held every morning, and evening parades with the regimental band were scheduled two to three times a week.[11]

Colonel Hayward naturally had concerns about how the local people were going to react to the presence of the regiment, and soon after the unit's arrival at the camp he called a regimental formation. Of gravest concern to him were the impact of the newspaper article objecting to the regiment being located in Spartanburg and reports of wild rumors circulating throughout the area's white civilian population about their safety and well-being in the wake of the 24th Infantry incident in Texas.[12] Hoping to quell racially motivated incidents involving the men of his regiment, Hayward appealed to the officers and men not to invite confrontations and, if necessary, to walk away from trouble if or when provoked.[13] Before he concluded the meeting Hayward extracted a pledge from the officers and men that none of them would engage in violence of any kind under any condition, however sorely tested they might be. To their everlasting credit, the officers and men kept their word to their colonel in the face of several unsavory incidents, which in some cases involved violent acts by local individuals against the enlisted men and some officers.[14]

In one galling case, Captain Marshall, the Harvard graduate and athlete, was insulted and thrown off a trolley. In another, a soldier was thrown from a sidewalk and then attacked and knocked into the gutter for not getting out of the way of town bullies. He refused to fight back, saying to his tormentors that he had promised his colonel he would not. Two white soldiers of the neighboring 7th Infantry of the 27th Division happened to see the incident and hear the black soldier's statement. One of them announced that he had made no such promise to his colonel and, followed by his companion, plowed into the bullies.[15]

Word of the shabby treatment of the officers and men of the 15th New York Infantry by certain townspeople of Spartanburg soon spread through the entire camp. Military organizations will always "take care of their own." So, one evening, several men from the 12th Infantry and the 71st Infantry of San Juan Hill, Cuba, fame made the rounds of a group of small businesses that had set up temporary stands on the outskirts of the camp to sell tobacco, soft drinks, candies, and similar items, asking each vendor if he would serve black troops. Shop owners who answered "no" found their shops boycotted by the entire camp.[16]

The most serious incident was one about which few of the townspeople or members of the camp ever learned. For reason unknown, a white truck driver from Spartanburg had told several men of the regiment who were walking along the road toward the camp that two men of the regiment had gotten into a fight with a policeman in town and that both had been hanged. The rumor spread like wildfire throughout the camp, followed by a report that two men had been absent from reveille call.[17] Some of the 15th New York Infantry troops, believing the rumors of a lynching to be true, headed toward Spartanburg to exact revenge. Sgt. Harry Leonard of Headquarters Company heard about the men going into town and immediately notified Hayward.[18]

An incident like that of the recent Houston mutiny was apparently averted by a narrow margin through the quick actions of Hayward. He grabbed the surprised sergeant by the arm and ordered the man aboard his car, next grabbed Lieutenant Europe, who happened to be close by, and then raced into Spartanburg to confront the wayward band of troops. He found a detachment of about forty-five men from the regiment standing in formation in front of the police station, in good order and discipline and with their rifles at order arms. Hayward approached the noncommissioned officer in charge, received a proper salute, and demanded an explanation.[19] Hayward later recounted the response: "The leader explained that they had heard that Privates 'Blank' and 'So-and-So' had been lynched by the police, and that, if it were so, they had come prepared to shoot the police—all of them if they could find them, and any other people of the town who might interfere or try to assist the police."[20] Hayward noted that the men were obviously under control and obeying the orders of their sergeants without question. He further learned that two of the men from the detachment were in the police station inquiring as to the whereabouts of the supposed missing men.[21] Hayward placed Leonard in charge of the detail and, with Europe in tow, entered the police station to find the two soldiers from his regiment standing at attention in front of the police sergeant's desk in conversation with the police officers. Hayward received salutes from the two men and proceeded to make his own inquiries about the missing men. He questioned the police officers closely and thoroughly, examined the police blotter, and inspected the jail, but found nothing to substantiate the rumor about the arrest of the missing men. Hayward also determined that no men of the regiment had been in trouble of any kind with the police to date.[22]

Hayward went back outside to find a small group of townspeople gathered around and watching the detachment with interest. He gave orders to Leonard to bring the detachment to attention and march them back to camp. The troops executed the sergeant's orders with such precision that the townspeople, unaware of what had brought the detachment to town and the closeness of disaster, applauded. Hayward later learned that Privates "Blank" and "So-and-So" had gotten lost returning to camp and had spent the night sleeping in a field.[23]

Not all of the townspeople of Spartanburg agreed with Mayor Floyd regarding the treatment of black soldiers. One evening after the regimental band had performed a concert for the townspeople on a large square near the main hotel, a representative for a group of businessmen approached Hayward and asked him and the senior officers of the regiment to meet with their party in a private room at a local hotel.[24] Accompanied by Little and Capts. Munston Morris and George F. Hinton, Hayward attended the meeting and was informed that Floyd did not represent "the true spirit of the conservative or responsible citizenship of Spartanburg."[25] The businessmen all expressed a belief that the War Department had in fact erred in sending a black regiment to train in a southern state, but as Little later put it: "They offered us full cooperation in striving to prevent the delicate situation from becoming an indelicate one."[26]

The responsible members of the Spartanburg community, both black and white, did work toward bettering racial relations and making the officers and men as comfortable as possible while far from home and in a hostile environment. Officers were invited to social events and clubs and various forms of arranged entertainment, while enlisted men were treated to church social events, dinners, and parties. As Little described the situation: "A social atmosphere of great promise was developing at Spartanburg."[27]

Yet, in spite of such progress, racial discrimination continued to plague the black members of the regiment. However sincere the group of businessmen may have been, others in Spartanburg were unwilling to accept black troops in their midst.[28] Racial incidents continued to occur between the black officers and men of the regiment and some members of the local population. Brig.

Gen. C. L. Phillips, commander of the post and of the 27th Division, finally concluded that the 15th New York Infantry was not going to be accepted by all of the people of Spartanburg regardless of how well the men behaved, and that at some point things could get out of hand.[29]

Phillips conferred with Hayward and determined that, although the regiment's training was not yet complete, the best solution was to pronounce the regiment ready for duty overseas based on the proven ability of the men to exercise discipline and self-control even when provoked. Phillips recommended moving the regiment to a debarkation point as soon as possible and making arrangements to complete whatever training was lacking after the men reached France. A few days later, Phillips and Hayward departed for Washington, D.C., to push orders through the War Department for immediate combat-readiness certification of the 15th New York Infantry and plans for shipment to Europe.[30]

An incident that occurred in Hayward's absence highlighted the need for this drastic measure. Drum Major Noble Sissle, a noted musician and baritone singer and a member of the regimental band, was walking through downtown Spartanburg one evening with Lieutenant Europe. Sissle entered the lobby of a hotel to purchase a newspaper and was verbally attacked by the proprietor and ordered out of the lobby. A large group of white soldiers of the 27th Division who had been lounging in the hotel lobby when Sissle was accosted began taking the place apart in reprisal and were about to inflict bodily harm on the proprietor when Europe entered the lobby to intervene and prevent any further damage or personal injury. The owner thanked Europe for saving his property and perhaps his life by cursing him and ordering him off the premises with the others.[31]

Phillips and Hayward argued their case well and succeeded in persuading the War Department to issue orders to move the regiment as soon as possible. Consequently, early on the morning of 24 October, not quite two weeks after its arrival at Camp Wadsworth, the regiment broke camp. After completing preparations to move, the entire regiment marched in a formal review parade for Phillips, then proceeded out the camp gate to Spartanburg and to the railroad yards to board their troop train.[32] The movement orders issued by the War Department were secret with regard to the regiment's destination, but everyone on the post knew that the 15th New York Infantry would be the first of the New York regiments to reach France. As the regiment marched through the camp, men of the 7th, 12th, and 71st Infantry Regiments lined the main street of the camp to cheer the 15th New York Infantry on its way and to wish it good luck.[33]

The troop train carried the regiment—less the 1st Battalion, which was still on guard duty in the New York City area—toward the northeast in three sections, one each for the 2d and 3d Battalions and one for regimental headquarters and the band and support detachments. Making good time even after several stops along the way for meals and leg stretching, the train rolled into Washington, D.C., about midnight to a much-appreciated welcome by Red Cross volunteers, who treated the men to hot coffee, sandwiches, and cake.[34]

The regiment reboarded the train and continued on toward its unknown destination, but the men began to see familiar sights on 26 October, when the train steamed across Jersey Meadows, New Jersey. Wild guesses abounded as to the final destination, and when orders were given to prepare to detrain, it appeared that the regiment would end up on the New Jersey side of the Hudson River. But the train continued on, passing through the Hudson River tunnel, through the Pennsylvania Railroad yards, and on through other tunnels and onto Long Island, New York. The train finally stopped at 9:00 PM at a siding of the Long Island Railroad, where the men learned that the ship that was to take the regiment to France had encountered some unknown problem and this siding was the transfer point for Camp Mills, near Garden City on Long Island.[35]

The regiment remained at Camp Mills for two days then moved into New York City to be quartered in several National Guard armories. For two weeks the men of the 15th New York Infantry worked long hours finding, drawing, and preparing for shipment the equipment required for overseas duty; getting inoculations; and completing piles of paperwork. The senior officers of the regiment spent a good portion of their time pulling strings, persuading, and in some cases almost begging the various supply agencies to provide the full complement of arms, equipment, and other essentials required to field an infantry regiment.[36]

The regiment had been kicked from pillar to post since leaving its armories in New York City for guard and construction duties, sent to South Carolina and back to New York City. During this experience the men had developed a distinctive sharpness and style in marching and executing the manual of arms. That factor and the outstanding band assembled and trained by Europe had gained the regiment the nickname "The Saluting Fifteenth." The men themselves, however, wearied by the constant moving from one place to another, had jokingly dubbed the regiment "The Traveling Fifteenth."[37]

Finally, Hayward received orders that the 15th New York Infantry was ready to leave for France. The regiment's equipment and baggage were moved by wagon, truck, and ferry to waterfront warehouses at Hoboken, New Jersey, and then loaded onto a troop ship, the SS *Pocahontas*. On 11 November 1917 the regiment marched by separate battalions to a pier on 96th Street and the East River. While police lines kept the general public away from the area, all personnel, carrying their packs and rifles, were loaded onto the excursion river steamer *Grand Republic*, which promptly departed the pier and headed down the East River, around the Battery, and up the Hudson River to the Hamburg America Line piers at Hoboken, New Jersey. The regiment debarked the *Grand Republic* and boarded the waiting *Pocahontas* to depart that night for France and for the war—or so everyone thought.[38]

CHAPTER 3

The "Eighth Illinois" Mobilizes

We will bring these colors back with honor or we will not come back
at all.

Col. Franklin A. Denison to Maj. Gen. George Bell Jr. when
presented with the 370th Infantry colors at Camp Logan, Texas

Whereas the 15th New York Infantry Regiment had the distinction of
being the newest black National Guard regiment of the yet to be designated 93d Division, the 8th Illinois Infantry Regiment was the oldest. When
the regiment went to France and then on to the front, it also became the most
controversial of the division's four regiments.[1]

The 8th Illinois Infantry dates back to 1890, when a group of black men led
by John R. Marshall, John C. Buckner, J. Bish, and J. Jordan came together
to work toward forming a separate battalion of militia in the Chicago area.
On 5 May 1890 the battalion was admitted to the Illinois State Militia as the
9th Infantry Battalion. On 4 November 1895 the 9th Infantry Battalion, with
eighteen officers and 407 enlisted men, was admitted into the Illinois National
Guard. The commanding officer was Buckner, promoted to major, and the
company commanders were Capts. John R. Marshall, Adolf Thomas, Charles
L. Hunt, and Robert R. Jackson.[2]

With the coming of war with Spain on 25 April 1898, President William
McKinley began federalizing National Guard units from various states. When
Governor John R. Tanner of Illinois did not include the 9th Infantry Battalion
in the president's first allotment call, the black population of the state and the
battalion members expressed their disappointment to their respective representatives in the Illinois legislature. Tanner responded to the requests of the
citizens not by mobilizing the 9th Infantry Battalion, but rather by calling John
Marshall into his office to suggest that Marshall raise and command a regiment
of black soldiers to be designated the 8th Illinois Infantry Regiment.[3]

Marshall accepted the challenge, was sworn in as colonel, and the regiment—with twelve letter companies—was still being raised and readied for
duty when the War Department called for the second allotment of troops.

Governor Tanner ordered the 8th Illinois Infantry to Camp Turner, the Illinois National Guard training post near Springfield, to complete recruiting and training for mobilization. While undergoing training at Camp Turner, and pursuant to the governor's instructions, the regiment quickly recruited enough personnel to reach its required war strength of 1,995 men and seventy-six officers.[4]

The 8th Illinois Infantry was mobilized to federal service and sent to replace the 1st Illinois Infantry, already on duty in Cuba and Puerto Rico, whose ranks and strength had been greatly depleted by yellow fever and malaria. On 14 August 1898 the regiment arrived in Santiago, Cuba, aboard the troopship SS *Yale* and took over occupation duties in the province of Santiago de Cuba. In the course of that duty, a promising young officer, Maj. Franklin A. Denison, an attorney with the Chicago prosecutor's office, was appointed judge of claims in Santiago. After a seven-month tour of duty that impressed both the local population and the Regular Army, the regiment returned home to march down Michigan Avenue in Chicago on 17 March 1899 to a rousing ovation from onlookers and admirers.[5]

After the regiment was released from federal service, Marshall continued as commanding officer, working with his officers to maintain and further build the unit until January 1914, when he was succeeded by Denison. In that same year, due mainly to the efforts of the recently promoted Colonel Denison, a new armory was constructed in Chicago for the 8th Illinois. The new facility was the first of its kind in the country to be dedicated to the sole use of a black National Guard unit.[6]

Black National Guard units always enjoyed the full support of the local black community, who took pride in the men serving their state and country in uniform. As a consequence, a backlog of applicants was always on hand whenever a slot became available, which allowed the National Guard unit to pick its officers and men from the cream of the community. The 8th Illinois Infantry was therefore able to recruit skilled tradesmen and college graduates who were draftsmen, designers, chemists, machinists, and mechanics, as well as professionals such as lawyers, physicians, and accountants.[7]

In 1916, during the border incident with Mexico, the 8th Illinois Infantry was again mobilized. After a short training period the regimental headquarters was sent to San Antonio, Texas, and the battalions were deployed south along the Rio Grande. Duty for the battalions consisted of patrolling the border hunting bandits and Mexican Army deserters who had turned renegade and were coming into the United States to raid ranches and small border communities.[8]

The 8th Illinois Infantry returned home after its release by the federal government on 3 July 1917 to find that orders had been issued for mobilization for

World War I. On 25 July all officers and men of the regiment reported to their respective armories for mustering in and preparation for equipping and training. At the time of the call-up, eight of the twelve companies, Headquarters and Headquarters Company, the machine-gun company, and various detachments were from the Chicago area. The other four companies were from Springfield, Peoria, Danville, and Metropolis, Illinois.[9]

Colonel Denison, the regiment's commander, was also it's oldest and longest-serving member. A native of San Antonio, Texas, Denison was a graduate of Lincoln University, Pennsylvania, and was the class valedictorian when he received a law degree from the Union College of Law in Chicago in 1890. He joined the 8th Illinois Infantry before entering college. Denison had already begun a promising private law career in 1891 when he was appointed an assistant prosecutor in Chicago by Mayor Hempstead Washburn.[10]

After the mobilization of the regiment, it became apparent that there were not enough open areas around the armories to perform the drill and training exercises required by the Regular Army. Denison, not one to wait for something to just happen, pushed forward with combat preparations anyway. Among other steps, he instituted a rigorous training program within the confines of the armories and the narrow streets around the armory buildings to make the best use of time while awaiting orders to depart to a proper training camp.[11]

The 8th Illinois Infantry soon received orders directing it to Camp Logan, near Houston, Texas—the site of the recent 24th Infantry "mutiny." There the regiment was to be attached for training purposes to the 33d Division, which was also composed of officers and men from Illinois National Guard units.[12] On 10 October 1917 the 1st Battalion departed as an advance party under the command of a promising officer, Maj. Otis B. Duncan. Two days later the remaining members of the regiment assembled at the armory in Chicago and marched to the railway station to entrain for the journey to Camp Logan to begin combat training. Regimental Chaplain William S. Braddan later described the event:

> The only [black] lieutenant of police in the world, Lieutenant Childs, paved the way with his baton in position of salute, led the procession, followed by nearly one hundred colored police officers in their tailor-made regular police uniforms, stepping to the martial music like so many trained soldiers, a beautiful sight to behold. The 370th Infantry entrained for Houston, Texas, by the glorious salute of a hundred thousand voices of our most patriotic citizenry, redoubled with the waving of flags and handkerchiefs out of windows all along the route from the armory to where the puff of the smoke from the engines which were waiting to carry them to their destination stood.[13]

The unfortunate incident with the 24th Infantry at Camp Logan would haunt the 8th Illinois Infantry in Texas just as it had the 15th New York Infantry in South Carolina. Influential citizens of Houston, fearing further violence from black troops, had lobbied the secretary of war to prohibit any black soldiers other than those mustered in Texas from training within the state's borders.[14] Concurrently, black leaders in Chicago pressed the War Department not to send the regiment to Camp Logan because they too feared the possibility of violent confrontations between the regiment and the civilian population. The War Department as a policy ignored such requests and stood fast in its decision, and in spite of objections from interested parties both north and south, the regiment was sent on to Camp Logan.[15]

A small contingent of Duncan's advance party had arrived at Camp Logan on 20 August 1917 to begin preparations to receive the main body of the regiment, and had thus been present on the post when the "mutiny" occurred. Sgt. Oscar Walker, a member of the small contingent, commented on the incident's effect on his companions:

A company of the 24th Infantry was stationed at Camp Logan as guards. It was a great pleasure to meet the men of the 24th and we soon felt ourselves a part of them. Our pleasure was soon blasted. The unfortunate incident which shortly followed caused many days of anxiety to our boys, and incidentally a test of discipline on our part. Uneasiness akin to despair swept our ranks.[16]

Of the decision to send the regiment to Camp Logan the *Chicago Tribune* wrote: "The regiment was sent into the South by an order that was not particularly notable for its wisdom, but the men went without a murmur."[17] The regiment's train trip from Chicago to Camp Logan was not exactly uneventful, however. Although the men may have gone toward the South "without a murmur," they did not respond quietly to the acts of racial bias they encountered along the way. The soldiers of the regiment chose to defy Jim Crow laws during stops in Arkansas and Texas, and in one case promptly looted a store when they were refused service. Fortunately, no incidents of that nature occurred between the men of the regiment and the civilian population of Houston during the stay at Camp Logan.[18]

A few isolated fights did happen, of course, mostly between the men of the regiment, and there were several knifings and shootings. Hostility and tension were certainly present, and in one case a civilian police officer shot a member of the regiment who interfered with an arrest. Yet, according to Chaplain Braddan, who was highly critical of both the Regular Army in particular and the white civilian population in general, the stay at Camp Logan proved to be the most pleasant of times for the regiment while away from home.[19]

The train carrying the main body of the regiment rolled into a railhead near Camp Logan in the foggy early morning hours of 18 October. By 10:00 AM the regiment had detrained, unloaded five boxcars of equipment, and marched eleven kilometers to the designated camp area. There, much like the experience of the 15th New York Infantry at Camp Wadsworth, the officers and men found nothing but a dense pine forest where the regiment's cantonment and training area was supposed to be. The solution was obvious, and Denison put his officers to work constructing their own camp. Under the direction of Capt. Charles Hunt, work parties began felling giant pine trees and clearing away underbrush to make room for tents, temporary wood structures, and drill fields. At the end of one week the job of clearing, filling in lowlands, and digging drainage ditches was near completion and the regiment, though still involved with the construction of several buildings, began its combat training in earnest.[20]

At some point after the regiment had arrived in Texas, the citizens of Houston requested a parade by the camp's host unit, the 33d Division, to be scheduled for the early part of November. Because the white civilians of Houston had objected so strenuously to the 8th Illinois Infantry's presence at Camp Logan, the officers and men of the regiment were undecided as to whether they should participate in the parade. The 8th Illinois was attached to the 33d Division only for training and support, not as one of its organizational units, giving the camp commander a ready excuse to exclude the regiment.[21] Denison approached Brig. Gen. H. D. Todd Jr., the acting division commander, and asked if the regiment should participate. Todd's response was: "The '8th' is part of Illinois' contribution to the mobile army designated to go over there, [so they will] see all the Division or none."[22]

The issue having been settled, Denison and his staff went to work planning the parade. To be doubly sure of making a good impression on the civilian population, the companies drilled until their execution of commands was flawless. The 8th Illinois Infantry marched past the Rice Hotel in Houston and presented arms with stunning precision, greatly impressing the onlookers with their discipline and reducing the fears of many white Houston citizens that an incident such as the one involving the 24th Infantry might be repeated.[23] Houston's black community rose to the occasion and came in droves to cheer on the marchers. The black citizens of Houston were so impressed by the performance of the 8th Illinois Infantry on parade that they virtually adopted the regiment and tried to outdo each other in making the officers and men welcome with parties and other entertainment during their five-month stay.[24]

Those five months, though arduous and often quite tense, were not without humorous and sometimes even bizarre occurrences. Perhaps chief among the latter was a memorable incident that came about when one of the unit's enlisted members became ill, was taken to the camp hospital for treatment, and was found to be a woman. Miss Johnson and her boyfriend, Private Gordon of Company A, had conspired to have her come to Camp Logan disguised as a unit member so they could be together until his departure for France. Miss Johnson's illness and the hospital medical examiner foiled their plans, and Miss Johnson went home on the next train while a saddened Gordon went alone to the guardhouse.[25]

On 1 December 1917 the entire 8th Illinois Infantry formed ranks on the post parade ground to be transferred to the National Army of the United States. Maj. Gen. George Bell Jr., the 33d Division's commander, read the official orders redesignating the 8th Illinois Infantry as the 370th Infantry Regiment, National Army of the United States, and handed the regimental colors to Colonel Denison.[26]

In order to remove the regiment from the still hostile environment in Houston and the possibility of racially biased incidents, the 370th Infantry was prematurely certified in late February 1918 by its Regular Army inspectors as ready for overseas duty. Still short of completing its cycle of training, the regiment left Camp Logan early in the first week of March on a slow, meandering train ride bound for the East Coast. After a long and exhausting trip, the regiment arrived on 10 March at its next post, Camp Stuart, near Newport News, Virginia, where the men worked hard to catch up on training missed at Camp Logan while at the same time preparing to sail for France.[27]

While the regiment was at Camp Stuart, Lt. Col. J. H. Johnson was discharged from service for medical reasons, and Major Duncan, who had led the advance party to Houston, was promoted to lieutenant colonel and placed in command of the 1st Battalion. At the same time Capt. Arthur Williams was promoted to major and given command of the 3d Battalion.[28]

Training at Camp Stuart was not all drill, field exercises, and kitchen police duty. The monotony of training schedules and waiting to ship out was broken when a contingent of four companies and the regimental band were invited to participate in a parade in Norfolk, Virginia, held to celebrate Washington's Birthday and to promote the sale of war stamps. The regimental band and the four companies of the 8th Illinois Infantry, with Denison and his staff at the front of the formation, were given the honor position of leading the parade of several thousand soldiers, sailors, and marines through the city of Norfolk. The affair was a pleasant and fitting cap to the regiment's accomplishments during its mobilization, recruiting efforts, and abbreviated training program while earning its deployment orders for overseas duty.[29]

CHAPTER 4

The Draftees of
the 371st Infantry

A black draftee, from a southern state, when asked if he was going to
France, replied, "No, Sir; I'm not going 'to France.' I am going 'through
France.'"

W. Allison Sweeney

When the U.S. Congress passed the resolution declaring war on Germany
on 6 April 1917, the War Department was faced with the overwhelming
problem of organizing and equipping a relatively small army about to expand
into millions of men. At that time the U.S. Army comprised 127,588 officers
and men of the Regular Army scattered in small detachments over the interior
and various overseas territories and dependencies. In addition, there were
80,446 officers and men of the National Guard still on federal service due to
the Mexican Punitive Expedition of 1916, and 101,174 men in state service.
Other trained or partially trained manpower included the Regular Army
Reserve of 4,767 men, the Officers' Reserve Corps of about 2,000, the Enlisted
Reserve Corps of about 10,000, the National Guard Reserve of about 10,000,
and an unknown number of graduates of the Reserve Officers' Training Corps
and other similar programs who were not commissioned or serving in any
organized military formation.[1]

No U.S. Army units larger than a regiment existed in April 1917, and officers and men were not equipped, organized, or trained for major operations at
brigade or higher levels of command, although many had participated in theo-
retical exercises in service schools. A number of the states had National Guard
units in regiments, battalions, and separate companies, all in varying levels of
training and preparedness. Even that force, when combined with the Regular
Army, would not be enough to satisfy the quotas set by General Pershing, the
newly appointed commander of the AEF. In his initial plans for combat in
Europe, Pershing projected the need for at least a million men in France by
May 1918, and at least three million by early 1919.[2] The staggering manpower

requirements Pershing set out would have to be met by conscription, which came with the passage of a draft act by Congress in May 1917. All male citizens between the ages of twenty-one and thirty-one were required to register; 23,779,997 men signed up, and 2,290,527 of them were black.[3]

What to Do with Black Draftees?

At the declaration of war against Germany, thousands of able-bodied young American men answered the call—through a sense of adventure, patriotism, or whatever motive they may have had—and lined up at local recruiting stations to enlist. Only a few of the black men who applied were accepted because there were only four black regiments in the Regular Army to which they could be assigned. Further, those four regiments were not slated to go to Europe, but instead two were to be deployed in the western United States, one in Hawaii and one in the Philippines.[4]

Another option for black citizens wanting to enlist in the service came later in the form of all-black pioneer infantry regiments, noncombatant engineer units that performed the unglamorous and dangerous jobs of digging trenches, building roads and fortifications, and handling ammunition and other materials at the front lines. It takes little imagination to understand the reluctance of anyone to expose himself to rifle and machine-gun fire armed only with a shovel or a pickax.[5]

As the War Department firmed up requirements for the number and composition of divisions to serve in France, its lack of confidence in the black soldier as a fighter became evident when no black combat units were designated in the mobilization plans. Leaders of the black community in America protested that black men were being called to serve as unarmed laborers rather than as combat soldiers. After continued pressure, the secretary of war instructed the War Department to plan for two National Army divisions to be made up of black troops. The tardiness of this decision is evident in the number designations of the black divisions: the 92d and 93d.[6]

By mid-1917, other than the formation of two black divisions, no decision had been reached as to how and where to employ the tens of thousands of qualified black men who were part of the draft and would soon begin arriving at induction stations throughout the nation. As a stopgap measure, War Department General Order 109, issued 31 August 1917, directed the commanding general of each of the sixteen National Army cantonments to organize one infantry regiment (colored) where sufficient black inductees were available. The order further designated that the 1st Provisional Infantry Regiment

(Colored) was to be formed at Camp Jackson, near Columbia, South Carolina, and was to be composed of black men from the first draft.[7]

The 371st Takes Shape

Col. Perry L. Miles, Infantry, National Army, and a major in the Regular Army, was appointed on 1 September 1917 to command the new 1st Provisional Infantry Regiment (Colored). Miles, born in Westerville, Ohio, and an 1895 graduate of the U.S. Military Academy, was a veteran of the Spanish-American War (in which he received the Distinguished Service Cross) who had later served in the Philippines. In addition, he was a distinguished graduate of the Army School of the Line with twenty-six years of active army service.[8]

On 19 September Lt. Col. Robert M. Brambila was appointed second in command of the regiment. A Regular Army officer of infantry, Brambila had spent nineteen years in service, including tours of duty in the Philippines in 1899 and 1911, and in China during the Boxer Rebellion. He was a graduate of the University of Nevada, having received a bachelor of science degree in 1897 and a master's degree in 1909. While at the University of Nevada he participated in the Reserve Officers' Training Corps (ROTC) and received his commission as a second lieutenant in 1898.[9]

The third field-grade officer initially assigned to the regiment was Maj. Joseph Benjamin Pate, Infantry, from the Organized Reserve Corps, a native of Tennessee who had graduated from Maryville College, Tennessee, in 1904 with a bachelor of arts degree. Pate was a well-qualified officer, having served in the Tennessee National Guard for several years before accepting a commission in the Philippines Constabulary, in which he served for eleven years and held the rank of captain. Pate was the first field-grade officer of the regiment to arrive for duty at Camp Jackson, and through his initiative, experience, and skill he had the regimental administration, officers' mess, and other routine operational matters organized and functioning when Miles arrived.[10]

The other notable officer with long experience in military service was Capt. Tobe C. Cope, who had served twenty-one years in the enlisted ranks in the Regular Army and was a first sergeant when he entered the officer training camp at Oglethorpe, Georgia. Cope had seen service in the Spanish-American War, the Philippines Insurrection, the Vera Cruz expedition in 1914, and had done a tour of duty in Alaska. Appointed the adjutant of the regiment, he would later command a battalion in France.[11]

Most of the remaining captains and a few first lieutenants were drawn from the army's supernumerary list of reserve and National Guard officers. Most of the rest of the regiment's junior officers, all second lieutenants and all from

South Carolina and surrounding states, were among the first graduates of the newly established officer training camps.[12]

Some of the officers, and especially a number of those from southern states, were disappointed when they learned they had been assigned to a black regiment, as most were of the opinion that drafted black civilians from southern states could not be made into effective combat soldiers. Few of the assigned officers had any experience with black troops or black culture. To compound the difficulties of organization, administration, and training, the army had neglected to assign the regiment any black noncommissioned officers from the four black Regular Army regiments.[13]

Given these negatives, the future of the regiment and its ability to function as an effective combat unit pivoted on the attitude of its commanding officer. Miles was up to the challenge. At his first officers' call, he informed his officers that black soldiers would be used as combat troops and that the Regular Army black regiments had always given a good account of themselves in battle. It seemed clear that Miles planned to organize and model his command after those black regiments. He did not believe at the time that his talk had much effect on his officers, but the seed was sown, and events would soon prove his approach to be the correct one.[14]

Miles's major worry was not with the enlisted men of his regiment but in his evaluation and expectations of his junior officers. To his field-grade staff Miles expressed real concern as to whether effective officers and leaders could be made from some of the inexperienced young men assigned to him as captains and lieutenants in the limited time available before the unit would be sent to France and into combat. "It was certain," he later wrote, "that if we did get into battle, what they had failed to learn would be paid for in casualties which knowledge could have avoided."[15]

To that end, Miles immediately organized training schools for his young officers where subjects learned in the officer training camps were relearned and subjects not covered were taught. In addition to performing their own unit operational tasks and other required duties, all junior officers were thus also required to participate in five hours of schooling per day, which Miles personally oversaw. His expectations of his officers were high, but no higher than those he placed on himself.[16]

A small contingent of fourteen draftees who had been assigned early due to an administrative error reported in from Pensacola, Florida, on 6 and 7 September 1917. No more draftees were scheduled to arrive until the middle of October because the draft of blacks had been delayed, the War Department having been led to believe that if the men were inducted earlier, a severe shortage of labor would be created in the South that would hinder the harvest of the 1917 cotton crop. The delay was fortunate in that it gave Miles and his officers an opportunity to work with the first fourteen arrivals and a few others who had somehow trickled into the regiment. The officers initially trained them as guides, orderlies, and messengers, but when the rest of the draftees began to arrive, most of the original arrivals, now considered "old-timers," were promoted to temporary noncommissioned officers.[17]

Camp Jackson was the training camp for the 81st Division, the regiment's initial assignment. Although the 1st Provisional Infantry Regiment was not an integral part of that division, the division's commander, Maj. Gen. Charles J. Bailey, and his staff provided assistance and attention as if it were. Thanks to their help, the regiment had a full complement of officers assigned, sufficient barracks prepared for use, and company mess halls manned with cooks from the cooks' and bakers' school standing by to serve meals when the first draftees arrived.[18]

The first large contingent to report on post was an eclectic group, to say the least. Capt. Chester Heywood, a company commander in the regiment, described the scene:

It was a sight never to be forgotten. There were big ones and little ones; fat ones and skinny ones; black ones and tan ones; some in rags and in tatters; others in overalls and every sort of clothing imaginable. They came with suitcases and sacks; with bundles and bandanna handkerchiefs full of food, clothing and knick-knacks. Many were barefoot. Some came with guitars or banjos hanging from their backs by strings or ropes.[19]

The inexperienced junior officers of the regiment were dismayed by the sight, which may well have reinforced their initial beliefs about a black regiment. Heywood would later remark: "The men were light hearted and practically always in good spirits and were accustomed to taking orders and doing what they were told. Discipline was easily attained and necessarily strict, but just. Clean clothes, well cooked food in quantity, systematic exercises and drill, regular hours, plus strict but intelligent and helpful discipline, soon worked wonders."[20]

Any experienced basic training sergeant would have seen nothing unusual in the results of the application of the above principles in the development of new recruits. Yet, without veteran sergeants to mentor and direct the new men entering military life, the younger officers were forced to learn the rudiments and effects of army basic training the hard way, the same as their charges.[21]

The draftees, as much strangers to army life as to their officers, responded so well and with such enthusiasm that the officers soon forgot their initial disappointment in their assignment and threw themselves into bringing the regiment to combat readiness. For his part, Miles continued to drive the officers hard, sometimes far into the night, long after the enlisted men were fast asleep in their barracks. This schedule became the norm for the officers until noncommissioned officers could be promoted from the ranks to take over much of the administrative work at the company level.[22]

The newly appointed noncommissioned officers proved to be hard workers and conscientious in their duties, yet, lacking veteran sergeant mentors to guide them, they sometimes resorted to unorthodox, and often humorous, commands and instructions as they drilled their squads and platoons. One of the new sergeants, while forming his platoon, was heard to bark out: "Dress right—." Forgetting the rest of the command, the sergeant reverted to language his charges could clearly understand. "Hey, you . . . , slick [your] eyes up and down that line." Another sergeant, when corrected by his officer in the procedure he was demonstrating for a drill movement, responded to his squad: "[I'm] doin' it wrong, but [I'm] tellin' you right."[23]

On 9 October 1917 orders came from the War Department that one thousand of the men from the regiment were to be sent to the stevedore regiment at Newport News, Virginia. The acting first sergeants may have been new at their jobs, but they had no difficulty figuring out which men to select for the transfer. The regiment got rid of a number of the sick, lame, and lazy, thereby instantly elevating its efficiency, and some of those who barely made the cut saw where the undesirables were headed and quickly sought to mend their ways. Unknown to all of those remaining, the orders assigning the men to labor units were a portent of things to come.[24]

The winter of 1917–18, one of the coldest in years, dragged by as training progressed and the regiment continued to show good progress toward its readiness goal. Heywood observed:

> Men and officers were happy and content. . . . The marching and the close order drill were excellent; the manual of arms unbelievably perfect. The men took the greatest pride in their uniforms and in their equipment. Their salutes were snappy; their carriage soldierly; and we were all proud, not only of our individual companies, but of the regiment as a whole.[25]

The training continued to be marked by unusual and sometimes amusing incidents, still reflecting the lack of old-timers in the regiment. The tyro soldiers sometimes showed remarkable initiative in trying to do things the right way, that being the "Army way." A case in point occurred one night when, after the posting of sentinels, an officer attempted to enter the regimental area and was challenged by a sentry:

> "Halt! Who goes there?"
> "Officer of the camp."
> Then came a long pause during which the officer grew impatient. "Well, what are you going to do next?"
> After a further wait the sentry responded, "You'll just have to mark time, Boss, while I [look] it up in my little book."[26]

As their skills and knowledge developed, the new sergeants and corporals took over the day-to-day operations of the companies. This allowed the officers to devote time during the day to other subjects of professional development, although Miles continued to require the night classes on advanced tactics and field operations. This was not easy at first because their officer counterparts from the 81st Division were less hard worked and could find time to spend in recreational pursuits in Columbia and surrounding areas. Yet, the officers were showing an increasing drive to excel, partly in response to the obvious efforts of their men to do their best, and partly from a desire to outdo the regiments of the 81st Division.[27]

By the end of November the effort put in by the officers and men to overcome every obstacle had developed a fine esprit de corps and built a nearly combat-ready regiment by stateside standards. But the War Department had now come to the first of several decisions regarding the disposition of black provisional regiments, and orders came to transfer all enlisted personnel in the 1st Provisional Infantry Regiment to the depot brigade in the camp to be assigned as laborers.[28]

The exceptional progress of the 1st Provisional Infantry Regiment had not gone unnoticed by Major General Bailey. When Miles went to Bailey to plead his case and ask for the regiment to remain as a combat element, he was informed that the general was way ahead of him. Bailey had already dispatched a lengthy telegram to the War Department citing the regiment's rapid advancement to combat status, the outstanding attitudes of the officers and men, and the need to retain the organization as a combat unit. Before Bailey and Miles could address the War Department in person, as Colonel Hayward, commander of the 15th New York Infantry, had done, another decision was made, that being to form the 93d Division with the 1st Provisional Infantry (Colored) as one of the divisional units. Within a few days Miles received General Order 33, dated 3 December 1917, from General Headquarters, Camp Jackson: "Pursuant to instructions contained in letter War Department, December 1, 1917, the designation of the First Provisional Infantry (Colored) is changed, effective December 1, 1917, and it will hereafter be known as the 371st Infantry. The assignment of the 371st Infantry to the 186th Infantry Brigade (Colored) is announced."[29]

And so the 371st Infantry Regiment became a regiment of the 186th Brigade of the 93d Division (Provisional), which was composed of three black regiments of the National Guard and now one of the National Army. Further, because the three National Guard regiments were already mobilized and being readied for movement overseas, the 371st Infantry had been placed on the priority list for shipment to France. The news electrified and elated officers and men alike. Heywood noted:

> Everyone simply knocked you down with a salute; sentinels came to the "present" with a slap that could be heard for yards: orderlies stood at statue-like attention when delivering messages, and about faced and stepped from the orderly room "by the numbers." . . . Everyone talked overseas, A.E.F., France, the Boche, and swanked about the camp and town as if they had already seen months of service in the trenches.[30]

Miles observed that "the officers who had at first bemoaned their assignment and at length had become reconciled to it now were more than happy with it. Indeed, they were the envy of many officers of the camp."[31]

Special attention was directed toward further development of elementary combat skills such as sighting and aiming drills, bayonet practice, and grenade throwing. British officers and noncommissioned officers arrived to instruct the men on trench warfare tactics and on some of the foreign-made machine guns and mortars they would be using. Through these events everyone became more acutely aware of and focused on the impending departure to France and the front lines.[32]

The regiment was still far from being "Regular Army." A story from the notes of a company commander describes the ingenuity of some of the men and their continuing lack of understanding of the army's way of doing things. Brig. Gen. George H. Harries, commander of the newly formed 186th Infantry Brigade (Colored), was ordered by Bailey to inspect the regiment and to report any deficiencies critical to movement to France. Harries decided to inspect the troops in ranks and had stopped in front of an obviously terrified private, who overcame his fear enough to bring his Springfield rifle smartly to "inspection arms." Harries, in proper form, snatched the rifle from the private, pulled the bolt, and glared into the chamber. The company commander recorded the following exchange:

"That's the way I like to see a piece kept."

The terrified private, in a sudden burst of confidence: "Yes sir, General, these new toothbrushes sure do get into the cracks and crannies."

"Toothbrushes are issued to clean teeth, not rifles," bawls the General, glaring at the Colonel, who glares at the company commander, who glares at the platoon commander, who indicates by his glare that there is a certain private who will most probably "die the death" shortly.[33]

A measure of Miles's dedication to building and supporting the 371st Infantry is evident in his handling of Lt. Chauncey E. Dovell, Medical Corps. Dovell was attached to the regiment, and Miles considered him one of the unit's most outstanding physicians. Just a few days before the regiment received orders to move to a port of embarkation, Dovell received orders from the post medical officer transferring him to the post hospital. Miles was upset that a capable officer had been transferred from his regiment on such short notice and on the eve of their departure for France. Miles told the chief of staff of the 81st Division that he intended to shanghai Dovell and take him to France with the regiment in spite of the orders, and he did just that.[34]

Dovell later received orders rescinding the original transfer, and he served with the regiment throughout the war, earning a Distinguished Service Cross for outstanding and heroic service. He remained in the army after World War I, served in World War II and the Korean War, and became one of the most decorated officers in the army. While commanding Eighth Army Medical Services in Korea, he was instrumental in instituting the concept of using helicopters as air ambulances.[35]

On 31 March 1917 a telegram arrived at 81st Division headquarters.

Confidential 4 DNA 36 GVT NEWPORT NEWS VA 1130 AM MCH 31 1918

Commanding General Camp Jackson Columbia S.C.

Send 186th Brigade Headquarters and 371st Infantry now at your camp so as to arrive at this port between one AM and five AM April 6th. The freight of organization must arrive by five AM April 5th, acknowledge receipt.

Hutcheson[36]

Movement of the regiment had been anticipated for several days, and friends in the other regiments of the division had been dropping in to say their goodbyes and complain about their own lack of orders. The men labored long hours to crate, seal, and load heavy items to be shipped by freight cars, and by the evening of 4 April 1917 all regimental equipment, packs, and personal items were ready for movement to the rail yard.[37]

In the predawn hours of 5 April the regiment was roused by an early reveille. Last-minute items of individual equipment were stowed away and a final policing of the camp area was made. Then, after a quick breakfast, the regiment assembled and marched out of Camp Jackson and to a nearby rail siding to board the troop train for Newport News and France.[38]

As the 371st Infantry left the camp, the officers and men could look back at the days spent in training at the post with considerable pride. They had labored hard, and their efforts had resulted in a well-trained and disciplined combat unit. In addition, they had accomplished that arduous task without causing any friction with the twenty-five thousand white members of the 81st Division and had received the compliments and applause of the citizens of Columbia, South Carolina.[39]

CHAPTER 5

The Composite 372d Infantry

When the regiment was organized at Newport News, Virginia, there arose at once a very poignant competition between all branches [units]. This brought about a standard of efficiency that never would have been accomplished had there been no competition.

Monroe Mason and Arthur Furr, 372d Infantry,
speaking of the competition between the two separate battalions
and four separate companies of the composite regiment

The first three infantry regiments of the 93d Division were each unique in origin, makeup, and history; the fourth regiment was no different. The 372d Infantry was constituted by the War Department on 16 August 1917 and came together in January 1918 at Camp Stuart, Virginia, as a composite of National Guard company-sized and battalion-sized units from several states. Once federalized, these units were augmented with officers from the Organized Reserve Corps, graduates of officer training camps, and enlisted draftees to bring the regiment to wartime strength.[1]

In late August 1917 Col. Glendie B. Young was appointed commanding officer of the 372d Infantry, with Albert W. Gale as his lieutenant colonel. There seems to be little on record of Young's previous service, although he is known to have served as a captain in the 1st Regiment, District of Columbia National Guard, when it was called up and sent to Cuba and Puerto Rico during the Spanish-American War. A note in the journal of Brig. Gen. George H. Harries, commander of the 186th Brigade, of which the 372d Infantry was a part, states that Young served as a captain under Harries in the Santiago campaign in Cuba. Colonel Miles of the 371st Infantry recalled that Young was "a prominent negro from Washington, D.C.," but other sources insist that Colonel Young was white.[2]

The National Guard units that made up the 372d Infantry were selected from five eastern and midwestern states and one southern state. The regiment consisted of the 1st Separate Battalion, District of Columbia; 9th Separate Battalion, Ohio; 1st Separate Company, Connecticut; 1st Separate Company,

Maryland; 1st Separate Company, Massachusetts; and 1st Separate Company, Tennessee. Each element had a distinctive origin and history as a black National Guard unit.[3]

Because one of the three battalions was made up of separate black National Guard infantry companies, that battalion's commander and his staff—as well as all of the officers of the machine-gun company, the supply company, Headquarters Company, and much of the regimental staff—were white officers drawn from National Guard and Organized Reserve Corps supernumerary lists or assigned as fresh graduates of officer training camps. This biracial officer corps makeup was to prove unfortunate. Some of the white officers were prejudiced and bigoted, and unwilling to treat their black colleagues as equals. Their conduct, which was not properly handled by Young, would have a negative effect on the morale and performance of the regiment shortly after its arrival in France.[4]

Each of the black National Guard battalions and companies had served its state for many years, and several had been called to federal service during the Spanish-American War and during the Mexican Punitive Expedition of 1916.[5] Typical of these units was the 1st Separate Battalion, District of Columbia. The unit was formed in 1863, during the Civil War, as a black battalion of two companies of volunteers designated the Butler Zouaves under the command of Maj. Charles B. Fisher. After the war, the battalion continued in state service as a militia unit in Washington, D.C. In 1880 another black company from the District of Columbia, the Washington Cadets Corps, was organized by Chaplain James H. Payne and commanded by Capt. George D. Graham. That unit soon grew into a battalion of four companies and came under the command of Maj. Christian A. Fleetwood. A third volunteer black battalion, the Capital City Guards, commanded by Maj. Frederick C. Revells, and also of four companies, was formed in 1882. In 1887 the adjutant general of the District of Columbia Militia designated the three organizations the 5th, 6th, and 7th Battalions of Infantry of the District of Columbia National Guard.[6] Various consolidations and reorganizations of the battalions occurred over the next nine years. Finally, by 8 April 1891, all had been consolidated into the all-black 1st Separate Battalion of Infantry, District of Columbia National Guard, with Revells commanding.[7]

The 1st Separate Battalion, Maj. Arthur Brooks commanding, was mobilized for the Spanish-American War but had not completed training by the time the war ended. In June 1916 the battalion was again called into federal service, under the command of Maj. James E. Walker, for the Mexican border incident. During its tour of duty the battalion patrolled the international border and guarded the waterworks near Naco, Arizona.[8]

On 25 March 1917, just before the United States entered World War I, the

1st Separate Battalion was called into federal service to guard government buildings and railroad lines in Washington, D.C., and surrounding states. The battalion reported for duty with fifty line officers, 929 enlisted men, five medical officers, and twenty-one enlisted medics. In early December 1917 the battalion was relieved of its guard duties, ordered to Camp Stuart, Virginia, and designated the 1st Battalion of the 372d Infantry.[9]

The 1st Separate Battalion, Ohio National Guard, traced its beginnings to the Duquesne Blues. The Ohio adjutant general's unit roster of 1874 lists the unit as a separate black company of the Ohio Militia under the command of Capt. Henry Harper. A second company, the Poe Light Guards, was organized and mustered into state service in 1878 under the command of Capt. Edward Brown. As the commanders changed, the unit was renamed the Palmer Light Guards and then the Duffy Light Guards. In 1881 the two companies were designated Companies A and B of the newly formed 9th Battalion, Ohio National Guard. The recently organized Martin Light Guards joined the battalion as Company C.[10]

The 1st Separate Battalion, Ohio National Guard, was mustered into federal service in the Spanish-American War but never left the continental United States. Called again for the Mexican Punitive Expedition of 1916, the battalion reported to a post near Columbus, Ohio, but was never deployed to the Mexican border.[11] In July 1917 the battalion was mobilized for World War I with a complement of fourteen officers and six hundred enlisted men, and one officer and seven enlisted men attached. The battalion reported to Camp Sheridan near Montgomery, Alabama, and performed various services and training exercises before reporting to Camp Stuart, Virginia, as the 2d Battalion of the 372d Infantry.[12]

In 1879 the Connecticut General Assembly enacted a law authorizing the adjutant general to raise four companies composed of black men. These companies would form the Independent Battalion of the Connecticut National Guard under the command of Maj. William H. Layne Jr. In February 1880 the Independent Battalion was redesignated the 5th Battalion (Colored). In 1890, for reasons not clear in the record, the 5th Battalion was disbanded, with two companies—the 1st and the 2d Separate Companies—surviving. The surviving companies were eventually disbanded as well, the 2d in 1896 after a court of inquiry of unknown purpose, and the 1st on 3 July 1899, again for reasons not clearly stated. Just over three months later, on 16 October, the 1st Separate Company, Connecticut Infantry, was reinstated and then completely reorganized with new officers.[13]

Mobilized for World War I on 25 July 1917, the company left New Haven and reported to camp at Niantic, Connecticut. After reorganization and re-equipping, the company was sent to Springfield, Massachusetts, on 3 September to perform guard duty at an arsenal there. On 22 November orders were received to report to Camp Green, near Charlotte, North Carolina, with the 1st Separate Company, Massachusetts National Guard. On 10 December 1917 the 1st Separate Company, Connecticut National Guard, was ordered to Camp Stuart, Virginia, to become Company M, 3d Battalion of the 372d Infantry.[14]

The 1st Separate Company, Maryland National Guard, began in 1879 as the Monumental City Guards under the command of Thomas H. Lewis; it was recognized by the adjutant general in 1882 and redesignated the 1st Separate Company. The company was mobilized for the Spanish-American War but never left the United States. In July 1917 the company was mustered into federal service to perform guard duties at the Allegheny Arsenal at Pittsburgh, Pennsylvania, and at Camp McClellan, Alabama. On 1 January 1918 the unit was ordered to Camp Stuart to become Company I, 3d Battalion of the 372d Infantry.[15]

The 1st Separate Company, Massachusetts National Guard, was founded in 1863 as an "unattached company" and became the 14th Unattached Company, Massachusetts Volunteer Militia, in 1864. In December 1878 the company became Company L, 6th Infantry Regiment of the Massachusetts Volunteer Militia. The 6th Massachusetts Infantry Regiment was mobilized for the Spanish-American War, at which time Company L was the only black company in the regiment. The regiment was brigaded with the 6th Illinois Infantry Regiment, National Guard, and the 8th Ohio Infantry Regiment, National Guard. The brigade proceeded to debarkation stations and sailed for Cuba, arriving on 10 July 1898, too late to participate in the battle of San Juan Hill and the siege of Santiago. The brigade next proceeded to Puerto Rico, where Company L helped to clear out the last hostile Spanish troops and served as occupation and constabulary forces fighting bandits and outlaws.[16]

When the 6th Infantry Regiment was mobilized in April and May 1917, Company L was separated from the regiment and designated the 1st Separate Company of Infantry. Under the command of Capt. J. H. Pryor the company was sent to Camp Green, North Carolina, and on 10 December 1917 the company was ordered to Camp Stuart to become Company L, 3d Battalion of the 372d Infantry.[17]

In 1886 the State Militia of Tennessee comprised nineteen companies, four of which were black—the Langston Rifles, the Sparks Rifles, the Chattanooga Light Rifles, and the Memphis Zouave Guards. During the period 1887–88 the number of black companies increased to twelve, but by 1899 only one remained in the reduced Tennessee National Guard. The remaining unit, one of three separate companies, was designated Company G, Colored, Unattached. In a striking contrast, the other two companies were known as Companies A and B, Confederate Veterans, Unattached.[18]

When the Tennessee National Guard was mustered into service for the Mexican Punitive Expedition on 19 June 1916, Company G, Colored, Unattached, was not included. Company G was mustered into federal service on 5 August 1917 for service in World War I; however, it was not incorporated into the 30th Division, which included regiments from Tennessee, North Carolina, and South Carolina. Instead, it was designated the 1st Separate Company with Capt. Charles O. Hadley commanding. On 1 January 1918 the 1st Separate Company reported to Camp Stuart as Company K, 3d Battalion of the 372d Infantry.[19]

When the individual companies and battalions had assembled at Camp Stuart in early January 1918, orders were received from the War Department stating that the regiment was scheduled to depart for France in early April. Colonel Young immediately ordered training stepped up to bring the companies and battalions together as a functioning regiment. Fortunately, all of the separate National Guard companies and battalions had begun training in individual and company-level combat skills after mobilization. Additionally, prior to call-up they had been organized and involved in rudimentary training in drill and other basic military skills at their home-state armories.[20]

During the three months of training at Camp Stuart, the officers and men of the regiment underwent the standard lectures, drills, and exercises preparing for deployment to France. A formal physical training program was instituted, as were off-duty events that included baseball, football, track, and other popular sports. Competitive drill formations and formal guard mounts were held to improve teamwork and unit integrity as well as morale and pride in the regiment. All of these events also provided entertainment for the civilian population, which at times even showed up early in the morning to watch the formal changing of the guard.[21]

The first contingent of enlistees and draftees, most of them from Michigan, Ohio, and Illinois, arrived in mid-February. The final group, the bulk from southern and midwestern states, arrived at the end of the month, bringing the regiment to near full strength.[22] The arrival of the new men generated some friction among the ranks. The national guardsmen had volunteered into units of long history and standing and considered themselves apart from and superior to the civilians who had waited to be drafted into service.[23] Because the new men had no military training and came late to the regiment, allowances were made to bring them up to the level of training of the national guardsmen. Fortunately, almost all of the draftees were literate and learned the missed portions of training easily. The very few who were unable to read or write were pushed hard by their peers to learn and soon developed enough literacy skills to become effective members of the regiment.[24] Eventually the new arrivals managed to fit in. On the positive side, many were professionals and skilled tradesmen able to fill critical positions in the regiment.[25]

During the month of March 1918, as the regiment was reaching wartime strength and nearing the completion of its training objectives, rumors began to flood the camp as to the exact departure date for France. Late in the month, all leaves were canceled and all of the regimental units began focusing on selecting and preparing for shipment all of the equipment essential to combat readiness.[26]

The impending departure for France was driven home hard to all personnel when postcards were issued to the men, already printed with the statement: "I have arrived safely overseas." Each man was required to address and sign his postcard and then turn it in to company headquarters to be held until the unit's arrival in France, at which time the cards would all be mailed home to signal a safe arrival.[27]

On 29 March 1918 orders were received at regimental headquarters to have all personnel and equipment on board the troopship *Susquehanna* no later than noon the next day. At 2:00 AM the following morning, reveille sounded throughout the camp. Officers and men fell out of their bunks to complete the tasks of loading equipment on carts and wagons, cleaning barracks, scrubbing mess halls, and policing the encampment prior to departing for the ship. At 6:00 AM the officers and men of the regiment formed up and stepped off from their cantonment area at Camp Stuart on the mile-long march to the docks at Newport News to load their equipment and then board the *Susquehanna,* bound for France.[28]

CHAPTER 6

The 15th New York Infantry Sails for France

Don't you see the black clouds rising over yonder
Like as though we're going to have a storm?
No, you're mistaken, them's "Loyal *black folks*
Sailing off to fight for Uncle Sam."

Anonymous

At the time of the armistice that ended hostilities in World War I, forty-three U.S. Army divisions were present in France. Eight were Regular Army, with a marine brigade consisting of two regiments serving with the 2d Infantry Division. Seventeen of the divisions were National Guard divisions or composite divisions made up of National Guard regiments from different states, as in the case of the famed 42d "Rainbow" Division. The remaining eighteen were National Army divisions composed primarily of draftees commanded at the platoon level by lieutenants from the newly established officer training camps. Regular Army officers normally manned upper-level positions while battalion, company, and nonkey division staff slots were often assigned to Organized Reserve Corps and supernumerary National Guard officers. Regular Army noncommissioned officers were assigned as a cadre to provide leadership and to train promising draftees, who were moved up quickly to corporal and the junior grades of sergeant.[1]

For reasons unknown, the 93d Division is counted in official records as a National Army division, although three of its regiments were of National Guard origin. Furthermore, the 93d Division is shown as reporting for duty at its port of debarkation in France on 5 March 1918, making it the seventh division to arrive in France although it was the highest-numbered division to go overseas.[2]

The 93d Division—like all of the divisions selected to be shipped to France—fell behind in the War Department's schedule for departure due in part to delays in organizing for mobilization and training, and further delays finding men, facilities, and equipment to accommodate the enlarged army.[3] Another

critical factor was the tremendous shipping losses inflicted by German submarines, which were waging unrestricted warfare. The losses in men and
materiél were proving devastating to the war effort and were of serious concern to U.S. war planners. Major losses of U.S. military personnel on troop-
ships sunk by German submarines would have been unacceptable to American
citizens.[4]

Immediately after the United States entered the war, Secretary of the Navy
Josephus Daniels sent Adm. William S. Sims of Spanish-American War fame
to establish liaison with Adm. Sir John Jellicoe, First Sea Lord of the British
Admiralty. Sims's mission was to determine how much Allied shipping ton-
nage could be made available to assist in transporting the AEF across the
Atlantic and what quantities and types of supplies were needed to sustain the
U.S. Army and meet the critical needs of the military forces and the civilian
populations of the Allied nations.[5] When he learned the actual figures of shipping lost to German submarines and of the critically low levels of food and
military supplies in England, Sims realized that the war was in danger of being
lost well before the U.S. Army could enter the trenches in France. A quick and
effective solution was needed to drastically reduce the submarine threat in the
Atlantic sea lanes.[6]

From the beginning of the war in 1914, the number of ships carrying raw
materials, food, and other strategic items from the Western Hemisphere to
England and France had drastically increased. The Allied war effort depended
on such supplies, and the Germans were determined to stop the flow. Lacking
sufficient surface vessels to blockade the English and French coasts and the
time to build them, the German Navy decided instead to build and deploy
long-range submarines with orders to sink all merchant shipping believed destined for Allied ports.[7] The British Admiralty answered the threat by assembling and deploying antisubmarine patrols of fast destroyers and small patrol
boats. The problem for the Admiralty was that most of the British destroyer
fleet was required to screen and protect the British Grand Fleet in anchorages
close to England, leaving few ships available to patrol the high seas to search
for submarines. Senior Admiralty officers proposed augmenting their antisubmarine patrols with U.S. destroyers to reduce the losses at sea. Sims disagreed,
realizing that there would still not be sufficient assets to find and defeat the
wide-ranging German submarine force in the vast expanse of the Atlantic
Ocean.[8]

A small group of less senior officers of the Royal Navy proposed a simpler
plan. Why not use the available antisubmarine assets to escort convoys of merchant vessels through the danger zone? They argued that the German submarines would be attracted to the convoys, where they could then be located

with ease and destroyed. The senior Admiralty officers were reluctant to implement such a plan, fearing that it would slow shipments, present consolidated targets, and cause collisions among the close-grouped merchant ships when under attack and maneuvering to avoid torpedoes.[9]

Sims concluded that the convoy strategy was the only viable approach to substantially reducing the German submarine threat. He went to Prime Minister Lloyd George and persuaded him to pressure the Admiralty into accepting the idea of escorted convoys. The plan was implemented, and the result was an immediate and drastic drop in ships lost to German submarine attacks. The convoy system also ensured that survivors of torpedoed ships would be much more likely to be rescued, with so many other ships close by. This point was proven when the SS *Tuscania* was torpedoed and sunk in February 1918 and 2,187 of the 2,397 U.S. soldiers on board were saved.[10]

With safer shipping lanes in the Atlantic, men and materials began to flow across the Atlantic to Britain and France. By war's end more than two million American servicemen had been transported to Europe, including all of the officers and men of the 93d Division.[11]

The 15th New York Infantry Sails
(and Sails . . . and Sails Again)

At about midnight on 11 November 1917, the blacked-out troopship *Pocahontas*, with the 15th New York Infantry on board, was helped out of its pier at Hoboken by harbor tugs and pushed into the mainstream of the Hudson River. The ship steamed down the river and into the Upper Bay to anchor with other ships waiting to form a large convoy. Sometime during the night the last of the vessels reported in, and with U.S. Navy destroyers as escorts, the mass of ships weighed anchors and moved eastward toward the open Atlantic. Soon the lights along the New York shoreline faded from the sight of shipboard lookouts and passengers hanging around at the railings too excited to sleep and wanting a last view of home.[12]

The *Pocahontas* was one day and 240 kilometers out to sea when one of its two steam engines suffered a burned-out crankshaft rod bearing. With only one engine for power the ship began dropping behind the convoy, and soon the other ships disappeared over the eastern horizon. Without the protection of escorts the *Pocahontas* would be vulnerable to attack by submarines or raiders in the danger zone, so the captain wisely reversed course and headed back to the dock at Hoboken.[13] Disappointed by yet another delay, the officers and men of the 15th New York Infantry disembarked on 12 November 1917 and marched to a rail siding where they boarded trains and traveled up the west shore of the Hudson River to newly established Camp Merritt near Engle-wood, New Jersey.[14]

While the crew of the *Pocahontas* made repairs to their ship's engine, the dejected officers and men of the regiment found themselves assigned to various construction and labor details at Camp Merritt. Most of the officers and men worked outside in extremely cold and wet winter weather, and soon rumors began to circulate throughout the regiment that it would continue to be used to provide labor to build camps in the area rather than going overseas to fight. Many of the men became demoralized and developed a strong desire to go home and see their families. More than several—in fact, about 850—went AWOL (absent without leave).[15]

Some of those who went AWOL and were far from home used rather ingenious methods of getting to their destinations. One enterprising young private who hailed from Pittsburgh simply boarded the first train he could find bound in that direction. When the conductor discovered that the errant private had no ticket and no means to pay for one, he had the man put off at the next station. The quick-witted private waited for the next train bound in his direction and repeated the process again and again until at last he reached Pittsburgh. He came out ahead again on train fare when he was picked up at his home by a detail of military police and transported back to Camp Merritt at the expense of the U.S. government.[16]

After three weeks of hard work in extreme weather conditions at Camp Merritt, the 15th New York Infantry received fresh orders. The regiment was to turn in its hammers and saws, move from Camp Merritt to arrive at Hoboken by 2 December, and once again board the *Pocahontas*. Colonel Hayward entered a short note on the movement in his journal: "moved secretly with colors eased and drums forbidden to play, at 10 AM by train to Hoboken and marched through the principal street to transport 'Pocahontas' at Pier 3."[17]

The men had just settled into berths in their cramped quarters belowdecks when a fire was discovered in a coal bunker. Although such fires were not uncommon in vessels carrying large quantities of soft coal for fuel, the ship's captain was forced to cancel the sailing and have all of the coal bunkers emptied, cooled, and reloaded with fresh coal. Hayward decided to keep the regiment in its cramped quarters on board the ship during the week to ten days that it would take to unload and refuel the *Pocahontas*, hoping to avoid both errant troops and the despised construction duties surely awaiting them if they returned to Camp Merritt.[18]

The regiment stewed for eleven cold, damp, and dreary days and nights on board the *Pocahontas*, waiting first for the coal to be exchanged and then for the next convoy to form. On the afternoon of 12 December, in a process becoming familiar to the regiment, the troopship backed out of its pier with the help of harbor tugs and moved down the Hudson River and into the Upper Bay to drop anchor a few kilometers off Sandy Hook, New York.[19]

The men's fear that the *Pocahontas* might be a hard-luck ship was confirmed during their first night at the anchorage. At about midnight, a blinding snowstorm blew in from the north, reducing visibility between ships to zero. The heavy winds and erratic high gusts caused a nearby British oil tanker to drag anchor, drift downwind, and collide with the *Pocahontas*. Damage reports confirmed that a large hole had been punched in a bow plate, and the captain prepared to issue orders again returning the ship to the dock for repairs.[20]

This time Hayward and the officers of the regiment had other ideas. They were determined not to undergo another delay if they could avoid it. Hayward and his officers held a conference with the captain and convinced him that with the assistance of an army machine shop unit on board the ship, adequate repairs could be made by the time the convoy was scheduled to depart. At first light, selected men of the regiment, assisted by the army machine shop unit, began the work of cutting out the damaged metal, fitting a patch, riveting it into place, and painting the repaired section. Battling heavy snows, high winds, and bitter cold, the crews managed to have the hole repaired and painted in just two days. On 14 December 1917, in blackout conditions and once again in a blinding snowstorm, the *Pocahontas* weighed anchor. On this third attempt, with the anxious but much-relieved 15th New York Infantry on board, the *Pocahontas* managed its second departure for France.[21]

To the great relief of everyone, the voyage was fairly uneventful, with only occasional abandon ship drills and a couple of submarine scares to relieve the boredom. On 26 December, near the coast of France, the convoy split up; one group headed southeast, and the remaining ships, including the *Pocahontas*, turned northeast, bound for Brest. Land was sighted at daybreak on 27 December, and at midday the *Pocahontas* entered the large, open harbor of Brest and dropped anchor close under its seawalls. After waiting a few more days on the ship for landing instructions, the regiment and its equipment debarked by lighter on 1 January 1918, entrained right at the waterfront, and departed for Saint-Nazaire, another seaport town.[22] Hayward reported in his journal: "December 27. Landed at Brest. Right side up."[23]

The train ride into Saint-Nazaire was the regiment's first encounter with the famous (according to some veterans, infamous) railcar of the French Military Rail Service known as *chevaus 8, hommes 40* (8 horses, 40 men), a name derived from the markings on the car side. The markings brought several derisive comments from members of the regiment who were fluent in French, including, "Well, it's all right about the forty men. It's going to be crowded; but that will help us keep warm. But after we all get in, where in hell are they going to put eight horses?"[24]

Hayward had not forgotten the meager three weeks of training afforded the regiment before its untimely departure from Spartanburg, South Carolina, and had expected the unit to go immediately into training prior to assignment to the front. Instead, he found to his displeasure that the officers and men of the regiment had been assigned to the Service of Supply, the rear-area support structure of the AEF. Many of the men were put to work unloading ships, hauling lumber, digging ditches, and doing other labor-intensive jobs. Some were transferred back to Brest to labor at laying down tracks and constructing feeder roads for a huge railroad yard. When that group did not have enough work to keep them busy, they were utilized unloading ships in the harbor.[25]

Then, as a final blow to the morale of the regiment, early in January the 3d Battalion was dispatched to the nearby town of Coëtquidan to guard a German prisoner-of-war camp, a bitter reminder of their earlier experience performing guard duties in and around New York City. To the officers and men it seemed that things had picked up right where they left off in the United States when the regiment left for France. Hayward, for his part, was discouraged because the men had not been sent into combat training, but he still believed that the present use of the regiment was only temporary. He was not aware that AEF Headquarters was thinking otherwise.[26]

Prior to the 15th New York Infantry's arrival in France, General Pershing sent a cable to Maj. Gen. John Biddle, the acting chief of staff in Washington, D.C., specifying his decision to disband the entire 93d Division and reorganize the four regiments as pioneer infantry units; that is, the men of all four regiments would become construction laborers rather than combat soldiers. Pioneer infantrymen were sent to the front lines to dig trenches and build bombproof shelters, dugouts, gun emplacements, and other fortifications and facilities in direct support of the front lines.[27]

By tradition, the National Guard and its predecessor, the state militias, had been formed and trained as combat units, and the officers and men of all federalized National Guard units expected that they would be employed to fight. One single factor distinguished the National Guard units from Regular Army and National Army regiments: the National Guard was a politically connected organization. Many National Guard officers were government officials, politicians, or, as with the case of wealthy Capt. Hamilton Fish of the 15th New York Infantry, enjoyed influential political contacts at state and federal levels.[28]

Colonel Hayward was a prime example of a well-connected National Guard officer. As previously noted, he was a lawyer by training and experience, had been the public service commissioner in New York City, and was a close friend and former campaign manager of Governor Whitman of New York State. Three of the four regiments of the 93d Infantry Division were

National Guard units, and one of the battalions of the 372d Infantry Regiment was from Washington, D.C. General Pershing, who was not known for his political sensitivity, seemed to be walking into a political minefield.[29]

It appears that the War Department was uncomfortable with Pershing's plan. During the first months of 1918, cables concerning the disposition of the four regiments of the 93d Division shot back and forth across the Atlantic between Pershing in France and Biddle at the War Department. Pershing was, in fact, facing what he perceived to be two irritating and diverse problems: what to do with the four infantry regiments of an incomplete division of black troops, and how to placate the French high command's demand that individual American regiments be assigned to their army.[30]

It is unlikely that Pershing was disposed to be critical of the performance of black troops. He had served with the 10th Cavalry, had commanded black troop units in 1916, and had made comments in his writings regarding his confidence and respect for them. On the other hand, there is ample evidence that some of Pershing's subordinate commanding officers thought that black troops would not be effective in combat and did not want them. Lt. Gen. Robert L. Bullard, commanding the Second Army, was most outspoken in his low opinion of the performance of blacks as soldiers. Such reluctance on the part of Bullard and other high-level commanders to accept black combat troops may well have hatched the original idea of converting the 93d Division's regiments to pioneer units.[31]

Pershing's other problem—the French high command's insistence on being given U.S. troops to command—would have a direct impact on the 93d Division's future. The French Army commander, Marshal Ferdinand Foch, had been grousing through back channels to the War Department and the White House over Pershing's continued refusal to parcel out arriving American regiments to the French Army. The policy of maintaining American forces intact and under the direct command of an American general had in fact been recommended and supported by Pershing and endorsed and put into force through policy statements by President Wilson. In spite of Pershing's resistance and the president's policy, Foch was becoming more and more insistent.[32]

Hayward was not yet privy to the maneuvering going on at AEF Headquarters regarding the disposition of his and the other three regiments of the 93d Infantry Division. He did know that the pick-and-shovel work being done by the 15th New York Infantry was destroying the morale of men who had come to France believing they were to serve in a fighting unit. Hayward, ever the alert commander, observed during this period that his soldiers "never saw their rifles except by candlelight."[33] Never a man inclined to sit around and wait for something to happen, Hayward wrote directly to Pershing about the present assignment of the regiment to the Service of Supply and its demoralizing effect on officers and men who had come to fight German soldiers, not to shovel French dirt.[34]

Perhaps Pershing was fortunate to have some astute political advisers on his staff able to exert some influence on his thinking, because soon after he received Hayward's letter a personal interview was arranged. It is not known what transpired in that meeting, because no record seems to have been made, but it appears obvious that Hayward was not told by Pershing at that time what decisions had been or might be made concerning the fate of the regiments of the 93d Division.[35] Soon after the meeting with Hayward, however, Pershing sent a cable to Biddle informing him that a decision had been made and approved by the War Department to send the four regiments of the 93d Division to serve with the French Army at Foch's discretion, thereby sealing their fate.[36] This order, although in direct contradiction to the intent of President Wilson's stated policy, was possible through an obscure loophole in Pershing's directive from Secretary of War Newton D. Baker that allowed U.S. Army units to serve under command of the French Army under "such minor exceptions in particular circumstances as your judgment may approve."[37]

It is not apparent what Pershing's thoughts were on the matter. He may have known or have been advised that there was no tradition of racial prejudice within the French military establishment. He may thus have believed, as was later shown to be true, that the French cared nothing about the color of the men of the American regiments, only about their fighting qualities.[38]

Although he had sent the regiments of the 93d Division to the French Army, Pershing continued to insist that he had ultimate control of U.S. Army units. He remarked in his memoirs that in a meeting with Prime Minister Lloyd George he had said, in rebuttal to a request for American regiments to be posted to British divisions, that "no people with a grain of national pride would consent to furnish men to build up the army of another nation."[39] Pershing soon found, however, that the French intended to keep the American regiments for the duration. Commenting on the "temporary" loan of the regiments of the 93d Division, Pershing would later remark: "Unfortunately, they soon became identified with the French and there was no opportunity to assemble them as an American Division."[40]

French divisions were composed of three regiments rather than the four that made up a U.S. division. Returning a regiment to U.S. control would thus have reduced a French division's strength by one-third. That two of the 93d Division's regiments were later assigned to a single French division seems to have ensured that the French could argue extreme hardship should Pershing ask for the return of the four American regiments.[41]

A further curious entry in Pershing's memoirs states simply that a visit from Hayward occurred in mid-June. A footnote explains, "Very naturally, the four infantry regiments of the 93d Division (colored), which have been assigned to four French divisions, were anxious to serve with our armies, and I made application for the organization and shipment of the rest of the division, but to no purpose and these regiments remained with the French to the end."[42]

Several attempts to get the regiments back were made following reports by American officers that French commanders were not giving the four regiments of the 93d Division proper support. Foch deftly blocked the efforts by claiming exactly what Pershing had anticipated. On 26 August, Foch wrote Pershing: "The General commanding the French Armies of the North and North East would be under the necessity of suppressing two of his divisions—through the inability of the moment to fill them up—which could not be considered."[43]

Whatever Pershing's real intentions were for the 93d Division, the situation turned into a neat solution for two of his problems: he was able to mollify Foch with a token complement of U.S. regiments and at the same time dispose of what seemed to be regiments unwanted by the U.S. Army in France.[44] Judging by later events, the U.S. Army was the loser.

The opinions of Pershing's commanders who doubted the combat ability of black troops did not square at all with the experiences of the Allies over the three and one-half years during which the French and British armies used them as combatants.[45] By 1917 more than 340,000 North Africans, most of them Berbers, more than 250,000 Africans from the Sudan and Senegal, and 30,000 blacks from the French West Indies were serving in the French Army. Many blacks held high command positions, including at least two general officers. Their incorporation was not an entirely smooth process. The early employment of blacks in combat by the French Army gave mixed results. Two battalions of Senegalese, for example, in combat for the first time and under fierce artillery fire, held their lines and then advanced under further heavy fire; yet, a regiment from West Africa broke in its first experience under fire.[46]

Rather than attributing the initial failures to black soldiers' inferiority, the French high command was open-minded enough to thoroughly investigate the West African regiment's experience and other such events and determined that several factors, including language barriers between the men and the officers, caused severe confusion at critical moments in combat. It was further determined that the units had been assembled in haste, and that some had not received proper training, and some lacked proper equipment. Climatic conditions also proved to be a significant factor in performance. The black troops from Equatorial Africa serving in the trenches on the Western Front during the bitterly cold winter of 1915–16 suffered enormously.[47]

Once the French Army had addressed and solved these problems, black soldiers demonstrated that they were extraordinary fighters. In fact, a Senegalese regiment is reported to share with a foreign legion regiment the distinction of being the most decorated unit of the entire French Army. The real testimonial came from the Germans who came to fear the French African troops, who preferred to fight at night in hand-to-hand combat with trench knives and bayonets and take no prisoners. The German high command tried to overcome the reluctance of their men to engage the black troops by offering a reward of four hundred francs for each captured black French soldier.[48]

On the other hand, the British War Office held a poor opinion of the black soldier as a combatant, and the British were less tolerant and thus less successful in finding the best way to utilize their colonial troops in combat. Although Britain did not deploy many black soldiers in France, they did have black units in the Dardenelles campaign, the Palestine and Jordan Valley campaigns, and in Cameroon. In all cases the black troops performed as well as white troops and held up much better physically in the tropical climates.[49]

Such experiences, in particular those of the French, contradicted the attitudes shared by the American high command and the American professional army officer in general. Had the facts been examined, the army would have found that black soldiers had served effectively in units of the U.S. Army since its beginning. Further, had the U.S. military officers in France cared to look about them, they would have found that black Americans were already serving with distinction in the French Army, the most notable perhaps being Eugene Bullard, the "Black Swallow of Death." Bullard, who hailed from the Deep South city of Columbus, Georgia, joined the French foreign legion in 1916 and later served with the French 177th Infantry Regiment, whose men became known as the "Swallows of Death" for their daring bayonet attacks. Twice wounded, Bullard transferred to the Lafayette Flying Corps, a French unit composed of Americans, and proved a daring and—too often for his commanders—reckless pilot in combat. When all American pilots were transferred to the U.S. Army Flying Corps, Bullard, already decorated with the Croix de Guerre, was refused a flying berth because the standing policy was "no blacks in the flying corps."[50]

Something the army high command knew nothing about, or if they did know could not prevent, were the so-called white blacks—those who could "pass" for Caucasian and did enlist and serve in white units. Notable among these men was PFC John Robert Kay, who served with a white separate combat engineer regiment. After the war he taught himself to fly and later barnstormed and flew in air races around California and Arizona. Tiring of that experience, he then got into auto racing, became a riding mechanic, and competed in the 1932 Indianapolis 500.[51]

The 93d Division thus faced an almost insurmountable obstacle in the U.S. Army, where prejudice and preconceived ideas that the black soldier could not or would not perform well as a combat soldier prevailed in spite of hard evidence to the contrary within both its own ranks and those of the other Allied armies. The army leadership continued to believe that the black man was best suited for menial labor in stevedore, construction, and pioneer infantry regiments, and this attitude prevented the proper treatment and utilization of a rich manpower resource for combat service in World War I.[52]

Hayward's efforts to retain his regiment's combat status in the U.S. Army may have set off the chain of events that led not only his regiment but also the other regiments of the 93d Division to serve out the war as a part of the French Army.[53] In any event, after all the maneuvering and decision changing, the 15th New York Infantry retained its combat status and received the long-awaited movement orders to entrain for a secret destination at the front.[54]

CHAPTER 7

The 15th Becomes
the 369th Infantry

The boys keep looking at the big flashes in the north, and saying, . . .
let's go, and we've formally adopted "Let's go" as the motto of this
brunette fighting outfit.

Col. William Hayward, 369th Infantry

Colonel Hayward's lobbying efforts with AEF Headquarters brought
secret orders to the 15th New York Infantry assigning it to the combat
zone as a fighting formation. While the other regiments of the 93d Division
were busy training in the United States and shipping across to France, the 15th
New York Infantry was well on its way to becoming the first regiment of the
"American Foreign Legion."[1]

The secret orders gave a departure date of 12 March 1918 and told where
the regiment was to go on the first leg of the trip but were sealed as to the regiment's final destination and assignment. In a letter to a friend, Hayward expressed his elation at receiving orders sending the regiment to a combat zone:

I loaded the wandering, saluting, laughing 15th N.Y., the only unit ever
in France with a state name, on about a million of these little French cars,
still carrying our state colors, and under sealed orders for the second half
of the journey, puffed away into the night on a strange mission—the
most wonderful adventure which ever befell a regiment in our army or
any other army since the war began.[2]

Whether it was because the French were showing their gratitude to the first
of the four American regiments to come under their control or simply because
no other accommodations were available, the regiment traveled in style on a
first-class French passenger train that was nothing like the "40-and-8" military
boxcars they had ridden from Brest to Saint-Nazaire. Hayward was even set up
in the bridal suite of a special coach, which had, as he put it, "everything that
went with it except the bride."[3]

The train traveled northeastward through a placid countryside dotted with tiny villages and farms, arrived at the initial destination given in the secret orders, and rumbled through without stopping. Soon the train was passing large artillery parks, supply dumps, ammunition depots, great artillery pieces mounted on railroad cars, military airfields scattered with aircraft, and other signs of war. "For the first time," Captain Little commented, "we saw a country devastated by modern warfare—wrecks of buildings, miles upon miles of meadow land torn and horribly disfigured by shell burst or by pick and shovel, the sole crop awaiting harvest, barbed wire entanglements."[4]

This initial glimpse of the battlefield was a sobering introduction to the destructive powers of twentieth-century weapons of warfare. Innovative and efficient machines such as rapid-firing artillery pieces that launched high-explosive and poison gas shells, airplanes and dirigibles, hand and rifle grenades, flame-throwers, and tanks graced the inventories of the modern armies of the day.[5] The effects of these modern engines of destruction on the human body were not lost on the officers and men of the 15th New York infantry. Little further commented: "We saw, also, little wooden crosses, marking the graves of patriots of the supreme sacrifice—thousands and tens of thousands—some carrying the wreath of the tricolor of France, some bearing marks identifying the dead of Germany; but all respected by the wonderful French, with their ideals of sentiment."[6]

These morbid signs of death and destruction were only a hint of the real side of war. The officers and men of the regiment received a much bigger jolt of reality after arriving at their destination. At 11:00 AM on 21 March, the train stopped at the town of Givry-en-Argonne, a village fifteen kilometers south of Saint-Menehould and halfway between Chalons-sur-Marne and the fortress city of Verdun, and the men stepped down from their small but comfortable coaches to the ominous rumble of heavy guns firing and the *boom-boom* of shells exploding to the north.[7]

Hayward was trying to get his bearings in the new and unexpected surroundings when a French officer approached him and asked if he was the "Trois cent soixante neuviéme Regiment d'Infantrie, Americain?" Only then did the commanding officer of the 15th New York Infantry learn that his regiment had been redesignated the 369th Infantry Regiment, Army of the United States, and attached to the French Army.[8]

The battalions of the newly designated 369th Infantry formed up and proceeded by foot from Givry-en-Argonne to their first billeting and training areas at the front. Regimental headquarters and the 1st Battalion were located at the village of Noileau, about a nine-kilometer march due west of Givry-en-Argonne; the 2d Battalion settled in at Saint-Mard-sur-le-Mont, about four kilometers southwest; and the 3d Battalion was at Remicourt, about one kilometer to the west on the road to Noileau.[9]

General Le Gallais, commanding the French 16th Infantry Division of Gen. Henri Gouraud's French Fourth Army, to which the 369th Infantry had been attached for training, welcomed the regiment to its new assignment. Le Gallais also informed Hayward that his regiment had carried the American flag farther north than any other unit of the U.S. Army. In truth, the regiment was also totally isolated from the other U.S. formations. Hayward reflected sarcastically: "We are *les enfants perdus* and glad of it. Our great American general simply put the black orphan in a basket, set it on the doorstep of the French, pulled the bell and went away. I said this to a French colonel with an 'English spoken here' sign on him, and he said 'weelcome leetle black babie.'"[10] It was apparent from the French colonel's response that the French Army was glad to have the 369th Infantry regardless of what the U.S. Army thought of the unit.[11]

The most immediate, unnerving, and surprising thing the regiment had to do in its new assignment was to turn in all American equipment and arms and reequip with French issue. The only items excepted from the exchange were boots, pants, shirts, jackets, overcoats, and overseas caps, all of which remained U.S. Army issue.[12] Most disagreeable of all was having to surrender the coveted Springfield model 1903 rifle, which used the powerful U.S. caliber .30-06 rimless cartridge. In its place the riflemen were issued the inferior French Lebel rifle, which used the equally inferior 8-mm rimmed cartridge known by the same name. Almost all of the men of the regiment had become highly proficient in firing the Springfield rifle, above standard U.S. Army range requirements, and they were not at all impressed with the French Lebel with its long, needlelike bayonet; three-round magazine; and relatively weak cartridge.[13]

At the time, the Springfield 1903 rifle was considered to be the finest individual shoulder weapon available to any army, and U.S. Army and Marine Corps servicemen believed exactly that. The Springfield '03 was an adaptation of the German Mauser bolt-action military rifle, for which, ironically, the U.S. government had paid the Mauser arms firm $200,000 for manufacturing rights. The powerful .30-06 cartridge had a muzzle velocity that exceeded any other cartridge used in the war except the Mauser 7.92 mm. Its rimless case made the cartridge easy to load and convenient to store and carry; and it used the highly effective and accurate "spitzer" bullet, another German development.[14]

The Lebel rifle, officially known as the 8-mm Fusil M1907/15, the French shoulder arm most in use in the French Army, was based on a bolt-action design developed by the well-known Lt. (later Gen.) André Berthier. The rifle used an adaptation of the Mannlicher clip-loading magazine and therefore was sometimes called the Mannlicher-Berthier rifle. The Mannlicher system required clips, and the Lebel rifle was limited to three rounds of 8-mm rimmed cartridges inserted from the top of the receiver. When the last cartridge was fired, the clip dropped from the bottom of the receiver to clear the way for the next clip to be inserted.[15]

The Lebel rifle was considered an inferior weapon by soldiers of the Allied and Axis armies alike, and it was certainly not a fair exchange for a Springfield rifle. Furthermore, the Springfield rifle played a key role in the organization of the infantry regiments of the U.S. Army, whose tactics were based on an open-warfare concept of fire and maneuver that relied on mobility, which perfectly fit the Springfield '03's long range, accuracy, and rapid-fire capability. In the hands of well-trained and organized riflemen, the rifle could deliver a lethal concentration of firepower in a battle.[16]

The French Army, fighting a stalemated and defensive form of trench warfare, had probably forgotten what mobility was. They had come to depend on large quantities of machine guns assigned to their infantry regiments to deliver heavy fire at a distance. For close-in combat in the trenches the French relied on bayonets, grenades, and knives. The Lebel rifle, with its length of 130 centimeters and its long, tricornered, and easily broken French M1915 bayonet, provided all that was needed for the French Army's form and method of trench-warfare tactics.[17]

To carry ammunition for the Lebel rifle, the men of the 369th Infantry received three French M1916 cartridge pouches of brown leather to be worn with the French M1903/14 leather belt. Each man wore two pouches in front, one on each side, and one pouch in the small of the back.[18]

All members of the 369th Infantry and its sister regiments arrived in France wearing the fedora-style felt hat with the crown shaped in what was known as the "Montana peak." The U.S. Army had not adopted a regulation steel helmet of domestic design and manufacture, so the men were given the helmet of issue in the French Army, the M1915 Adrian helmet, an adaptation of a design long used by firemen in Metropolitan France. The helmet, painted a dull blue-gray, was adorned with a ridge running from the top to the lower rear rim. A representation of a flaming bomb or grenade, the badge of the French Metropolitan infantry, was fastened on the front of the helmet just above the short brim.[19] The Adrian helmet was made of cold-pressed mild steel, making it quite inferior to the German M1916 *Stahlhelm*, which was hot-pressed of silicon-nickel steel and much harder, tougher, and more resistant to penetration by shrapnel or projectiles. The narrow skirt of the Adrian helmet provided only a little more protection to the wearer's neck than did the flatter British Brodie helmet, and far less protection than the full-skirted German helmet. Adrian helmets were cheap to manufacture, however, and more than three million of them were made before 1915. Because of their ready availability, they were worn by the armies of several Allied countries.[20]

The standard uniform clothing of all U.S. Army enlisted men consisted of the M1917 tunic with stand-up collar and M1912 semibreeches, both in olive drab. A dull bronze disc with "US" embossed on it was worn on the right collar, and a similar disc with crossed rifles and the regimental number was worn on the left collar. These clothing items, along with U.S. Army issue boots, would be worn throughout the 369th Infantry's assignment with the French Army.[21]

Two items of equipment—one French and one U.S. Army issue—would create serious problems for the officers and men of all the regiments of the 93d Division. The first problem was with the individual soldier's equipment-carrying arrangement. The French Army issued a small backpack for extra boots, mess gear, and tent items; and a small haversack for rations. Each French soldier was also provided with the French M1914/15 greatcoat, which contained numerous large pockets for carrying whatever other items might be needed; later-model greatcoats even included special ammunition pockets. The U.S. Army supplied its men with a large-capacity backpack that could carry almost everything required to live and fight in the field. The U.S. Army overcoat lacked the generous equipment-carrying capacity of the French greatcoat. The result of the issue of the French backpack in combination with the U.S. overcoat was a lack of carrying capacity, and items essential for comfort and survival in the field often had to be discarded.[22] In addition to the backpack and overcoat problem, the U.S. Army issued to each man three blankets, whereas the French army issued only one blanket. The French soldier was trained to use his versatile greatcoat, with its long length and enormous collar, and the one blanket to provide warmth when bedding down in the field.[23]

Footwear for the men of the regiment consisted of U.S. issue M1917 canvas webbing leggings and M1917 brown leather boots with hobnail soles. The canvas leggings proved to be inadequate for trench warfare and, as they wore out, were replaced with cloth wrap-puttees of French design. The U.S. Army issue boots would continue to be supplied by the U.S. Army and worn by the men of the regiment throughout the war.[24]

For a convenient source of water in the field, the modern U.S. Army M1910 canteen, which clipped onto the M1910 belt, was replaced by the French Army M1877 canteen, an outdated two-liter enameled steel bottle with a cork stopper. The bottle was covered with horizon blue uniform cloth and hung over the shoulder by a leather strap. An enameled steel cup was issued as well and was usually tied in place with the canteen's cork stopper string.[25]

The one item of French equipment that the men of the 93d Division found to be a definite improvement over U.S. Army issue was the gas mask. The issue mask of the U.S. Army, of British manufacture and design, required a clamp to be applied over the bridge of the nose to seal properly. Unfortunately, the mask could not be made to seal tightly around the broad, flat noses of many of the black soldiers. However, the French ARS design, referred to in the field as the "pig nose," did not require a nose clamp and fit fully and comfortably over all shapes of noses and faces.[26]

The French rations also proved to be a problem. French soldiers received a diet high in carbohydrates, whereas the Americans were accustomed to a high protein intake. Soups and breads were the major components of meals served in the French Army, but American troops were accustomed to meat stews, steak, cornbread, cooked vegetables, and other more substantial items.[27] Arrangements were made to provide additional supplies of more appropriate types of food from the American commissaries, and the scheme worked as long as the regiment was in one place for an extended period. When the regiment was in the trenches or on the move, the men often had to make do for long periods with what the French were able to supply, which was usually insufficient in quantity and quality, and it materially affected morale.[28]

The men of the 369th Infantry were surprised to be issued a liter of wine, usually claret, with each day's ration. Customarily, the French soldier drank a small portion of his wine issue at each meal and in the evening before bedding down. The American troops, never having been issued wine before, had not developed that habit, and many were inclined to consume the full liter at one sitting. This sometimes resulted in the strange and inexplicable appearance of German troops in trees and on rooftops. These apparitions caused sudden calls to action and were an annoyance for the many sober individuals who had to take cover from the rifle bullets whizzing around their heads.[29] The wine issuance had to be discontinued, much to the understandable disappointment of a number of the American troops. For reasons unknown, a brown barley sugar ration was substituted. The impromptu gun battles ceased and the troops went back to being sober most of the time, but it is also likely that by war's end many of the men had developed an aversion to brown barley sugar.[30]

Pay continued to come from the U.S. Army, and there arose some confusion as to the exchange rate from American to French currency. At first, many of the men could not believe that the French currency—small, torn, dirty bills that looked like used soap wrappers—was worth anything. Once they overcame that misconception, some of the more resourceful individuals began to take in a bit more than their allotted salary. Payday gambling, an activity frowned on by higher command, has been customary in armies since time began. In the U.S. Army, that gaming often consisted of shooting craps. The objects used to play the game were referred to, with some affection by those most skilled in their use, as galloping dominoes, and in the Regular Army black regiments as bones—to wit, dice.[31]

The French troops received a paltry sum on payday compared with the American troops' pay, but that did not stop the American soldiers from going after it. The Americans became expert at drawing unsuspecting French soldiers into playing what to them appeared a strange yet fascinating and friendly game of chance. Within a few days the French soldiers had lost all of their pay, and the majority of the money was in the hands of a few individuals who seemed to have bones that could magically perform their bidding.[32]

Once all the administrative work and reequipping had been completed, the next project for the 369th Infantry was to reorganize on the French regimental system. The French regiment was made up of three battalions, each consisting of three rifle companies and one machine-gun company. The regimental Headquarters Company contained all supply, medical, signal, and other support personnel.[33] In comparison, an American regiment had three battalions of four rifle companies each and a single separate machine-gun company. There was also a separate supply company; each battalion had a medical section attached; and all signal communications functions were provided by a platoon attached from the divisional signal company.[34]

The new organization for the 369th Infantry, and eventually for the other three regiments of the 93d Division, consisted of reducing the three battalions to three rifle companies each. A French division has three machine-gun companies, so two of the three excess rifle companies were turned into machine-gun companies, and the regular machine-gun company made up the third company. The remaining rifle company was set up as a reception company tasked to train and assign replacements as they came up from the replacement depots. A signal section was established, trained, and assigned to Headquarters Company, while the supply company remained separate and functioned as it would in a regular American regiment.[35]

The only weapons the 369th Infantry had brought to France were the Springfield rifles carried by each soldier as his shoulder weapon. All crew-served weapons, mainly light and heavy machine guns and mortars, had to be supplied by the French Army. Under the new reorganization the regiment would require three times the number of machine guns assigned to a U.S. Army regiment. Some training had been provided on French crew-served weapons during the 369th Infantry's short stay at Camp Wadsworth in Spartanburg, but intensive training by French advisers would have to begin immediately.[36]

The machine guns available to the French Army, and which the 369th Infantry would use in combat, consisted of light assault weapons and heavy defensive weapons. The standard-issue light machine gun was the M1915 Fisul-Mitrailleur CSRG, commonly called the Chauchat, or "sho-sho," by American troops. The common name came from a Colonel Chauchat who headed up the French arms commission that adopted the weapon for use by the French Army. The initials CSRG stood for the development group—

Chauchat, Suterre, Ribeyrolle—and the manufacturer, Gladiator. The gun incorporated a design worked out at the turn of the century by a Hungarian named R. Frommer, who developed the long recoil system for automatic weapons. The long recoil system worked quite well in semiautomatic shotguns and even fairly well in pistols, but it worked poorly when designed into machine guns, and the Chauchat suffered miserably from that design misapplication.[37]

Two other factors also contributed to the Chauchat's poor performance. The first was that the contract to produce the gun in France was awarded to the firm of Gladiator, a bicycle maker with no experience in arms building. Gladiator's machine guns were so poorly manufactured that parts could not be interchanged on many of the weapons and parts breakage became almost endemic.[38] To further compound matters, the Lebel 8-mm rimmed cartridge was adopted as the ammunition for the gun. Rimmed cartridges used in machine guns are notorious for poor feeding, which results in malfunctions in firing. The rimmed cartridges also take up more space in magazines than do rimless cartridges, thereby reducing the capacity of the magazine. All of these factors add up to poor performance in combat.[39]

The heavy machine gun in use and initially issued to the 369th Infantry was the French Hotchkiss M1914. In both performance and effectiveness in combat it was the antithesis of the Chauchat light machine gun. The Hotchkiss was developed after the beginning of the war when the French Army realized the need for dependable heavy machine guns in defensive warfare, and was in full production by 1916. The machine gun proved highly reliable even though, like the Chauchat, it was designed to use the Lebel 8-mm cartridge with its rimmed case. The weapon's major drawback was its feed system. Rather than a belt, the Hotchkiss used a magazine of a rigid metal rack design, which limited the number of cartridges that could be loaded and fired at one time and thus reduced the gun's rate of fire.[40]

Within each battalion, a Stokes mortar section, commanded by a lieutenant, was organized from the few men who had trained on the weapon at Spartanburg. The Stokes, a British lightweight, short-range trench gun, was available in 3-inch and 4-inch shell size. The 3-inch model threw a shell weighing 10 pounds, and the 4-inch model could toss a shell weighing 25 pounds; both could fire shells a maximum distance of 1,250 meters. The gun, developed in 1915 by Sir Wilfred Stokes, consisted of two parts: a smoothbore barrel with a light, bipod mount and a metal base plate to absorb shock. When the shell was dropped into the tube and hit bottom, a percussion cap located on the shell base hit a fixed striker at the end of the tube that ignited the propellant charge and fired the shell out of the tube. Firing rate was determined by how fast the crew could drop the next shell into the gun after the previous shell had cleared the tube. Some well-trained teams could load and fire the mortar at such a fast rate that the gun tube overheated and required external means of cooling before firing could continue.[41]

The 369th Infantry and its sister regiments would later acquire the French 37-mm infantry gun, a direct-fire weapon used to supplement the trench mortar. Commonly called a trench gun, the weapon had a range of 2,400 meters but was seldom effective beyond 1,500 meters. The gun was useful in assaults because the ammunition was lighter than that used in mortars, it could be easily manhandled, and it could attack machine-gun nests and bunkers with more accuracy by direct fire.[42]

Although not a component of the regiment, the field artillery batteries are worthy of note as a major supporting element supplying entrenched battalions with defense and assault troops with covering fire.[43] The most common close-support weapon of the French artillery batteries, and the most successful in the war, was the French model 1897 75-mm field gun. This well-designed gun, commonly called the French 75, fired either a 16-pound shrapnel fixed round or an 11¼-pound high-explosive fixed round to a distance of 9,000 meters. Its rapid rate of fire made the gun the favorite of the French and American armies. A well-trained crew could deliver fifteen to thirty rounds per minute in emergency conditions.[44] In conjunction with the vaunted French 75, the French Army employed guns and howitzers ranging from 105-mm close-support guns to railroad car–mounted long-range weapons such as the 520-mm Schneider howitzers and 270-mm guns.[45]

As soon as the 369th Infantry completed rearming and reorganizing to the French regimental model, the men began adjusting to and training with their new French weapons prior to moving into the trenches.[46] Grenade practice became one of the more exciting activities. The French M1916 CF grenade, the most commonly used, was activated by striking the base on a hard surface, igniting a time-delay fuse of five seconds' duration. If the grenade were thrown right after igniting the five-second delay fuse, the enemy might have time to pick it up and toss it back at its previous owner—or at least out of harm's way. The practice was thus to count "one" as the grenade was struck against a hard surface, "two" as the throwing arm was extended, and "three" as the grenade was launched at the enemy position, allowing two to three seconds for the grenade to pass through the air and reach the target before exploding. Obviously, the timing was critical; too long a wait could result in the loss of a hand.[47] There were naturally some rather anxious trainees in the grenade pits. One individual threw his grenade on the count of "one." When his platoon leader jumped on him for an explanation, his response was: "Yes, Sir. I knew to wait until 'three' but I had to throw it 'cause I could . . . feel that thing a-swellin' in my hand!"[48]

Training in the use of French arms continued until 6 April, when the 2d Battalion was moved to the north to the vicinity of Maffrecourt, Remicourt, and Hans. The rest of the regiment followed on 13 April. The new billeting areas positioned each battalion close enough to the front to be easily rotated in and out of the trenches. It was here that the officers and men of the regiment, integrated into seasoned French battalions, began their training in earnest.[49]

Certainly, Hayward and his officers had not anticipated being deployed as a combat regiment in a French division. Nevertheless, they had achieved their major goal of being sent to the front line as a combat unit and were about to see the true culmination of their efforts as the regiment headed into its first action in the trenches.[50]

CHAPTER 8

The Rest of the 93d Division Ships Out

You ask me if the men were sea-sick. Well if you could have seen them lying around the deck and hanging on the rail you would not have asked the question. Speaking about feeding the fish, the majority of them must have had a contract to feed whales.

Chaplain William S. Braddan, 370th Infantry

Less than a month after the 369th Infantry took up its station at the front, the other regiments that would eventually join it to form the 93d Division received their own orders to embark for Europe.

The 370th Infantry

On 6 April 1918 Colonel Denison received orders to bring the 370th Infantry on board the troopship SS *President Grant*, scheduled to depart that very night. The plan called for the troopship to meet its convoy and escorts two days later in the Atlantic Ocean near Cape Henry, Virginia.[1] The regiment began departing Camp Stuart, Virginia, at 5:00 AM and marched to Pier 3 at the Norfolk docks to load onto the troopship. Although the departure time and date were supposed to be secret, hundreds of friends and relatives were at the pier waiting to say good-bye to the regiment. By 11:00 AM the entire regiment along with a pioneer battalion was on board the ship, where they settled in to await loading of the 371st Infantry Regiment, which had also received orders to embark on the *President Grant*.[2]

The 371st Infantry followed the 370th Infantry aboard later that day, bringing the ship to its full troop-carrying capacity. Just before midnight, the *President Grant*, pushed along by tugs, left its pier, turned into the river stream, and moved out into Hampton Roads. At around 4:00 AM, in the spirit of the 15th New York Infantry's accident-plagued transport, the ship ran aground on a sandbar in the channel. A navy board of inquiry that came on board the ship the next day determined, much to the relief of the civilian captain, that the government charts defining the channel were at fault.[3]

After the crew spent two days off-loading fresh water to lighten the ship, a bevy of tugs pulled the *President Grant* off the sandbar. After being resupplied with fresh water, the ship renewed its journey, but without the protection of a convoy and destroyer escorts. Fortunately for all on board, the vessel sailed its particular Atlantic sea lane without encountering any enemy submarines or surface raiders or experiencing any further mishaps. The men of both regiments were anxious to see some kind of action during the tedious journey, but initially, abandon ship drills and morning alerts that required standing by lifeboats in the event of a submarine attack provided the only breaks from the boredom.[4]

Some excitement did come in the form of a severe gale that struck the ship in mid-Atlantic. Heavy ship handling resulted in a large number of seasick troops. On 14 April a bit more excitement was generated when another troopship joined up with the *President Grant*. On 20 April, as the ship was nearing the European continent, another short-lived thrill came when several American destroyers and a French dirigible came out to escort the ship on the last and most dangerous leg of the journey.[5]

The *President Grant* arrived in Brest on 22 April, maneuvered into the anchorage, and dropped its hook in the harbor near the town and seawall. While the ship was being secured, both regimental bands assembled on the forward deck and played to a nearby fleet of cargo ships, most of which were flying the Stars and Stripes.[6] In spite of the bouts of seasickness experienced during the trip, the men seemed to be in high spirits, as expressed by Sgt. Oscar Walker of Company G, 370th Infantry: "If there was any discomfort aboard *President Grant* from crowded quarters, never a word was spoken, not a murmur was heard. These men, seasoned to hardship and privation, were soldiers."[7]

On 23 April the 370th and 371st Infantry Regiments were transported to the docks by lighters and then marched to the old Pontanezen Barracks of Napoleon fame on the heights beyond Brest. For the next two days the men of both regiments occupied themselves with getting rid of their sea legs and gathering up the baggage and equipment being unloaded from the *President Grant* and dumped on the docks.[8]

On 25 April the 370th Infantry departed Pontanezen Barracks by train in 40-and-8 freight cars for a trip clear across the interior of France to Grandvillars (Haut-Rhin) in the quiet Vosges Front region near Belfort. The short stay in the post area of Brest was both fortunate and unfortunate for the officers and men of the regiment. They had little opportunity to accustom themselves to the strangeness of a foreign country, but neither were they exposed to the racial bias or manual labor assignments that had befallen or would befall the other regiments of the 93d Division who were quartered in the area for several days or weeks.[9] Once at its destination at the Vosges Front, the regiment moved quickly to transition into French equipment and the French system of organization, and then on to training areas for combat training in the trenches.[10]

The 371st Infantry

When the 371st Infantry arrived in Newport News, Virginia, on 6 April, the 370th Infantry was, as previously noted, already on board the *President Grant*, as were General Harries and his brigade staff.[11] The regiment detrained at a dock siding and the men began loading themselves and their equipment onto the ship, less three companies and a separate complement of nineteen officers. The nineteen officers had to be detached from the regiment due to lack of space on the troopship. They were to be sent over in style and comfort on the SS *Great Northern*, a first-class luxury liner of the Pacific trade, which made them the envy of the officers' mess of the 371st Infantry. The nineteen officers reached Brest a few days after the main body of the 371st Infantry and had to suffer the jeers and scoffs of their envious fellow officers when they caught up with the regiment.[12]

The three companies that did not make the trip—a machine-gun company and Companies A and F, consisting of twenty-two officers and 404 enlisted men—were left behind in quarantine at Camp Jackson under the command of Lieutenant Colonel Brambila because a few cases of mumps and measles had developed within their ranks. Finally, on 8 April, the three companies were released from quarantine and moved to Camp A. P. Hill, Virginia; on 10 April they were moved to Newport News.[13]

Brambila's detachment, reduced to twenty-one officers and 365 men, and joined by a few casuals from the 370th and 372d Infantry Regiments, boarded the troopship SS *Matawaska*, the former German liner *Koenig Wilhelm II*. The vessel left Newport News on 15 April, met a convoy of seven ships and a naval cruiser, the USS *Seattle*, at sea, and arrived at Saint-Nazaire on 28 April. The detachment, after a change in destination orders, finally joined up with the regiment on 5 May.[14]

The 371st Infantry, minus the nineteen officers coming on another ship and the companies quarantined in the United States, departed Pontanezen Barracks on 26 April on a French train made up of 40-and-8 freight cars. Their orders were to go to Givry-en-Argonne, a town close to the front lines, but no other information was provided.[15] The train journeyed through the French countryside for two days and nights, arriving at Givry-en-Argonne to find no American staff officers or billeting officers waiting to meet them. Even more puzzling to Colonel Miles, the French stationmaster was surprised to see American troops at his depot. Miles ordered the train run back a few kilometers to a junction with telephone communications so that he could call AEF Headquarters at Chaumont for clarification and instructions.[16]

When they reached the junction, a French railway transportation officer approached Miles to inform him that his destination was a town called Vaubecourt a few kilometers up the other branch of the railroad. Miles thanked the man for the information but still called the adjutant at AEF Headquarters. He informed the staff officer of the circumstances and told him that a French officer at the station had told him that the regiment was to proceed to Vaubecourt. When the adjutant asked why Miles had not taken the regiment on to Vaubecourt as instructed, Miles replied, "This is the first information that I have had that I am to obey any French Army officer that I happen to find at a railway station or anywhere else."[17] The adjutant then told the shocked Miles the news that General Pershing had turned the regiment over to the French Army and that he was to do whatever the French transportation officer directed.[18]

The train carrying the regiment arrived at Vaubecourt station at 1:00 AM on 29 April to find a cluster of French staff officers waiting. The French officers were aghast at the amount of arms and equipment the regiment had brought with it. But, of course, they knew what Miles and his officers did not know—that the 371st Infantry, like the other regiments of the 93d Division, was to be issued French arms and equipment and be reorganized into the French regimental formation.[19] The French officers were not at all pleased at having to find secure storage for two thousand Springfield rifles and tens of thousands of rounds of .30-06 ammunition. The French and American officers immediately began trying to overcome the language barrier and make order of the chaos caused by the lack of prior coordination between the French and American authorities. Meanwhile, the men crawled out of the tiny French freight cars into a drenching rain and began a long and dreary march toward the billeting towns and their first real taste of war.[20]

The 372d Infantry

Early on the morning of 30 March 1918, the officers and men of the 372d Infantry shouldered their rifles and packs at their cantonment area at Camp Stuart, Virginia, and started on the march that would take them ultimately to France. Their destination on this day was the SS *Susquehanna*, an old German freighter formerly called the *Rhine*, which had been taken as enemy contraband at the declaration of war. By 7:00 AM the regiment had marched the long mile from their barracks to the *Susquehanna* and started boarding. By mid-afternoon all troops had been assigned sleeping berths and all equipment was stored on board. Shortly after 4:00 PM the ship left its dock to move into Hampton Roads to anchor near another vessel on its way to France.[21]

Family members and friends watched from the shore as the ship moved away from the dock. Monroe Mason and Arthur Furr, who served with the regiment, later recounted the contrasting feelings of the men on board the ship and those left behind:

> A number of curious onlookers had gathered on the outside of the pier to witness the sailing. Many of them were friends of the men who were confined to the bowels of the ship and they looked in vain for a last glance or a last smile. A sad feeling predominated on the shore, while the feelings on the boat could scarcely be classified. Some felt the spirit of adventure, some joy in the change of location, some sadness in leaving their friends; others wondered about the future and what it had in store for them.[22]

At lights-out that evening, the men settled into the crude temporary wood bunks in their quarters belowdecks to get some sleep, trying to ignore the cramped space, poor ventilation, and strange creaks and groans of a ship at anchor.[23]

The next morning, which was Easter Sunday, the officers and men of the regiment awoke to find that they were on the high seas out of sight of land, and that other ships had joined up into a large convoy shepherded by a gray U.S. warship. Like the voyages of the 372d Infantry's sister regiments, the first part of the trip was mostly routine with the exception of some rough seas generated by a twenty-four-hour storm on the tenth day out.[24] After the storm had passed and almost everyone had recovered from the seasickness it caused, the monotony began again but was cut short by some real excitement. On the eleventh day a vessel believed to be a submarine appeared on the horizon, and alarms clanged throughout the ship. The regiment's officers and men had donned their life preservers and gone to their bunks when a loud explosion shook the ship from bow to stern. Imaginations ran wild, and rumors soon raced throughout the belowdecks compartments that the ship had been torpedoed and was in danger of sinking. A collective sigh of relief was breathed when the word came down that the explosion was the noise of a 3-pound gun on the stern of the ship that had been practice-fired by the ship's naval gun crew.[25]

After twelve days at sea, fourteen fast destroyers came up from the east to take the convoy on to France. The single escort warship saluted the new arrivals, turned the convoy over to the destroyers, and headed back to the United States. Toward late afternoon the coastline of Europe was sighted, and on the morning of 13 April the convoy entered the Loire River channel and docked at Saint-Nazaire.[26]

The following day, under an overcast sky and intermittent rain, the regiment disembarked and marched five kilometers to Base Section No. 1, an area with temporary barracks where they set up camp and settled in for the first night of rest on shore for nearly two weeks.[27] The next morning, still under overcast skies, the men of the 372d Infantry were loaded onto trucks and sent to work as stevedores handling cargo on the docks at Saint-Nazaire and in the railroad yards at Montoir, a few kilometers away. The men, for the most part, did not object to the required work, although many began to fear that they might end up as laborers and not go to the front as combat troops at all.[28]

One of the first incidents of racial discrimination suffered by a member of the 93d Division in France occurred while this regiment was in the Saint-Nazaire area. One of the men engaged in stevedore work complained of being ill. A white officer, not of the regiment and believing the soldier was feigning illness, kicked him, and other soldiers in the area came immediately to his defense. White noncommissioned officers supervising the workers produced firearms and ordered the troops back to work. Word was sent to the officers of the regiment, who investigated the incident and registered a complaint with the commanding officer of the port. The officer promised a prompt investigation and a court-martial if conditions warranted. Colonel Young was duly notified and registered his own concern, but what action was taken in the matter—if any—is unknown.[29]

That same day, an incident occurred in the camp area that directly reflected Young's failure from the very beginning to deal effectively with issues of racial discrimination and bigotry within his regiment. When the black officers returned to their billets that evening they found that someone had partitioned the spacious one-room building, confining the black officers to a small area at the back. Although the black officers complained to Young, no action was taken to have the partition removed, and most of the black officers found lodging in other parts of the camp. This incident, compounded by Young's removal and transfer of several black officers without apparent reason before the unit left the United States, further eroded the morale of the black members of the regiment.[30]

After ten days at Saint-Nazaire, orders came in attaching the 372d Infantry to the French 63d Infantry Division of the French XIII Corps for training.

The regiment was ordered to move to a new station nearer the front, and on 22 April the men marched to Montoir and boarded a train bound for Vaubecourt-en-Barrois (Condé-en-Barrois). The regiment had the pleasure of riding in comparative style since the train, like that of the 369th Infantry, was made up of small passenger coaches and not the 40-and-8 freight cars used by the 371st Infantry—which is not to say that the accommodations were spacious. Each section of the French train was intended to transport a French battalion, but an equivalent U.S. Army battalion was much larger, and eight to ten soldiers with all of their equipment had to be crowded into coach compartments designed to carry six.[31] Further, the weather happened to be quite warm at the coast at that time, the train lacked lights and sanitary facilities, and the tracks were so much in need of repair that the train could travel no faster than twenty-five to thirty kilometers per hour. The trip became quite uncomfortable for men forced to eat, sleep, and live in the cramped compartments for two long days.[32] As the train progressed toward the front lines the weather conditions turned cooler, making the trip more comfortable. And the trains stopped from time to time at villages along the way where the men could jump down for a quick breath of fresh air and some morale boosting in the form of warm greetings by the local townspeople.[33]

The first section of the train arrived in Vaubecourt-en-Barrois on 24 April at 7:00 PM, and the second and third sections arrived at 9:00 and 10:00 PM. The men stepping down from their cramped cars saw flashes of light from intermittent artillery fire and the ghostly glare of illuminating flares floating in the sky at the front to the north. Even over the barking of noncommissioned officers and the noise of the men assembling, a low rumble could be heard from the direction of the front. An artillery duel between French guns just a few kilometers away and German guns countering their fire was escalating. German shells searching for the French guns were dropping in and exploding behind the French lines. The apprehensive officers and men of the 372d Infantry were seeing and hearing their first signs of a new and strange adventure called war.[34]

CHAPTER 9

The 370th Starts
Combat Training

Everywhere there were double lines of barbed wire stretched in our path in every conceivable way, and the constant rattle of machine-gun fire was like the constant rain-drops in a storm.

Sgt. Oscar Walker, 370th Infantry, at Saint-Mihiel

On 15 april 1918 the officers and men of the 370th Infantry Regiment left their cramped but dry quarters at the Pontanezen Barracks in Brest to spend the next two days riding in the cramped, cold, rattling 40-and-8 freight cars.[1] Traveling at a snail's pace, the regiment rode all the way across France, finally arriving at the village of Morvillas, near Belfort, in the Vosges Mountains region close to the border of Switzerland and the old boundary with Germany. After detraining and getting organized, the officers and men of the regiment marched on for four more kilometers to the town of Grandvillars and comfortable billets in the homes of the townspeople.[2]

Colonel Denison was quickly informed that the 370th Infantry had been turned over to the French Army and attached to the French 73d Infantry Division. As the men of their sister regiments had done, his men spent the next few days exchanging American equipment and arms for French issue, reorganizing from an American regiment into the makeup of a French regiment, and then training in French tactics.[3]

The regiment made good use of the training time and on 19 May was transferred to the French 133d Infantry Division. On 1 June the regiment received orders transferring it to the French 10th Infantry Division. After the last transfer, the regiment moved forward to occupy a quiet sector in the front lines near the town of Montbéliard on the Swiss border to gain experience in the trenches. Less than two weeks later, after getting little more than a bare feel for life in the front lines, the regiment boarded a train on 12 June and moved back toward the west bound for Lignières in the Saint-Mihiel sector. There, on 17 June, it joined the French 34th Infantry Division, which was holding the tip of the Saint-Mihiel salient (see map 1).[4]

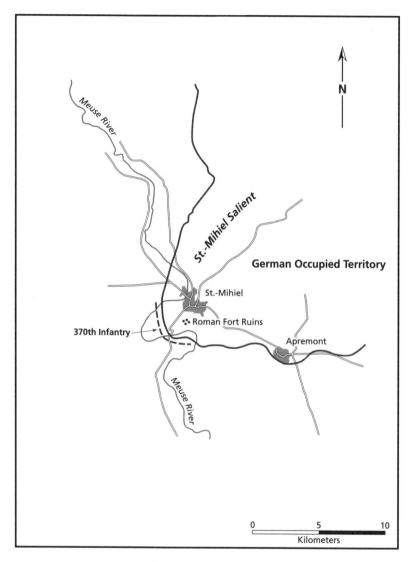

*Map. 1. 370th Infantry Operations at Saint-Mihiel,
22 June to 3 July 1918*

On 21 June the 1st and 2d Battalions began moving into the trenches at the tip of the salient, a much more active area than they had been exposed to in the Vosges. The regiment completed the move on 24 June, locating just south of the town of Saint-Mihiel near the site of an old Roman fort. The battalions were cycled in and out of the front lines, intermingling in the trenches with the platoons and companies of the battle-hardened French 325th Infantry Regiment, which afforded an excellent opportunity for close-in training with combat-experienced troops.[5]

Sgt. Oscar Walker found the front line in his sector overwhelming: "The hill afforded natural protection for enormous guns of every description and in unlimited quantities—they were skillfully placed. Saint Mihiel forest, here large trees of every description help to make this place the 'Gates of Hell!'"[6] For the moment the sector was quiet. Only sporadic shelling, scattered rifle and machine-gun fire, and the occasional patrol assignments and manning of forward outposts broke the monotony. Beyond these activities, little of special interest occurred during the regiment's stay in the lines in the Saint-Mihiel area, and fortunately the regiment suffered no serious casualties.[7]

The regiment was relieved on the line on 1–3 July and moved to the vicinity of the town of Lignières in the Meuse-Argonne. After a short rest there, the men were moved by train to an area near the Argonne Forest. They detrained at the town of Les Islettes, which was located in the middle of the Argonne Forest and in the valley of the Biesme River. The officers and men then marched through Clermont-en-Argonne to Rarecourt in the vicinity of Auzeville and the Aire sector, about twenty kilometers southwest of Verdun, where, on 6 July, the regiment joined the French 36th Infantry Division for an extended period of training in the lines.[8]

Maj. Rufus Stokes's 1st Battalion moved into reserve positions at Brabant and prepared to man frontline trenches at Subsector Hermont. Maj. Charles Hunt's 2d Battalion billeted at Rarecourt with forward positions designated at Locheres, where companies of the battalion were slated to begin moving into the lines on five-day training cycles. Maj. Arthur Williams's 3d Battalion was billeted at Vraincourt and placed in reserve, with only Company M directed to take up frontline positions at Buzemont from 7 to 14 August. The experience gained in this sector was to be the 370th Infantry's final training; the next scheduled move would put the regiment into full frontline service on its own at the highly active Château-Thierry sector near the Marne River.[9]

At some point within this time frame, prior to 12 July, Colonel Denison apparently became concerned about the level of training the regiment had received to date. When Denison received his orders to move to the Château-Thierry sector, his reply to the general commanding the French 36th Infantry Division was to the effect that "his men were not competent to take over a sector of such an important front, that they were neither American or French soldiers, being in a transitory state; having been deprived of American equipment and without sufficient time to master the French equipment they were not half as good as an American or French soldier."[10] The immediate result of Denison's statement was that the 370th Infantry was excused from frontline duty at Château-Thierry and ordered to remain at Rarecourt.[11]

Denison was relieved of his command soon after this incident, causing a storm of controversy within the regiment over the intent of General Pershing and AEF Headquarters regarding the command structure of the regiment.[12] Among the rumors circulating through the regiment was one that Denison was ill and his health would not allow him to withstand the rigors of a frontline command. Col. Thomas A. Roberts, assigned to the 370th Infantry by AEF Headquarters as an official observer and destined to command the regiment, had, in fact, expressed concern about Denison and had questioned Chaplain Braddan about Denison's physical health relative to his ability to handle combat duty.[13]

Denison was fifty-six years old, but no official record seems to exist regarding the condition of his health; nor is there any indication that his age affected his ability to do his duty. There was, however, a policy in force within the AEF aimed at weeding out older officers who were not, or seemed not to be, mentally, physically, or emotionally capable of standing up to the rigors of modern warfare. Pershing was adamant about having fit commanders, to the point of excluding some men who had once been his staunch supporters. He also had his own model of what a senior officer should be, and that did not necessarily include being outspoken about the facts at hand.[14]

In his service memoir Braddan accused Colonel Roberts of maneuvering the situation to obtain a combat command for himself. It is true that Roberts monitored the activities of the 370th Infantry and one other regiment of the 93d Division for AEF Headquarters, had the ear of higher command, and could well have influenced the decision. Braddan was also very outspoken in his belief that Roberts was bigoted and hated blacks. Roberts was, Braddan said, the "arch enemy, vilifier and traducer of the Negro soldier."[15]

If Roberts was indeed such a bigot, it is difficult to comprehend why he would have wanted command of a black regiment. W. Allison Sweeney of the *Chicago Defender*, who was also in a position to observe the events, had a different view of Roberts: "Colonel Roberts, a veteran cavalryman, was very fond of his men. He has repeatedly paid them the highest compliments, not only for their valor and soldierly qualities, but for their quick intelligence, amenity to discipline, and for the clean living which made them so remarkably free from disease."[16]

Braddan further accused Roberts of intending to replace the entire officer corps of the 370th Infantry with white officers, but that seems not to have been the case either. When Roberts took command, he brought with him only two white officers, and he added only one other at a later date.[17]

A report on the regiment submitted to AEF Headquarters may well have been the pivotal factor in the relief of Denison. The report, by Capt. George Marvin, the regiment's liaison with AEF Headquarters, was made on 14 June and stated various shortcomings, concluding: "From all of the above it is clearly evident that this regiment is unavailable for service at the front now and, in my opinion, will not be fit for two months to come, if ever. It was plainly evident that there had been a serious loss of morale throughout the entire regiment."[18]

Notwithstanding Braddan's opinion and the rumors that Denison was relieved because of ill health, his replacement seems to have had more to do with timing and with the French Army's lack of attention to the training needs of the regiment, although AEF Headquarters apparently made no effort to step in and correct the situation. Two other factors may have been involved as well: Pershing tended to follow a "one strike and you're out" policy with subordinate commanders, and he may have wanted to replace all National Guard officers with the rank of colonel and above with Regular Army officers.[19]

There seems to be no doubt that the regiment lacked the training necessary to survive in the trenches. Since its arrival in France, the 370th Infantry had been shipped across the entire country to the eastern border in the Vosges Mountains and then back to several points in between. During that time the regiment had been shifted from one French division to another and had been with the French 36th Infantry Division only six days when Denison was relieved. Marvin, in his report, expressed concern about poor liaison between the regiment and its French advisers due to language barriers and the change in instructors and equipment three times in three weeks. These factors and others mentioned in Marvin's report were not the fault of Denison and must have been an enormous hindrance to training. Furthermore, the unit had no experience with liaison and had not had a chance to develop a working relationship with the new division headquarters. The officers and men of the regiment were acting under a severe handicap when they tried to handle the new and unusual requirements being thrown at them by the French Army command.[20]

Denison, who was certainly aware of these problems, and of Marvin's report as well, had cause to ask that his regiment be excused from the anticipated heavy combat in the Château-Thierry sector to be given further training. As a reward for his moral courage and integrity in stating the facts, Denison seems to have been made a scapegoat to cover the embarrassment caused by the failure of both the French commanders and AEF Headquarters to properly handle and prepare the regiment for a major combat assignment.[21] The three sister regiments of the 93d Division, it should be noted, serving under a different French command structure, fared much better in their training and preparation for combat.[22] What a galling experience it must have been for Denison. After guiding the regiment through the mobilization process, overcoming training problems at home, and then bringing his officers and men to France to fight, he found himself relieved of command just as his efforts should have been reaching their culmination.[23]

Col. Thomas A. Roberts, Cavalry Corps, a Regular Army officer and graduate of the U.S. Military Academy, took command of the regiment on 12 July 1918.[24] At the time Roberts assumed command, Majors Stokes, Hunt, and Williams, all black officers, commanded the battalions of the regiment. In the course of events these positions would be reshuffled and some officers replaced, but in spite of Braddan's accusations that Roberts and AEF Headquarters were intent on replacing all of the black officers of the regiment with white officers, Roberts brought with him, as previously mentioned, only two other white officers. Maj. W. H. Roberts of the Regular Army, Roberts's brother, would serve as operations officer; and 2d Lt. M. F. Stapleton was assigned to the 1st Battalion as adjutant. One other white officer joined the regiment at a later date, but all of the black officers remained with the regiment throughout its combat experiences in the war, and two of them served as battalion commanders.[25]

Shortly after 12 July, the regiment began moving battalions into the lines; the men continued to train in combat situations in the Auzeville area up until 18 August. The 1st Battalion, which had already moved into reserve positions on 6 July at Brabant (S. Groupement Courcelles), was ordered into the front lines at Subsector Hermont. The 2d Battalion moved into the area of Rarecourt and then on to Locheres, where companies were sent into the lines on five-day tours in the trenches. The 3d Battalion was held in reserve at Vraincourt, with Company M moving into the lines for fourteen days of training at Buzecourt.[26]

The men performed the usual frontline activities—manning outposts and sending patrols to work in no-man's-land, the area between the Allied and German front lines. During this time the officers and men remained under constant incoming artillery fire and sporadic machine-gun and rifle fire, yet casualties were fortunately light; when the regiment left the area it had suffered only one soldier killed, one captured, and four wounded.[27] The man who was killed, the first for the 370th Infantry, was Pvt. Robert Lee of the 2d Machine Gun Company; he was buried at Vraincourt. His death came about just before noon on 14 July when heavy German artillery fire, marking the beginning of a German offensive, landed on the regiment's positions.[28]

After the additional training in the trenches, the officers and men of the regiment began to feel more at home with their new surroundings and equipment. On 1 August the Stokes mortar platoon commanded by Lt. Robert A. Ward was detached and sent into the lines in Subsector Vaquois to support a French force in a coup-de-main scheduled for 4 August. Ward's platoon was charged with giving fire support to the attacking forces by filling in gaps as they developed during the covering French artillery barrage. The platoon fired more than three hundred rounds on targets in the zone. At the completion of the mission, the French division commander commended Ward and his men for their work.[29]

On 15 August the 370th Infantry was again reassigned, this time being placed under General Vincendon's French 59th Infantry Division, a part of General Mangin's Tenth Army, where it remained until the end of the war.[30] The French 59th Infantry Division had recently been ordered out of the front lines and into reserve in the vicinity of Mareuil-de-Ourcq at La Ferté–Milon after being badly mauled during battles at Chavigny, Leury, and the Bois-de-Braumont. The division was gravely under strength, and Vincendon began immediate reorganization by bringing two of his French regiments—the 232d Infantry and the 325th Infantry—up to strength with the remnants of a decimated third regiment. The general assigned the newly arrived 370th Infantry as the third regiment of his division. At the time it reported for duty to the division, the 370th Infantry was twice the size of each of the two reconstituted sister French regiments, and as a consequence, much of the heavy work that lay ahead was to fall on the shoulders of the Americans.[31]

The French 59th Infantry Division moved back of the lines to the Bar-le-Duc area on 18 August. The 370th Infantry marched east to the village of Rampont to board a train, which took it to the vicinity of Fains to participate in open-warfare training. After completing training, the regiment moved on 1 September to the vicinity of La Ferté–Milon, sixty kilometers northeast of Paris, where it arrived on 4 September with the rest of the French 59th Infantry Division to rejoin the French Tenth Army.[32]

On 11 September Majors Hunt and Williams were relieved as commanders of the 2d and 3d Battalions, reportedly due to illness and injury, and sent to the rear. According to Chaplain Braddan, they were both demoted to captain, although there is no note of that in the official records. Capt. John H. Patton, previously the regimental adjutant, was assigned to command the 2d Battalion, and Lt. Col. Otis B. Duncan was assigned to command the 3d Battalion. Both officers proved to be excellent choices for battalion commanders; they were capable, courageous, efficient, and energetic in their new assignments.[33]

The French 59th Infantry Division enjoyed nearly a month of rest and training, mostly for the benefit of its two exhausted French regiments, but also giving the 370th Infantry time for further training and indoctrination. At the end of the month-long rest, the division received orders to return to the front lines to join the French XIII Corps of the French Tenth Army. On 15 September the officers and men of the 370th Infantry boarded trucks, locally known as "camions," near the village of Mareuil-sur-Ourcq and arrived at dusk at a destroyed town called Saint-Bandry.[34]

The men bedded down for the night as best they could, although there was little hospitality to be found in the ruins of the town. Pvt. Isaac Fisher of Company G described the move to the front; his description mirrors the experiences of all of the officers and men of the regiments that served at one time or another in France:

> September 14th we were resting in a small village named Maroles, when we received the order to move on to Soissons front. That was a very hot front at that time. France had just started her 1918 fall drive. The next day they loaded us on trucks driven by Frenchmen and we were carried within 30 kilometers of Soissons to a small shell-shattered town, Ambreny. Here we rested over night. The next day we began the hike which carried us into the danger zone. We arrived there about 2:00 AM We were told to stay in the trenches by Captain Johnson until morning. It was dark and cloudy but no rain. At the end of the trench there was a dead Fritz. Of course, I did not like him there but there was nothing for me to do but remain with him until morning. Being worn out and tired I fell asleep. In about an hour I was awakened—the Frenchmen were throwing a barrage. It was raining also and we were wet to our skins.[35]

Fortunately for Fisher and the rest of the officers and men, the regiment remained in the vicinity of Saint-Bandry for the next two days, resting and bringing in supplies and equipment to come to battle readiness. The division had already received orders to prepare to move north to a forward position and then into the trenches.[36] Artillery and air bombardments kept everyone aware that the front was just a few kilometers away, yet few knew or guessed that the regiment was about to undergo its first real test in combat along the Canal l'Oise–l'Aisne and the Bois de Mortier.[37]

CHAPTER 10

The 371st Goes into the Trenches

4 hours off—2 hours on—
And not a thing to do but think,
And watch the mud and twisted wire
And never let your peepers blink.
Two hours on—4 hours off—
The dug-out's slimy as the trench;
It stinks of leather and stale smoke—
You wake up dopey from the stench.

Four hours off—2 hours on—
Back to the same old trick again,
The same old noth'n' to do at all
From yesterday till God knows when.
On post or not it's just the same.
The waiting is what gets your goat
And makes you want to chuck the game
Or risk a trench knife in your throat.

Two hours on—4 hours off—
I s'pose our job is not so hard,—
I s'pose sometime we're going to quit—
. . . .
The ghosts we leave—do they stand guard?

"That Quiet Sector," Pvt. Hilmar R. Baukhage,
371st Infantry, Avocourt sector, France, 1918

After stepping down from the 40-and-8 freight cars at the railhead at Vaube-court on 30 April, the officers and men of the 3d Battalion, 371st Infantry, formed up and marched six kilometers in the predawn darkness through pouring rain to the village of Rembercourt-aux-Pots. The 1st and 2d Battalions had arrived at Vaubecourt the previous day and were now quartered at Maratsla-Grande and Marats-le-Petite. All of the villages were between thirty and forty kilometers from Verdun, and the faint booming of artillery fire off to the north brought the war to the forefront of everyone's thinking.[1]

The regiment, like its sister groups, was here introduced to the system of billeting commonly used and accepted by the French people but foreign to American soldiers because the practice is outlawed in the United States. The enlisted men were quartered in barns and other available buildings, and one or two officers were placed in each home, usually in a single room, for which the owners were well paid.[2]

The U.S. Army's practice of keeping troop quarters in the cleanest possible condition caused some conflicts with the local inhabitants. The well-manicured manure piles kept in and around barns were important to the local people for fertilizing gardens, but they conflicted with the U.S. Army's ideas of sanitation and tidiness. And the centuries of accumulated cobwebs in the barns seemed to have some kind of intrinsic value for the French while to Americans they were a sign of poor housekeeping. Attempts to remove both items brought vigorous protests from the landowners, and for the time being, the fastidious requirements of the first sergeants of the U.S. Army in barracks living had to take a backseat to international goodwill.[3]

Colonel Miles learned through conversation with the French officers who had met the train at Vaubecourt that his regiment was at present an independent unit of the French Army attached to the French 154th Infantry Division of the French XIII Corps. Since all orders were being received at the regiment in French, Major Coupé of the French Army and two enlisted men were assigned to regimental headquarters to ensure that the orders were understood. Likewise, a high-level noncommissioned officer was stationed at each battalion and a private was sent to each company to serve as both interpreters and advisers in the ways of the French Army.[4]

Immediately after the arrival of the French advisers the 371st Infantry went through the same procedures the other regiments of the 93d Division either already had or would experience. The officers and men exchanged rifles, helmets, packs, and other equipment for French issue; received ARS gas masks, Chauchat and Hotchkiss machine guns, and other strange arms and items; and the regiment was reorganized on the model of a French infantry regiment.[5] With French advisers assigned, French equipment issued, and reorganization completed, the regiment plunged into training. The training area was close enough to the front for the men to hear artillery firing; at night, flashes from guns and exploding shells could be seen in the distance toward Verdun. To further the awareness of what was in store for the regiment at the front, officers were sent up in two groups at separate times to spend a twenty-four-hour period in the trenches with French counterparts.[6]

One group's visit to the sector of the village of Esnes proved more exciting than anticipated because it coincided with a series of German attacks in support of the Aisne offensive in May. The attack that occurred in the Esnes area proved to be a demonstration of no more than two German battalions. However, the heavy artillery support for the attack continued throughout the twenty-four-hour period, with a number of shells falling close to a command post occupied by some of the regiment's officers. It was a hair-raising experience, and more than the group had bargained for, as they had been told they were going to a quiet sector.[7]

On 2 June the French XIII Corps sent orders to the 371st Infantry to proceed to an area at the extreme tip of the Saint-Mihiel salient to relieve a French regiment and take over a sector. The regiment had started toward the sector when a change in orders on 6 June directed it to march north to Sivry-la-Perche, Bois Bourrus, Vigneville, and the Bois de Bethlainville instead. The regiment had been reassigned to the Verrières sector between the Aire and Meuse rivers; once there, it became a permanent regiment of the French 157th (Red Hand) Infantry Division commanded by Brig. Gen. Mariano F. J. Goybet.[8]

On arrival in the assigned sector, the regiment was detailed to the French 68th Infantry Division for further training and the men took up support positions behind the lines. On 16 June the regiment was ordered into the Avocourt subsector to prepare to relieve an Italian regiment of the Garibaldi Brigade attached to the French 68th Infantry Division.[9] To facilitate the inexperienced 371st Infantry's movement onto the line, Goybet arranged with the commanding general of the French 68th Infantry Division to have his French 344th Infantry first relieve the Italians. The French regiment then remained in the trenches for several days while the officers of the 371st Infantry became acquainted with the area. After the entire regiment moved on the line, the French company commanders remained for another twenty-four hours to ensure that all was going well. The regimental operations officer had published well-prepared and detailed orders, and the transition progressed so well that the German units facing the regiment were not aware of the change until several days later.[10]

The subsector manned by the 371st Infantry was defined on the extreme right by the destroyed village of Avocourt in the Hesse Forest. The line then extended east, roughly along La Buanthe Rau to the left boundary line near Vauquois Hill. At some places along the front the opposing trenches were only forty meters apart. Beyond the right boundary of the subsector was Hill 304, which was located just north of Esnes and of some fame in the area. To the north of Avocourt was the village of Montfaucon, atop the hill of the same name. In this area Crown Prince Wilhelm of Germany, commanding an army group named after him, had placed a high observation post that made any movement in the open during daylight hours extremely dangerous. Anyone foolish enough to expose himself above the trench parapet for very long could expect to receive fire from artillery, machine guns, and snipers.[11]

Just after dark on the 371st Infantry's first night on its own in the trenches, rifle and machine-gun fire broke out on part of the regiment's front. Before regimental headquarters could get a messenger up to the line to find out what was happening, French artillery shells began roaring overhead. As no German artillery shells were falling on the lines or around the regimental command post, Colonel Miles realized that a ghost fight initiated by the inexperienced troops of the 371st Infantry was in progress.[12] Miles had decided to wait for the battalion commander to reach the same conclusion when Coupé, the French adviser, grabbed the field telephone and excitedly called the French adviser at the battalion, ordering him to stop the firing. The gunfire along the line soon dwindled and then ceased. Coupé's call, however, was in direct interference with Miles's command and soon got him relieved of his duties. Coupé's replacement, Capt. Anton Lebre, proved to be a much abler officer with a cooler disposition under fire.[13]

The battalions were scheduled to cycle into the lines for two weeks and then back to rest and recuperate for one week. When their turn came, the officers and men of each battalion quickly settled into the routine of living in the trenches. During the day the men went on sentry duty or work details such as repairing trench walls damaged the night before by artillery activity. When not on some kind of work detail, they ate their meals, cleaned their weapons, slept, wrote letters, and played poker or craps if anyone had money left to bet. The officers inspected trench conditions and weapons dispositions, wrote reports, read and prepared orders, and planned raids; when they were done with their official duties, they engaged in writing letters or in other personal activities.[14] Observers peered across no-man's-land—either through carefully concealed observation ports or through periscopes—trying to see what was happening at the German trench line. No one dared raise his head above the trench parapet because German snipers equipped with rifles with telescopic sights were hiding at concealed points along the line. These sharpshooters lay quietly watching through ports or periscopes, waiting for some careless soldier to show himself long enough for a shot, which was always accurate and almost always fatal.[15]

As soon as night fell, the heavy activity began. In addition to occasional raiding parties and patrols going through the wire, work details repaired the forward sides and parapets of trenches or dug and fortified new outposts. Wire parties went forward into no-man's-land to install and repair wire entanglements. Behind the trenches, supply details brought rations, ammunition, engineering materials, and mail up from the rear. The occasional flare, sporadic machine-gun fire, or random artillery shell would cause everyone in the open to drop to the ground or scurry for cover, only to rise and continue his work as soon as the threat had subsided. As dawn approached and the sky began to grow light in the east, the men exposed above ground rushed to complete their tasks and get to their trench or dugout. By the time there was enough light to see across the battlefield, no human form remained visible to the observers watching from the trench lines looking for any significant changes made by the other side in the battlefield during the night.[16]

Although the front along which the 371st Infantry was deployed was considered a quiet area, raids of various sizes were conducted to acquaint the officers and men of the regiment with life in a combat zone. The primary intent of such raids was to capture German officers or noncommissioned officers for interrogation in order to determine what was happening across the wire that might be of interest to intelligence officers. Of major importance were changes made in infantry units, construction of new fortifications, addition of artillery units, and other unusual occurrences that might indicate a major German offensive action along what was normally a quiet front.[17]

The division commander sent word that the 371st Infantry was to be given additional training in anticipation of a major raid to be made into the German lines. Execution of this unique raid would require exact timing of all of the assets being employed but laid a particularly heavy responsibility on the artillery and mortar batteries. Their success in executing the plan would determine whether the raiding party could get through German wire obstacles and then safely past the machine-guns emplacements to reach the target area.[18] In order for the raid to be successful, the supporting artillery would have to fire its missions in sequence. The guns would first attack and destroy any machine-gun posts protecting the target area and the route of the raiding party. When the raid commander judged that those threats had been sufficiently suppressed, the artillery, supported by Stokes mortars, would deliver a box barrage around the target area to isolate it and cut through protective barbed-wire entanglements. When the raiding party was positioned and ready for its attack, the artillery would move to its third mission. All guns would mount a barrage behind the target area to prevent any occupants from escaping back to the German trenches and to deter reinforcements. If necessary and available, the artillery assets could also engage in counterbattery fire.[19]

The raid was ordered for the night of 5 August, to be conducted by elements of the French 333d Infantry Regiment, the 371st Infantry, and the 372d Infantry, which had joined the French 157th Infantry Division as its third regiment. The attack was to be made in an area northwest of Avocourt known as the Triangle. Lt. Allen G. Thurman, Cpl. Arthur Floyd, and Cpl. Alonzo Kearse of Company C of the 371st Infantry and a lieutenant and two corporals of the 372d Infantry were detailed to accompany the raiding party. The complete raiding party was made up of seventy officers and men led by a French captain assisted by two French lieutenants. The two French lieutenants and Thurman made a preliminary reconnaissance of the sector on 24 July. Using the information they gained, miniature trenches and outposts were laid out to scale, and training over the mock area continued for another two weeks. At the end of the training period the members of the raiding party felt confident that they were prepared to execute the raid.[20]

A platoon of the Stokes mortar battery of the 371st Infantry under Lt. Joe Roddey, assisted by Lt. Norman Thayer, was designated to assist the French Stokes mortar team in cutting the first and second of the three lines of wire in front of the targeted German position. A platoon from the 372d Infantry under Lieutenant Hames was also assigned to the team.[21] At the time the raid was ordered, no member of the 371st Infantry's Stokes mortar battery had even seen a Stokes mortar being fired, much less fired one; their training had consisted of using wooden sticks as props for mortars. Lieutenant Gouin, the man in charge of the French Stokes mortar team participating in the raid, had his men demonstrate how to operate the two guns to be used by the 371st Infantry in the raid, and a few rounds were fired for practice. That was all the training the platoon would receive before the raid. Fortunately, someone at headquarters decided this was a problem, and at the time of the raid the platoon was integrated into and assisted by the French Stokes mortar team.[22]

The fifth of August was a dreary day, with cloudy skies and intermittent but heavy rain falling throughout the afternoon. At 9:05 PM French 75-mm artillery batteries opened up as planned to deliver fire on machine-gun nests and other firing points along the route of the raid. At the same time, the Stokes mortars began their barrage on the first and second wire lines at the targeted German position. French artillery also attacked rear-area targets as a diversion, and in the process exploded an ammunition dump, causing an unexpected bit of excitement. The initial barrage continued for nine minutes, although the ten Stokes mortar teams had done their work within six minutes, in that short time expending around nine hundred rounds of ammunition.[23]

At about 9:15 PM the artillery batteries shifted their fire to lay a box around the targeted German position while the raiding party moved into position in front of the objective. The artillery batteries then lifted the portion of the barrage aimed at the front of the box, and the raiding party moved forward to attack the objective. As the party advanced, they found that the first and second lines of wire had been completely severed by the Stokes mortars. The third line, however, had not been completely cut by the 75-mm guns, and much of the wire was still intact.[24]

As the party tried to find a way through the entanglement they were detected; German machine guns that had not been suppressed by the artillery opened fire. At the same time, German artillery shells began to fall on the raiding party, resulting in about thirty casualties before the raiders could reach their objective. Of the 371st Infantry participants, Corporal Kearse was killed by a shell fragment wound to the stomach, and Corporal Floyd was severely wounded. The officer and both corporals from the 372d Infantry were wounded as well. The party was ordered back to its trenches, suffering further casualties as German shells continued to fall on the retreat.[25]

In after-action reports, controversy emerged over the origination point of some of the shells that rained down on the party at the wire and in the retreat. Accusations were made that the shells came from the Stokes mortar team, and French authorities gave some support to the accusation by theorizing that the heavy rains had caused the mortars to deliver short rounds. Further analysis of the reports indicated that the Stokes mortars were not responsible. The mortar teams had completed their mission at 9:14 PM and had already retired to their dugouts under a German artillery attack before the raiding party had started on its way toward the target. In the final analysis, it was determined that the Germans had simply saturated the area with artillery fire and that no casualties had been caused by friendly fire.[26] The mission's failure was attributed to the French artillery's failure to cut the last line of wire and suppress the supporting German machine guns. In his report to his French commander, Lieutenant Gouin commended the Stokes mortar sections of both the 371st Infantry and the 372d Infantry, citing their coolness and ability to accomplish their first mission while struggling with guns unfamiliar to them.[27]

The attack was a costly failure and a harsh lesson for the officers and men of the two American regiments. Yet, the lesson was not taken to heart by division headquarters. The two regiments were ordered to participate in a similar operation with the French on 18 August, which failed for the same reasons. Although no one in the 371st Infantry was injured on that raid, one of the 372d Infantry's officers, Lt. James E. Sanford, who was either wounded, lost in the confusion, or both, was captured by the Germans and spent the rest of the war in a prisoner-of-war camp.[28]

Lieutenant Roddey's platoon, this time with four guns in action, again performed well; the determination of his gunners was demonstrated in one notable occurrence. After expending about twenty rounds, mortar number four slipped out of position because the ground beneath it was too soft to support it. The crew leader, Cpl. George Byrd, stopped firing, shored up the mortar, and then continued his mission. When the mortar again slipped out of position, Byrd jumped astride the gun tube and held it with his legs for the rest of its scheduled fire. He was awarded the Croix de Guerre with Palm for his coolness and resourcefulness in action. Byrd paid a personal price for his courage and boldness, suffering permanent hearing loss in his left ear and hemorrhaging in his right ear.[29]

After the two large-scale raids using artillery failed, division headquarters considered using small-scale raids to gain their objective. The normal practice in such raids was to use ambush patrols: a small group would enter no-man's-land, hide, and wait for an unsuspecting German to pass close by, then subdue him and bring him back to the trenches for interrogation. These patrols were at best hit and miss, and had not been very successful. Division headquarters next decided to try sending in a deep-penetration patrol backed up by a large raiding party. If the deep-penetration patrol failed in its attempt, then the back-up large-scale raiding force would follow with a broad sweep of the entire area.[30]

During the first part of September, division headquarters ordered the new approach to be executed in the hope that the deep-penetration patrol would be able to enter German trenches and capture German officers for interrogation. The raid was to be conducted entirely by the 371st Infantry. Lt. John B. Given of Company H was selected to lead the smaller patrol, and Capt. William (Shag) Thorn was to conduct the follow-up large-scale raid in the event the smaller deep-penetration patrol was not successful.[31]

Given selected a force consisting of one other officer, Lt. J. L. (Pooch) Nelson; five noncommissioned officers; and twenty privates for the patrol action, which was scheduled for the night of 7–8 September. The plan called for the deep-penetration patrol to cross no-man's-land to the enemy wire and find an entry point. The entry point would be covered by Nelson and twenty men while Given went through the wire with five men and entered the German trenches to try to capture a German officer or high-level noncommissioned officer. The penetration patrol was to travel extremely light, each man carrying only a pistol with loaded magazine, a bolo knife, and six French O. Feuilette model 1915 rifle grenades for arms. In addition, two members of the party carried insulated wire cutters. Rations were to consist of a canteen filled with wine (obtained from the French since the regiment no longer received a wine ration) and a cheese sandwich.[32]

As the patrol set out on schedule, a severe lightning storm broke out, upsetting Given's compass and making land navigation impossible. The penetration patrol had already cleared its own wire and was moving forward when Given ordered it back and canceled the operation.[33] Given and his patrol tried again the next night but were foiled once more, this time by the Germans, who had apparently observed Given and a sergeant reconnoitering the area in front of the wire that afternoon and had guessed that something was going to happen. When the patrol left the forward trench to move into no-man's-land, German "potato masher" hand grenades fell among the group, followed by gunfire. Conjecturing that the Germans had sent out their own force to cut off the patrol and fearful that casualties would be incurred before even getting started,

Given again called off the action.[34] By this time both Miles and Given's battalion commander, Major Greenough, under pressure from division headquarters to capture prisoners for interrogation, were becoming impatient. Miles was considering conducting a full-scale raid with Captain Thorn's group, but Given argued for the original plan and was granted permission to try again.[35]

Given took his patrol out for the third time on 9–10 September. The weather was good for patrol action that night. There was a slight breeze from the German lines, and an overcast sky was producing rain, although on occasion the moon peeked through holes in the clouds. After about two hours spent crossing no-man's-land, Given had his patrol right up against the German wire in an old apple orchard. There he formed Nelson's covering force into a V with Nelson positioned at the point, which was touching the wire. Given, followed by Sergeants Ballard and Duncan, Corporal Logan, and Privates Grant and Green, then began crawling along the wire looking for a break. He soon found an opening that appeared to be used by the Germans for sending their patrols out into no-man's-land, and led his patrol through the gap into enemy-held territory.[36]

Given discovered an abandoned trench and crossed to another unoccupied trench, which appeared to have been in use during daylight hours. Germans could be heard talking nearby as the patrol crossed another vacant trench, passed between two lookout posts, and entered a vacant mortar emplacement. Soon thereafter Given found the connecting trench he was searching for. After lying in wait with his patrol for about fifteen minutes with no results, he took the patrol down the connecting trench until he found an unoccupied lookout post.[37] He continued to the next traverse and found another empty lookout post, from which he could hear Germans talking as they set up flares in some nearby location. He had started to go around to the next traverse when footsteps were heard approaching the patrol from behind. Given stationed his men on each side of the trench. When the first German soldier came near enough, Duncan stunned him with a haymaker to the face. The rest of the German party saw what was happening and beat a hasty retreat back the way they had come. The captured German appeared terrified and must have thought the black men with Given were Senegalese who were going to knife him on the spot. Instead, the patrol gathered up their prize and beat their own hasty retreat back to join the rest of the patrol. As the alerted Germans threw up flares and randomly fired machine guns, Given and his group crossed no-man's-land to the safety of the French lines.[38]

After turning the German prisoner, a sergeant, over to regimental headquarters for interrogation, Given related a story that added a flair of comic amusement to the whole operation: "One of my men said to me as we were bringing our prisoner back across no-man's-land, 'Lieutenant Given, . . . have we done gone and got twisted 'round and captured us a frog soldat?' Upon being assured that this certainly was a Boche and not a Frenchman, he said, 'Well, he sure smell[s] like one.'"[39]

For their actions in the successful execution of the penetration patrol, Given and the six men who captured the German sergeant were awarded the Croix de Guerre. In addition, the twenty-six members of the patrol divided up the sum of one thousand francs awarded by division headquarters along with ten days' leave in Paris.[40]

During the three months the 371st Infantry spent in the area west of Verdun, Colonel Miles had his headquarters located first at the Hermont command post and later, when the regiment shifted to the right in the line, at the Verrières command post. These command posts had once been used as division headquarters and contained spacious underground chambers that easily housed the entire regimental headquarters as well as the reserve battalion. The battalion was quartered in a two-story dugout capable of accommodating more than eight hundred officers and men, with separate quarters for the officers.[41]

Because the dugout had once been the division's headquarters, the regimental command post was located much farther from the front than Miles preferred to be. To ensure good communications whenever he made a trip to the lines, Miles took along a message runner from each battalion who knew the routes to take to get to his own battalion. When Miles was in the area of a particular battalion he would take with him a runner from each company, and so on, down to the outposts forward of the trenches.[42] The major duty of the runners was to carry official orders and messages between headquarters locations.

A runner's job is one of the most risky and dangerous in any army because it exposes him to artillery, machine-gun, and rifle fire as he crosses the open terrain going from place to place. Some of the bravest acts of heroism in combat have involved runners carrying critical messages to their commanders while under fire. The job requires a special kind of courage.[43]

Miles had noticed that one of the runners assigned to regimental headquarters seemed to lack the requisite courage to carry out his duties. Although the headquarters command post was located well behind the lines, German artillery shells frequently dropped into the area, and French guns located behind and around the command post fired missions around the clock. Every time a loud explosion occurred, whether it was generated by friendly or enemy artillery, the runner in question would leap into the nearest dugout and stay there, if permitted to, until the shooting ceased.[44]

Miles knew that the runner was efficient and conscientious and tried to do his best, and he wanted to keep him at his job, but he feared that under extreme combat conditions the man might prove unreliable. Miles suggested to Captain

Blossom, the regimental adjutant, that a twenty-four-hour stint with a company in the trenches might be a good lesson for the runner. Miles hoped that the experience would convince the man that his job at regimental headquarters was nothing compared with the hazards of a frontline runner and might calm him down.[45] When the man returned to the comparative safety of the regimental command post after his stay in the trenches, however, nothing had changed. Each time a German artillery shell fell or French guns in the vicinity fired, he would make for the nearest dugout unless on an assignment, in which case he would do exactly as ordered and deliver the message. For reasons unknown, perhaps because the runner performed his duties admirably in spite of his obvious fear, Miles let him remain a runner.[46] Miles never named the man in his memoirs, but he did mention that he had cited the runner as the bravest man he had ever seen—significant testimony coming from a man who himself had earned the Distinguished Service Cross.[47]

The list of awards and decorations for World War I mentions only one runner serving with the 371st Infantry. When the regiment was in the thick of its most violent action during the latter stages of the war, Pvt. Reuben Burrell earned the Distinguished Service Cross for the following:

> Disregarding personal danger he carried numerous messages across areas swept by the enemy's machine-gun and artillery fire on Hill 188, September 28, 1918, and by his fine spirit of courage served as an example to other members of his group. He was painfully wounded in the knee by a bursting shell on September 30, 1918, but refused to be evacuated as he said that there would not be enough men left in the group if he went to the rear.[48]

One can only wonder whether Burrell was the runner mentioned by Miles.[49]

By September the 371st Infantry had been in the Meuse-Argonne region for nearly four months and had enjoyed the good fortune of never having been attacked along its front by a major force. In the main, the activities of the battalions in the trenches consisted of numerous small patrols and two major raids. All in all, the regiment had gained valuable experience and seasoning in trench warfare while stationed along a quiet front. But things were about to change. Reports coming into regimental headquarters indicated the continuing deterioration of conditions within the German Army and on the German home front, and the buildup of American divisions in France. It was evident that a major action was soon to come.[50]

CHAPTER 11

The 372d Gets Its First Taste of Combat

The trees have long since been stripped of their bark and foliage and the bushes and shrubbery lie on the ground dead and withered, either dug up by the artillery or cut to pieces by shrapnel and machine-gun fire.

Monroe Mason and Arthur Furr, 372d Infantry

At about midnight on 24 April 1918, the battalions of the 372d Infantry completed detraining at the railhead at Vaubert-en-Barrois, formed up, and then stepped off on the march to their billeting area at the village of Condé-en-Barrois. The weather was quite cool, and the light from flares and artillery rounds exploding to the north reflected against the overcast sky.[1] The regiment had progressed less than three kilometers along the road when the sky opened up with a drenching rain. Under the heavy load of rifles, wet packs, and equipment, and with ankle-deep mud sucking at their feet, the rain-soaked and shivering men were soon exhausted, and some began falling out along the road. Fortunately for the stragglers, trucks carrying the regiment's baggage and equipment running between Condé-en-Barrois and Vaubert-en-Barrois were able to pick them up the next morning.[2]

Those hardy souls who completed the miserable nineteen-kilometer march to Condé-en-Barrois found that billeting had not been arranged for them, and they had to scramble about the village looking for any kind of shelter that would provide some protection from the heavy rain.[3] When the sun rose the following morning, the citizens of Condé-en-Barrois awoke to find soldiers in strange uniforms lying in abandoned hen coops, pigsties, haylofts, cattle pens, woodsheds, horse stalls, and anything else that could protect them from the rain. Those who could not find shelter had slept in the street, crowding up under the slight protection offered by building eaves. The crowded, stuffy— and warm and dry—train compartments must have become a fond memory during that night.[4]

The 372d Infantry was to remain in the area for thirty days while training under the wing of the French XIII Corps. Billeting arrangements were worked out the next day to accommodate the regiment for the training period, but many of the men found that the same shelters they had quickly settled into to get out of the rain would be their homes for the near future. Cleaning up the dirt and filth became the first order of business, and many cartloads of refuse were carted away before the makeshift quarters were livable.[5] Fortunately, a stream ran through the village, giving the men a place to wash up and refresh themselves after their housework.[6]

The next two days were given over to reorganizing on the French regimental pattern and trading in U.S. Army equipment for French issue. French instructors arrived from a Moroccan unit, and although most did not speak English at all and the few who did were not proficient, training got under way on 29 April. As with the other regiments of the 93d Division, the training consisted mainly of trench and outpost construction; handling and throwing grenades; learning to use the strange and clumsy French Lebel rifles, the temperamental Chauchat automatic rifles, and the excellent Hotchkiss machine guns; and learning to wear ARS gas masks. The troops progressed well and rapidly, bringing favorable comments from the French instructors and the regimental officers.[7]

On 3 May, while training was in progress in the field, the regiment got its first view of aerial combat when four German aircraft passed overhead on what appeared to be a reconnaissance and bombing mission. Four French aircraft came up to engage the Germans, and French antiaircraft guns joined in the fight. An aerial show progressed with airplanes climbing, diving, chasing, and shooting at each other while the antiaircraft guns banged away enthusiastically but with no noticeable effect. Finally, the German aircraft turned back toward the lines with the French planes in hot pursuit, and soon all had disappeared into the distance. The excitement provided fuel for lively discussions among the men for days afterward.[8]

On 14 May General Pershing inspected the ranks of the entire regiment, examining each officer and man and checking every detail. He must have been pleased with what he found, for he remarked: "These men are the making of a very able regiment."[9] By 18 May the French instructors and commanders considered the 372d Infantry's training sufficiently complete to send selected officers and men to serve for two weeks in the trenches with their French counterparts to get firsthand combat experience prior to committing the entire regiment on the line. While those select few spent time in the trenches, the remainder of the regiment continued training in the rear areas and waited for orders to move up. During this time, chilling news came back that the unit's first casualty had occurred: a lieutenant had been severely wounded at the line.[10]

On 27 May the regiment was ordered to move closer to the front to temporarily join the French 63d Infantry Division and to begin cycling battalions into the line for training under fire. The officers and men fell out at 5:00 AM the following day, boarded French camions, and after a dust-choked ride arrived at their destination a little after noon. Their new post was in the Aire sector on the Meuse-Argonne Front running from the Aire River to Le Four de Paris. The regimental headquarters was at the village of Les Senades in the valley of the Biesme River, which cuts through the center of the southern half of the Argonne Forest. Les Senades was about eight kilometers from the front and within easy German artillery range, although the Germans gave the village little attention. From Les Senades several units of the regiment marched to other villages close by for billeting and again found shelter in barns, sheds, and other farm buildings.[11]

On 1 June orders arrived from the French command designating the 372d Infantry an organic regiment of the French 63d Infantry Division, and Colonel Young received instructions to bring the regiment's equipment load to combat level and condition. Excess equipment and baggage was stored in warehouses in the billeting villages; the men carried with them only their combat load of rifles, gas masks, canteens, grenade carriers, packs, blankets, and ration bags with hardtack and canned meat.[12] The 3d Battalion went into the lines at Courtes Chausses during the night of 4 June while the 2d Battalion occupied the reserve station at Camp Kapp in the valley near La Chalade. The 1st Battalion went into division reserve farther down the valley at La Noue and Les Islettes, and the supply company settled in at Le Neufoin.[13]

When the 3d Battalion left its billeting area and began its march up the Biesme Valley road to take its place at the front lines, the night was so dark that the men were unable to see the road ahead or who or what was just in front of them. Pvt. Sumler Parran, Company I, later recalled the difficulty of the march:

> About 2 o'clock at night, we were going up a dark road to the front. The Germans must have been suspicious that an attack was underway and opened fire on us. We all scattered, of course. They knocked out a French cook wagon, and some light artillery—about 75 or 80 men were killed. This was our baptism of fire. With the aid of French interpreters, everyone was rounded up and carried to some dark forest. We found our way to a place called the "700 dugout." The next morning we could see where we were, we were in the trenches.[14]

The "dark forest" where Parran and his companions found themselves was the middle of the Argonne in the area of Le Four de Paris. The terrain was made up of low, thickly wooded mountains. Numerous streams running down from the northeast had cut small valleys through a shallow ridge along the east side of the Biesme River. All of these terrain features made the area extremely difficult for maneuvering, easy to defend, and easy for those unfamiliar with the terrain to get lost.[15]

On 7 June Young took command of the entire Subsector Argonne-Quest (Meuse), and on the night of 8 June the 2d Battalion moved up to Center of Resistance (CR) Chalet to relieve the 4th Battalion of the French 305th Infantry Regiment, which then moved back to division reserve at Camp Kapp. The next night the 1st Battalion moved to Camp Kapp and relieved another battalion of the French 305th Infantry Regiment, placing the entire 372d Infantry either on the line or in direct support of battalions on the line.[16]

During the regiment's first days on the line, the Germans sent over numerous observation aircraft to see what was happening in the area. Those airplanes, some harassing artillery shelling, and intermittent bursts of machine-gun and rifle fire were the only excitement until 19 June, when a German patrol of about twenty men intent on taking prisoners conducted a night raid on a forward outpost. The men at the outpost discovered the patrol before it could execute a surprise attack and used grenades to fight off the raiders while suffering one slight casualty. The fight was a lesson of the need for vigilance on the front line, and it also gave the men a boost of confidence by affirming that they could handle situations in the lines without their French trainers.[17] After that brief affair, little action occurred for the next week other than a few casualties caused by shrapnel wounds from artillery rounds.[18]

On 21 June the 372d Infantry was transferred to the French 35th Infantry Division after that division had relieved the French 63d Division. From 27 June through 1 July the regiment was relieved by battalions of the French 123d Infantry Regiment and then shifted its position to take command of the entire Vauquois subsector in the Aire sector, east of the Aire River.[19] The new sector was quite different from the Argonne in that the area was open and the devastation caused by artillery shelling and airplane bombing was far more apparent. The Butte de Vauquois was a heavily contested hill with tunnels, emplacements, and barbed-wire entanglements everywhere. Shell holes covered the area, and the trees had been completely denuded by artillery bursts and poisonous gas. Movements were easily detected, and all visible approaches to the front lines were covered by German machine-gun fire and registered by their artillery batteries. This sector forced the officers and men to exercise more care in conducting their duties while at the trenches.[20]

On 2 July the regiment was placed under the command of Brigadier General Goybet's French 157th (Red Hand) Infantry Division, where it remained, along with its sister regiment, the 371st Infantry, for the rest of the war.[21] The Americans serving with the French Army did not lose all touch with their countrymen. On 4 July, in celebration of Independence Day, an American aircraft circled the sector several times and then dropped a bouquet of flowers near regimental headquarters. The men closest to the drop site made a mad scramble for the bouquet. By the time the bouquet reached headquarters, the flowers had lost a great number of their petals, taken as souvenirs by the rescuers.[22]

On 11 July the 372d Infantry was relieved in the Vauquois subsector by the French 49th Infantry Regiment and moved back to rest before moving to a new sector. While the unit rested, French Army intelligence discovered that a major German offensive was scheduled to occur on the night of 13 July. The French answered the attack with a preemptive strike, and a major battle took place, but the action was in sectors west of the regiment's location. The division moved to the Verdun sector to relieve the French 68th Infantry Division on 14 July, and the battalions of the regiment were dispersed across the area, with the 1st Battalion at Bois-de-Feucheres, the 2d Battalion at Brabant, and the 3d Battalion and regimental headquarters at Locheres.[23]

On 14 July Colonel Young was relieved of command of the regiment. No official reason was given for his removal, but some army records indicate that he was doing a less than satisfactory job. Col. Thomas A. Roberts, in a telephone report made on 9 July to AEF Headquarters, expressed his opinion of the condition of the regiment and of Young: "There is rather a serious state of disorganization there. . . . Here I received the same impression that the field officers had given me, that is, he [Young] should not be trusted with the command of a regiment in war time." Roberts also reported that Goybet was considering taking direct command of the regiment in case of an attack. Roberts indicated that three of the field-grade officers of the regiment had complained to him that orders were not being received in time for execution or were contradictory. Further, Young's failure to act on earlier incidents involving conflicts between some bigoted white officers of the regiment and the black officers must have had a devastating effect on the morale and performance of the latter, and of the regiment as a whole. Whatever the final reason, AEF Headquarters decided to remove him from command of the regiment.[24]

Col. Herschel Tupes, Cavalry, Regular Army, was Young's replacement. Tupes, a native of Ohio, had graduated from the U.S. Military Academy in 1896 and from the University of Missouri in 1910. He served as a 1st lieutenant with the 1st Infantry Regiment in Cuba in 1899, and later in the Philippines Insurrection. Tupes came to the 372d Infantry from assignments as chief of staff of the U.S. 32d Division on the Alsace Front and as the inspector general of the U.S. 1st Division at Cantigny.[25]

The 372d Infantry moved again on 18 July, this time to relieve the French 92d Infantry Regiment in Subsector 304 in the Verdun sector (see map 2). The 2d Battalion occupied the village of Vigneville, the 3d Battalion took over Camp Normandy at Bois-e-Bethelainville, and the 1st Battalion moved into

Subsector West. On the night of 24–25 July the 1st and 2d Battalions moved up to take over CR Lorraine and CR 304, respectively, from battalions of the French 333d Infantry Regiment while the 3d Battalion remained in reserve at Camp Normandy. The displaced French 333d Infantry Regiment shifted its positions to the left flank in the Bois de Malancourt between the villages of Avocourt and Malacourt.[26] To the right flank of the 372d Infantry was its sister regiment, the 371st Infantry Regiment, which had joined the French 157th Infantry Division on 16 July. The 371st Infantry had its hands full in the area of Hill 295, which was known as "Mort Homme," or "Dead Man's Hill."[27]

The nearby fortress city of Verdun was no longer a prime objective of the German high command, so the sector taken over by the French 157th Infantry Division had not been occupied for some time. Many of the fortifications were either totally demolished or in bad repair. After a reconnaissance of the area the 1st and 2d Battalions of the 372d Infantry moved onto the northern slope of Hill 304 to take over the positions that remained usable. The other positions were repaired and new ones were constructed to make the area defensible and habitable. The construction work was completed within two weeks, and most of the men retired to the reserve positions to rest between stints in the forward trenches and outposts.[28]

The Germans opposite the Americans occupied the valley just south of the village of Bethincourt, with their front lines strung along a road on the north side of the Rau de Forges, a stream running down to the village of Forges-sur-Meuse at the Meuse River. During the day the Germans occupied the high ground north of Bethincourt in the Bois de Forges, and at night they dropped down into the valley to their forward posts and sent patrols across the stream to probe the American lines. Few conflicts occurred, however, and the sector remained peaceful; most of the excitement came from aerial combat bouts, which entertained the troops who happened to be outside their dugouts during the day, and from an occasional artillery duel between French and German batteries.[29]

Tupes's style of leadership came to the forefront one afternoon when he and his French army adviser, Captain Drouhin, were observing the village of Bethincourt through field glasses and debating whether it was actually occupied by the Germans. Tupes was of the opinion that it was not occupied; Drouhin argued that it was, and that a patrol should be sent out for confirmation.[30] That night, Drouhin retired to his dugout not knowing that Tupes had taken his advice and was leading a patrol to probe the village.[31] A few hours later Drouhin was awakened by heavy German machine-gun fire and sporadic French artillery fire. He went back to sleep, only to be awakened again by a disheveled and mud-caked Tupes standing at the foot of his cot. Tupes said simply, "You were right. The village is occupied," then turned and walked away.[32]

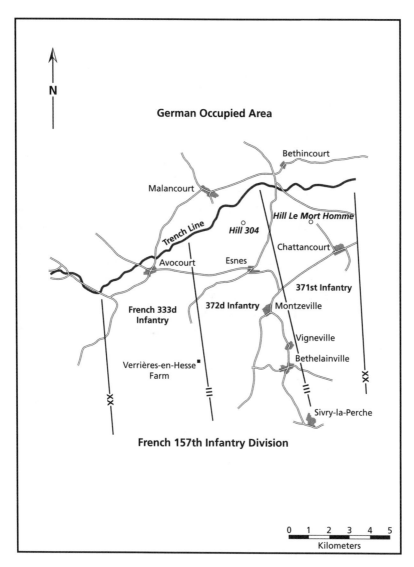

N

German Occupied Area

Bethincourt

Malancourt

Trench Line

Hill Le Mort Homme

Hill 304

Chattancourt

Avocourt   Esnes

371st Infantry

French 333d Infantry   **372d Infantry**   Montzeville

Vigneville

Bethelainville

Verrières-en-Hesse Farm

Sivry-la-Perche

French 157th Infantry Division

0 1 2 3 4 5
Kilometers

*Map 2. 371st and 372d Infantry Operations in the Verdun Sector,
16 July to 14 September 1918*

Battalions of the regiment shifted back and forth between frontline duty and reserve duty at the rear at Camp Normandy. Those off the front lines began training in open-warfare techniques; in particular, the men were taught the niceties of aggressive patrolling methods. After a week of detailed instruction by French noncommissioned officers, the trainees were sent on reconnaissance patrols to practice storming enemy outposts for the purpose of gathering information and taking prisoners for interrogation.[33]

On 8 August a severe shelling occurred with Hill 304 and the village of Montzeville as primary targets. The next day the French artillery answered with a monstrous reprisal barrage. From that day on, German artillery bombardments became more intense and more accurate in the sector and the regiment began to take casualties. Although several wounds were serious, there had as yet been no deaths.[34]

Toward the end of August, reports from observation posts, aerial patrols, and other means of monitoring enemy activity indicated a great deal of movement far back of the German frontline trenches. Heavy French artillery guns were brought up and situated at the bottom of Hill 310, which was at that time the site of regimental headquarters. Once in place, the French guns delivered a concentrated barrage on an area about twenty kilometers behind the German lines. The men of the regiment had been ordered to stay deep in their dugouts to avoid the concussion from the guns, but some were forced to leave their shelters when the firing of the guns caused several of the dugouts and trench lines to collapse. At the end of the artillery action, those men on Hill 304 still in their shelters came out to watch a large German ammunition dump blaze up into the night sky. The fireworks display was punctuated by brilliant flashes of exploding shells and, as a grand finale, a solid wall of smoke climbing against the fire-lit horizon.[35]

A few days later the Germans responded with a terrific artillery attack, which included mustard gas shells, across the front of the French 157th Infantry Division. The gas shells had no effect due to good gas mask discipline and effective gas curtains on shelter entrances, but the high-explosive shells damaged the shallow dugouts and shelters. For the rest of their stay at Hill 304 the men slept in the deepest shelters available, some of them fifty feet underground.[36]

Tupes, a well-trained, well-educated, and experienced officer, had somehow reached the conclusion that many of the black officers in combat positions in the regiment were not capable of performing their duties. In a letter to AEF Headquarters requesting replacement of the black officers by white officers, he stated: "The racial distinctions which are recognized in civilian life naturally continue to be recognized in the military life and present a formidable barrier to the existence of that feeling of comradeship which is an essential to mutual confidence and esprit de corps." That lack of esprit de corps was the direct result of Colonel Young's failure to recognize and correct the bigotry mentioned earlier, which had resulted in a lack of cooperation and efficiency that had become ingrained in the officer corps of the regiment. Unfortunately, Tupes did not have the luxury of time to rebuild his officer corps into a functioning team; he had to act quickly to accomplish combat readiness, even if that meant replacing some of his officers.[37] In his after-action report of 26 March

1919 to Col. Allen J. Greer, General Staff, War Department, Tupes confirmed the problem when he stated: "Immediately upon joining the regiment it was recognized that its condition could never be improved with mixed white and colored officers, and steps were immediately taken to eliminate the colored officers and replace them with white."[38] The report mentioned only medical and dental officers, chaplains, and a commander of the depot company as performing their duties satisfactorily.[39]

During the later part of August and into September, AEF Headquarters ordered that boards composed of white officers of the 371st and 372d Infantry Regiments be convened to determine the qualifications and fitness for duty of the black National Guard officers brought onto active duty with the various separate battalions and companies that had formed the 372d Infantry.[40] Twenty of the black National Guard officers of the regiment were disqualified for service due to lack of mental capacity or inadequate military training; transfers or discharges were recommended as the appropriate actions in those cases.

As the boards were meeting, rumors began to circulate among the enlisted men that some or all of the black noncommissioned officers of the regiment were to be replaced by white noncommissioned officers. Although no official records confirm that Tupes at that time intended to replace any of the noncommissioned officers, that belief and the removal of almost all of the black officers further devastated the morale of the enlisted men of the regiment.[41]

That this extreme disruption of the officer corps of a serving frontline regiment occurred on the eve of its being committed to its severest test in combat may well indicate the extent of the disorder resulting from Young's lack of leadership. His actions, or the lack thereof, may have so demoralized the black officers that they were not emotionally capable of effectively following another white commanding officer. The other courses of action Tupes may have had available to him are not known, but obviously he felt that drastic action was necessary to make the best of the situation he had inherited.[42]

Some outside observers simply could not understand Tupes's actions. One French officer said, "The French liaison officers could not understand why Americans should treat one another so harshly and cruelly when it was momentarily expected that the division would be plunged into battle."[43]

How Tupes and AEF Headquarters found enough officers qualified to fill the empty billets and able to adjust to performing their duties effectively in the short time left before being committed to severe combat conditions is also not reported. The sudden absence of officers that the men knew and trusted from long association must have placed a heavy burden on the noncommissioned officers to provide the required leadership in the interim.[44] To their credit, the men of the 372d Infantry Regiment performed their duties admirably, and in the upcoming battles acquitted themselves well.[45]

CHAPTER 12

The 93d Division's
First Heroes

If ever proof were needed, which it is not, that the color of a man's skin
has nothing to do with the color of his soul, this twain then and there
offered it in abundance.

> Reporter Irvin S. Cobb on the exploits of
> Sgt. Henry Johnson and Pvt. Needham Roberts

On 13 April 1918, while the 370th, 371st, and 372d Infantry Regiments were
still en route to France or engaged in reequipping, reorganizing, and
training for combat, the 369th Infantry moved closer to the front and into billeting areas for training in the trenches. The regiment, less the 2d Battalion, left
Herpont and Herpine to march north to the vicinity of Maffrecourt, Remicourt, and Hans. The 2d Battalion had moved to the front a week ahead of the
other battalions and was already in training in trenches in the Afrique sector,
west of the Argonne Forest and north of Saint-Menehould. After marching
about eight kilometers, the two battalions arrived at the town of Auve; headquarters and the 3d Battalion moved northeast to Maffrecourt to establish a
base of operations, and the 1st Battalion went due north through the village of
Hans to billets at Camp des Peupliers. The 1st Battalion's new location was so
close to the front lines that shells from French long-range guns located to the
rear could be heard rumbling overhead in flight to targets on the German side
of the front.[1]

As with other moves made by the regiment, the march to Maffrecourt,
Remicourt, and Hans was not without amusing incidents. One involved the
regimental color bearer, Sergeant Cox.[2] The identifying flag, or colors, of a
military formation has served since the beginning of organized warfare as the
point on which the formation forms and moves on the field of combat. The
responsibility for carrying the colors was placed with a trusted senior noncommissioned officer stationed at the front of the unit to best indicate its direction
of movement as ordered by the commander. The color bearer was normally an
individual of tall stature and sufficient stamina to be able to carry the heavy and
awkward staff and colors for long periods high enough to be seen by all mem-

bers of the unit. Soldiers in armies everywhere recognized that should the color bearer be struck down, the man closest to him must pick up and carry the colors so that the formation would know where to rally and in which direction to move. It was also well known that disabling the color bearer and thus grounding the colors of an enemy force was the quickest and easiest way to cause a commander to lose control of his unit.[3]

Stories abound of men taking up the fallen colors and rallying a unit to victory on the field. One such incident in the U.S. Army involved Maj. Gen. Arthur MacArthur, father of General of the Armies Douglas MacArthur. As a lieutenant in the 24th Wisconsin Regiment he won the Congressional Medal of Honor for recovering the fallen regimental colors and leading an attack at the Battle of Missionary Ridge on 25 November 1863.[4]

Foremost among valorous color bearers in the history of black units of the U.S. Army stands Capt. Andre Cailloux, commanding officer of Company E, 1st Regiment of the Black Phalanx, and the men who preceded him as color bearers. As his regiment was attacking a Confederate stronghold at the Battle of Port Hudson, Louisiana, in 1863, the regimental color bearer was struck down; as the standard was picked up, the new bearer was struck down. Again the colors were picked up, and when the flag went down for the third time, Cailloux, who happened to be the closest, picked it up and rallied the men to him to carry the attack to the Confederate works. As the assault forces swept up the front of the breastworks, Cailloux was mortally wounded. The Black Phalanx did not carry the Confederate works that day, but the rallying powers of Cailloux and the color bearers before him were evident in the fighting tenacity of the men of the 1st Regiment, who refused to stop until the regiment was nearly destroyed.[5]

It is not known whether Cox of the 369th Infantry knew of Cailloux and the other fallen color bearers of the 1st Regiment of the Black Phalanx, but he certainly understood, and was dedicated to carrying out, the responsibilities and traditions of his office.[6] The area just behind the front lines, in which the 369th Infantry was at that time marching, was called the "zone of advance." Regulations required all troops in the zone who were in the open to take cover whenever German airplanes were sighted. If cover was not available, the troops were to spread out, drop to the ground, and remain still.[7] The 3d Battalion, under the command of Major Dayton, was leading the regiment on the road toward Remicourt when unknown aircraft appeared overhead and the order was given to disperse and lie down. Seconds later the entire battalion was prone . . . with the exception of one color bearer—Sergeant Cox.[8] Dayton called back to Cox and ordered him to lie down. Cox did not move. Dayton called again asking if Cox had heard his order. Cox answered yes, he had heard it. Dayton then got up, went up to Cox, and asked why he had not obeyed his order. Cox, a powerfully built man fully six feet tall and of soldierly bearing, remained at rigid attention and replied that he was very sorry, but he could not obey the order.[9] Dayton demanded to know why.

"Sir, Major, Sir, I'll just tell you," Cox replied.

> Long time ago, more than a year ago, maybe a year and a half, way back at home in New York State, right out on 5th Avenue, down in front of the Union League Club, Governor Whitman, the governor of New York State, done handed me these colors. And the governor, he says to me, "Sergeant, don't you ever let this flag here touch the ground." And Sir, Major, Sir, so long's my legs is stiff enough to hold me up straight, and so long's my hands is strong enough to hold this staff, Sir, Major, Sir, this here flag ain't never agoin' to touch the ground!"[10]

On hearing that explanation Dayton gave in to the inevitable, ordered Cox to carry on, and returned to the head of his battalion and lay down.[11]

After a one-night rest in Camp des Peupliers, the 1st Battalion, commanded by newly promoted Major Little, received orders to move into the front lines to start training. The battalion marched to the north on 14 April and spent that night at Camp des Haut Batis, a protected post just behind Secteur Citadelle de Saint-Thomas. The camp was located in a ravine and had wood-frame barracks for the men and huts for officers. The hillside along the north side of the camp provided some protection from direct shelling, but bomb shelters had been dug into the embankment as an added precaution. Just before dinner, thirty German shells fell randomly into the area, putting members of the regiment under direct fire for the very first time.[12]

Little asked the sector commander, Colonel de Villiers, if the Germans knew that the 369th Infantry had moved into the area. De Villiers replied that the Germans most certainly knew: "They gave you a welcome. They have not shelled that camp for many, many months."[13]

That first shelling caused no casualties or damages, but it did result in another amusing incident. All personnel had been ordered to carry their gas mask packs on them at all times. Soldiers in one bomb shelter, convinced that the shells dropping on the camp contained poison gas, began to don their masks. Someone who had disobeyed orders and left his mask behind was running around looking for it. In a frantic plea, he shouted: "Has anybody got two masks?" One of his bunkmates unsympathetically called out: "Wait a minute brother, wait 'til I [get] mine on, and I'll put my hand over your mouth!"[14] No one was hit in the attack and, luckily for the man who was without his gas mask, the shells were all high-explosive loads.[15]

The men were instructed to move up to their trenches at night through zigzag communications laterals. Once there, they found three lines of firing trenches extending along the front that were connected by more communications laterals. The trench line nearest the enemy, the frontline trench, extended anywhere from fifty meters to nearly a kilometer from the German frontline trench.[16] Several hundred meters behind the frontline trench ran the support trench, and a few hundred meters farther back was the reserve line; all were classified as firing trenches. Shallow trenches called "saps" ran out from the frontline trench into no-man's-land to connect with observation posts, machine-gun positions, and listening posts. All three of the well-built firing trenches zigzagged like the communications trenches and contained firing steps on the side closest to the enemy. At random intervals bombproof command post bunkers and troop shelters were dug deep into the ground on the side away from no-man's-land. Forward of the frontline trench, massive, rusty barbed-wire entanglements defaced the landscape.[17]

The officers and men of the 369th Infantry had gained helpful knowledge from their French trainers in the arts and skills of trench warfare in practice trenches in the rear area. Yet, as the battalions of the 369th Infantry began rotating into the frontline trenches, the men found that nothing had prepared them for what they experienced there. They soon learned that the ordinary duty of manning the trenches and outposts and going on patrols was a mixture of extreme boredom punctuated by moments of sheer terror.[18]

The first taste of real excitement came when Lt. Marshall Johnson of the 2d Battalion led a patrol into no-man's-land and captured a German prisoner. For his actions Johnson received a Croix de Guerre; it was the first decoration for the regiment and the 93d Division.[19] The very next night a platoon commander caught several men armed to the teeth with knives and grenades preparing to go over the trench parapet and into no-man's-land without authorization. When the lieutenant demanded an explanation, the leader replied: "Sir, Lieutenant, Sir, I was just going over there to get one of them Bush Germans, so's to get one of those 'Qua di gairs' for my gal."[20] Orders immediately went out to all platoon commanders to be on the lookout for overambitious members of their commands looking to sneak into no-man's-land to earn pretty baubles for their girlfriends back home.[21]

On 11 May the 1st Battalion came up from the regimental rest area at Maffrecourt to relieve the 2d Battalion in the Montplaisir sector. This was a familiar sector to the battalion; the men had been there with a French battalion under Lieutenant Colonel Josse during their first indoctrination tour in the trenches. Immediately they were faced with a problem. Weaknesses in the layout of the defenses had allowed German snipers to infiltrate to positions where they were able to fire on the battalion's observation posts from the rear.[22] To counter this harassing tactic, the battalion commander ordered out daylight patrols to sweep and probe the areas between the trench line and the observation posts for signs of sniper activity. The patrols soon discovered several well-used entrance points and abandoned shallow dugouts that showed signs of recent use by the Germans. The dugouts and any obvious hiding places for snipers were destroyed, and that evening at battalion headquarters plans were laid to set ambushes at entrance points to trap German patrols and take prisoners for interrogation.[23]

At dusk on 12–13 May, ambush parties crawled forward of the trench lines and into no-man's-land to set up at three entrance points. Once in position the men settled in and waited. The night passed, with the only excitement being several false alarms, some stray rifle shots, and a few flares illuminating the landscape. When dawn arrived, the tired and disappointed patrols crawled back to their own trenches, found their bombproof shelters, and fell into their bunks to get some sleep.[24]

The next night three patrols made up of fresh personnel went out and set up at three different entrance points. At about 2:30 AM a German patrol could be heard working its way through the lines. But the Germans, intending to capture one or more of the strange new black men facing them across their lines, came in force through one of the entrance points that had been set up for ambush the night before.[25] The German party of about two dozen men made their way about 150 meters through the first barbed-wire line to the rear of Combat Group 29, an isolated forward observation and listening post manned by four privates and a corporal. The observation post had a small bombproof shelter where the off-watch relief could sleep in relative safety. From the observation post, a narrow lateral trench ran several meters north to a fortified forward listening dugout with prepared positions for two men to stand watch. About 50 meters to the west was Combat Group 28, a strongpoint garrisoned by about one-half of a platoon commanded by Lt. Richardson Pratt and constituting the support element for Combat Group 29.[26]

Pvt. Needham Roberts was on duty at the isolated forward observation and listening dugout of Group 29 when he heard strange noises to the rear of his position. He slipped across to the far side of the fortified enclosure and, motioning him to silence, brought his watch-relief partner, Sgt. Henry Johnson, to his side of the dugout. They waited and listened. Moments later the sounds were repeated and both men realized that the strange noise was wire being cut just behind the dugout. Johnson responded to the threat by shouting, "Corporal of the Guard," and discharging an illuminating flare into the night sky.[27]

Both men had a ready supply of grenades laid out at their positions, and they started throwing them in the direction of the sounds while still shouting for the corporal of the guard. German potato masher grenades came sailing out of the darkness and tumbled into the small enclosure. The grenades ex-

ploded, knocking Roberts and Johnson to the ground and wounding both soldiers. Meanwhile, the corporal of the guard and the two watch-relief men had
heard Johnson's calls and had seen the flare go up. They tried to come out of
the observation post and into the lateral trench to render assistance but were
pinned down by German rifle fire and grenades thrown into the lateral.[28]

Roberts, badly injured in one arm and a hip from grenade fragments,
crawled over to his position, propped himself up against the side of the dugout,
and started throwing grenades over the side of the enclosure with his good
arm. Meanwhile, Johnson had recovered his senses. He struggled back on his
feet, again shouted, "Corporal of the Guard," and stumbled to his position just
in time to meet a group of Germans charging over the parapet and into the
enclosure. He emptied his three-shot Lebel rifle into the first three Germans,
dropping them into the dugout. The fourth German, an officer, came over the
parapet shooting at him with a pistol. Johnson grabbed his empty rifle by the
barrel and swung it around, striking the officer in the head.[29]

Still shouting for the corporal of the guard, Johnson whirled around to see
that two of the German raiders had Roberts by the shoulders and feet and were
trying to heave him out of the dugout, intent on taking him prisoner. Johnson
charged at the two and attacked the nearest—the one who had Roberts's shoulders—with his trench knife and cut him down. The second German dropped
Roberts's feet and scrambled out of the enclosure. By then the German officer
had recovered his senses enough to aim and fire three shots at Johnson with his
semiautomatic pistol. Johnson realized he was hit when he felt pain in his left
leg, his right hip, and right forearm. He dropped to his hands and knees,
lunged at the officer, and thrust his trench knife into the man's stomach. This
time the German officer stayed down.[30]

Johnson could hear more Germans shouting somewhere over the parapet.
In spite of severe pain, he managed to crawl back to his position to a box of
grenades and started throwing them in the direction of the shouting. A few
moments later, Pratt and a relief party entered the enclosure of the listening
post of Combat Group 29. Private Johnson looked up at the lieutenant and was
just able to mumble, "Corporal of the Guard," before he passed out.[31]

At about 3:30 AM the battalion sergeant major woke Major Little to inform
him that a fight had occurred at the left *point d'apuis;* two men had been
wounded, and it appeared that they were dying. When Little reached the aid
station, both men were conscious, although in great pain and weak from their
severe wounds and loss of blood. Both had been given a cup of rum from a
supply kept in the company dugout and were plainly starting to feel the relax-
ing effects of the alcohol.[32]

These were the first severe casualties the regiment had suffered during the
several weeks it had spent on the line, and although he tried to keep his face

passive while interviewing the two wounded men, Little was visibly shaken. Johnson, who was watching Little, detected his concern and motioned for him to come nearer. The battalion commander knelt by Johnson's stretcher and bent down to hear the private say, "Sir, Cap'n, Sir. You all don't want to worry about me. I'm all right. I've been shot before!"[33]

At dawn, Little went out to the remote post and examined the dugout and the ground around it, and then followed the escape route of the surviving Germans. Four of the enemy soldiers were known to be dead. Blood trails and discarded medical wrappings found along the route were proof that several of the retreating German patrol had been wounded, and more may have died and been carried away. The recovered German equipment left in and around the outpost included forty unused potato masher hand grenades, seven long-arm wire cutters, three Luger semiautomatic pistols, three service caps, and other odd pieces of German equipment.[34]

On 16 May the following communiqué arrived from Headquarters, French 16th Infantry Division (translated from the French):

Argonne-Vienne–La-Ville
16 Division
May 16, 1918
Order No. 697

General Gallais Cdt of the 16th DI cites to the order of the Division the soldiers of the 369th R.I.U.S.

1st: Johnson, Henry, No. 103348, soldier in the said command: Doing double night sentry duty, was attacked by a group of a dozen Germans and put one out of the fight by gunshot and seriously wounded two with a knife. In spite of having received three wounds by revolver shots and grenades at the start of the action, went to the help of his wounded comrade who was being carried away by the enemy and continued the strife until the rout of the Germans. Gave a magnificent example of courage and energy.

2nd: Roberts, Needham, No. 103369, soldier in the said command: Doing double night sentry duty was attacked and seriously wounded in the leg by a group of Germans; continued the strife by throwing grenades, in spite of having fallen to the ground, until the enemy was put in rout. Good and brave soldier.

The General requested that the citation for soldier Johnson be changed to the citation of the Order of the Army.

2A Chief of Etat Major Boye
General Cdt. of the 16th DI
Gallais[35]

Thus did slight, mild-mannered Henry Johnson, once a redcap porter at the New York Central Railroad station at Albany, New York, come to be one of the first private soldiers of the U.S. Army in France to receive the Croix de Guerre with Bronze Palm for gallantry.[36]

As the officers and men of the 369th Infantry were receiving their first blooding in the trenches, Gen. Erich Ludendorff, commander of German forces on the Western Front, was learning the hard way what the American troops were made of. He launched a diversionary offensive during the early hours of 27 May 1918 with the point of attack on the Aisne front between Anizy-le-Château and Berry-au-Bac, west of Rheims. Forty-six hundred German guns opened fire at dawn along a thirty-nine-kilometer front, and forty-one German divisions went over the top, beginning the Fourth Battle of the Aisne.[37] Ludendorff's initial attack was at a point defended by eleven weak and battered French divisions, and the German assault units penetrated deep behind the French lines. The German divisions advanced to within sixty kilometers of Paris before the Allies could halt them, creating a salient extending to Château-Thierry. The city of Rheims was able to hold against repeated attacks, narrowing the German breakthrough and causing a slight Allied salient north into the German main line.[38]

While this battle was going on, all of the 93d Infantry Division's four regiments were either in transit to the front or being trained by the French Army in areas not subjected to the attack.[39] Other American troops were in the battle, however, in the first offensive action of a U.S. Army unit in World War I, near Montdidier on the Somme. One American unit would be the first to demonstrate to the German military leaders how wrong they were in their low opinion of the fighting ability of the American soldier. A full brigade of four thousand men of the U.S. Army's 1st Division, supported by French artillery, air cover, and flamethrower teams, counterattacked and captured the town of Cantigny on 27 May and held it for three days against violent and sustained attempts by the Germans to recapture it.[40]

On 1 July the U.S. Army's 2d Division was transported by truck to the front and entered the lines northwest of Château-Thierry, establishing itself across the approach route to Paris and effectively stopping the German advance in that direction. The German commander who faced the 2d Division during this period gave the unit high marks: "The personnel must be called excellent.... The spirit of the troops is high.... The 2d American Division can be rated as a very good division.... The nerves of the Americans are still unshaken."[41] The German high command quickly became aware that the Americans were not a rabble of amateurs stumbling into battle, as had been first reported. The regiments of the 93d Division would further prove that point even as they operated with an army not their own.[42]

Attacks and counterattacks continued between Allied and German forces west of Rheims. Combat actions along the front controlled by the French Fourth Army, to which the French 16th Infantry Division and the 369th Infantry were assigned, consisted of patrol and counterpatrol actions across no-man's-land and isolated feints by the Germans. On 12 June, in the Bois d'Hauzy on the left fringe of the Argonne Forest, the Germans fired a heavy artillery barrage in preparation for an isolated infantry attack. The men of the 369th Infantry called the barrage a "million dollar raid," as they were of the opinion that the shells alone must have cost at least that much.[43]

The Germans may have justified the extra heavy expenditure of shells in the belief that the American black soldiers would break under the pressure of sustained bombardment, as some of the French Moroccan and Senegalese troops had done earlier in the war. But when the Germans advanced into the line, they found themselves faced with accurate rifle fire, heavy Stokes mortar barrages, precision grenade attacks, and well-positioned and well-manned machine-gun posts. In that action, Sgt. Bob Collins so effectively deployed his machine-gun section that he was awarded the Croix de Guerre.[44]

The steadiness and confidence being gained by the officers and men of the 369th Infantry through their first experiences in combat were typified by the nonchalant and somewhat cavalier attitude of the cooks manning one of the regiment's rolling kitchens. The kitchen was under random German artillery fire, but the cooks continued to go about their duties. When several French soldiers ran up to the kitchen and tried to get the cooks to take cover, one replied: "Oh, that's all right, boss. They ain't hurting us none."[45] Throughout the remainder of June, the battalions of the 369th Infantry continued to be shifted in and out of the frontline trenches as the officers and men became hardened to combat.[46]

During this period it became clear to the men of the 369th Infantry that the German "million dollar raid" shelling reflected increasingly intense artillery bombardment along the entire front of the Fourth Army. The number of gas attacks was higher than normal as well, some with the dreaded yperite. German patrols were becoming more numerous and were penetrating deeper into the lines, and German air reconnaissance flights were coming over the trenches more than ever before. Something big seemed to be building in front of the French Fourth Army, and the officers and men of the regiment began to understand that the hard lessons and combat experience thus far gained in the trenches might soon be put to the test.[47]

This monument on the crest of Mont Blanc near Sommepy, France, raised by the U.S. government, includes an inscription commemorating battles fought by the 369th, 371st, and 372d Infantry Regiments of the 93d Division at Ripont, Sechault, Ardéuil, and Trières Farm, from 26 September to 6 October 1918.

AMERICAN BATTLE MONUMENTS COMMISSION

Pvt. E. E. Ewing, 372d Infantry, wearing his Croix de Guerre at the dock in New York City on his arrival home from France on 11 February 1919.

U.S. NATIONAL ARCHIVES AND RECORDS ADMINISTRATION

Brig. Gen. Roy Hoffman,
Commanding General, 93d
Division.

U.S. NATIONAL ARCHIVES AND RECORDS
ADMINISTRATION

Sgt. Lee R. McClelland, Medical Detachment, 371st Infantry, receiving the Distinguished
Service Cross from Maj. Gen. Eli. A. Helminch at Brest, France.

U.S. NATIONAL ARCHIVES AND RECORDS ADMINISTRATION

*Officers of the 369th Infantry standing with Major General Lebouc,
Commanding General, French 161st Infantry Division. Left to right:
Maj. E. W. Whittemore, Medical Officer; Col. William Hayward, CO,
369th Infantry; Maj. Arthur W. Little, CO, 1st Battalion; Major General
Lebouc; Capt. John H. Clark, CO, 2d Battalion; Maj. David A. L'Esperance,
CO, 3d Battalion.*

U.S. NATIONAL ARCHIVES AND RECORDS ADMINISTRATION

*Lt. George S. Robb, Platoon
Leader, 369th Infantry Regiment,
was awarded the Congressional
Medal of Honor, French Legion of
Honor, Croix de Guerre, Purple
Heart, Italian Military Cross, and
a citation from Montenegro.*

HARRY ROBB WELTY

Lt. William Warfield, Sgt. Lester Fossie, and Pvt. Alonzo Walton, all of the 370th Infantry Division, wearing their Distinguished Service Crosses. Fossie is armed with a U.S. 1903 Springfield rifle; Walton holds a U.S. 1917 Enfield rifle. U.S. NATIONAL ARCHIVES AND RECORDS ADMINISTRATION

Officers of the 370th Infantry on board the ship taking them home. All are wearing the Croix de Guerre, the Distinguished Service Cross, or both. Left to right, kneeling: Capt. G. M. Allen, Lt. O. A. Browning, Capt. D. J. Warner, and Lt. Roy B. Tisdell; standing: Lt. Robert P. Hurd, Lt. Col. Otis B. Duncan, Maj. J. R. White, Capt. W. B. Crawford, Lt. William Warfield, and Capt. Matthew Jackson.

U.S. NATIONAL ARCHIVES AND RECORDS ADMINISTRATION PHOTO, COURTESY OF JOHN LISTMAN

Officers and men of the 372d Infantry prior to boarding ship for home. The fifth soldier from the right has a souvenir German helmet hanging from his belt. All of the enlisted men are armed with U.S. 1917 Enfield rifles with covers over the actions. The men are wearing the 93d Division shoulder patch with the French blue Adrian helmet.

U.S. NATIONAL ARCHIVES AND RECORDS ADMINISTRATION PHOTO, COURTESY OF JOHN LISTMAN

Monument to the 371st Infantry located near Ardeuil-Montfauxelles. Most of the upper pyramid was later blown away during World War II by a German artillery shell.

U.S. NATIONAL ARCHIVES AND RECORDS ADMINISTRATION

Monument to the 372d Infantry Regiment at Monthois, France. The chains surrounding the monument were later removed, probably for use as scrap metal in World War II.

U.S. NATIONAL ARCHIVES AND RECORDS ADMINISTRATION

Brig. Gen. Perry L. Miles, former CO, 371st Infantry.

ASSOCIATION OF GRADUATES,
U.S. MILITARY ACADEMY

Gen. Henri Joseph Etienne Gouraud, commander of the French Fourth Army, implemented the elastic defense strategy in the Second Battle of the Marne, in which the 369th Infantry participated.

U.S. NATIONAL ARCHIVES AND RECORDS ADMINISTRATION

The Victory Monument, 8th Infantry Regiment, Illinois National Guard (370th Infantry) at the parkway at Martin Luther King Jr. Drive, Chicago, Illinois.

BOB THALL, COMMISSION ON CHICAGO LANDMARKS, DEPARTMENT OF PLANNING AND DEVELOPMENT

*Col. Robert M. Brambila, former
executive officer of the 371st
Infantry.*

MILDRED BRAMBILA

*Maj. Joseph Benjamin Pate,
Battalion Commander, 371st
Infantry.*

COL. WILLIAM H. KERN, FROM THE ISAAC J.
NICHOLS PAPERS

Two soldiers of the 369th Infantry flanking a French soldier at a sentry box outside regimental headquarters. Note the Lebel rifle, the French Adrian helmets worn by the Americans, and the gas mask cases slung over their shoulders. The warning horn attached to the wall at the left is a gas alert siren.

U.S. NATIONAL ARCHIVES AND RECORDS ADMINISTRATION

A soldier of the 371st Infantry receiving a postcard from a young lady of the Salvation Army at the docks in New York City on 11 February 1919. The postcard was to be sent home announcing safe arrival in the United States.

U.S. NATIONAL ARCHIVES AND RECORDS ADMINISTRATION

Cadet Herschel Tupes, West Point Class of 1896, became the colonel commanding the 372d Infantry in France in 1918.
LIBRARY OF THE U.S. MILITARY ACADEMY

Maj. Franklin A. Denison in Cuba during the Spanish-American War, 1898. Colonel Denison commanded the 370th Infantry in France in 1918.
GARY VAN DIS, CONDÉ NAST, AND KEN DENISON

CHAPTER 13

The Elastic Defense
and the 369th

The first thing I knew all there was between the German Army and Paris
on a stretch of front a little more than four miles long was my regiment
of Negroes. But it was fair enough at that. All there was between us and
Berlin was the German Army.

Col. William Hayward, 369th Infantry

The French Fourth Army's commander, Gen. Henri Gouraud, was known
and respected by his officers and men for developing and using tactics
designed to cause the least number of casualties to his troops and the most to
the Germans. To defeat the anticipated German offensive, Gouraud, after con-
sultation with Marshal Pétain, the commander of the French Army, adopted
an elastic plan of defense. Gouraud had learned of the defensive maneuver
through Marshal Foch, who had developed the concept from tactics previously
employed by his German opponent, General Ludendorff.[1] Foch's adaptation of
the plan created a buffer zone to absorb a massive German attack with minimal
losses to his forces while inflicting heavy casualties on the Germans; his troops
would then revert to the attack when the Germans were isolated in no-man's-
land and most vulnerable.[2]

Gouraud, following Foch's lead, sent out instructions to units of his command, including the French 157th Infantry Division, which included the 371st
and 372d Infantry Regiments, and the French 161st Infantry Division, with the
369th Infantry under its command. The regiments were to begin preparing an
elaborate trap for the Germans by constructing rear-area fighting trenches
between two thousand and three thousand meters behind the main line. In this
line Gouraud would place his fighting divisions, less a few battalions left
behind in the original trench line as a ruse. The German Army commanders
had a habit of beginning an attack with a concentrated artillery barrage at midnight followed by an infantry attack just before dawn. Gouraud's orders thus
called for the few French combat battalions still in the forward lines to fall back
to the rear-area trenches to join the main force when the Germans' heavy
artillery barrage began.[3]

Small "camouflage teams" composed of volunteers from each regiment would remain behind in carefully prepared and hardened positions in the frontline trenches and forward outposts. When the German infantry attacked at dawn across no-man's-land and closed on the outpost positions, the teams would trigger obsolete heavy machine guns rigged to fire on their own until they ran out of ammunition and would fire signal flares and other pyrotechnic devices and throw grenades to make the outposts appear fully manned. When the Germans came close enough to overrun the outposts, the teams would beat a hasty retreat back to the original main trench line.[4]

At the original main trenches the teams would repeat the deception and would also open poison gas canisters to flood the dugouts and trench bottoms with chlorine gas. As the Germans came up to attack the original main trenches, the teams would fall back again, this time to the rear-area lines to join the main body of French forces waiting to attack the exposed German troops. The entire French Fourth Army's artillery assets would then open a concentrated barrage on top of the German troops, driving them to seek shelter in the gas-flooded French main trenches and dugouts. After a thorough bombardment, the French artillery would range out toward the German lines, behind the trapped Germans, and the French forces would then counterattack from the rear-area trenches to destroy the survivors caught against the wall of the French artillery barrage.[5] The plan was set in motion as Gouraud's army, including the three regiments of the 93d Division under his command, went about building the trap for Ludendorff's army.[6]

On 3 July 1918 the 369th Infantry received orders from Headquarters, French 16th Infantry Division, to prepare for their part in the elastic defense plan by moving to a new sector near Minaucourt, south of Butte du Mesnil. Their march took them through escalating heavy barrages of German artillery fire of all types, but the regiment made the trip without any serious injuries.[7] On their arrival in the new area, Colonel Hayward deployed his three battalions on the line in the new defensive positions already prepared by pioneer infantry regiments in accordance with Gouraud's plans. In the sector near Minaucourt, these positions were about three kilometers behind the French forward trench line (see map 3). According to Major Little's memoir, the regiment was deployed as follows: the 1st Battalion was entrenched on the slope of a hill to the north of Courtemont, overlooking the River La Bionne and the main road leading from Hans through Courtemont toward the front lines; the 2d Battalion was dug in on a hill to the right and rear of the 1st Battalion, about halfway between Maffrecourt and Courtemont; the 3d Battalion was at Berzieux, to the right of the 1st Battalion, straddling the main road from Saint-Menehould to the front.[8]

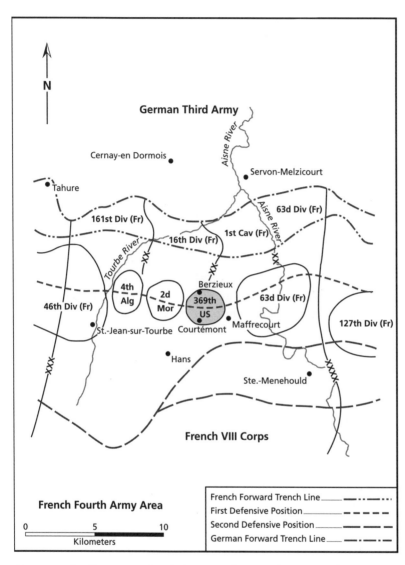

Map 3. 369th Infantry Operations during General Gouraud's Elastic Defense Strategy, Morning of 15 July 1918

Shortly after arriving at the new positions, the 369th Infantry and all regiments of all divisions of the French Fourth Army received orders from Gouraud to expect an attack at any time from 4 July forward. All formations were to be on alert and in their fighting positions ready to execute the elastic defense plan from 10:30 PM until 3:00 AM each night.[9]

On 7 July Gouraud issued informal orders to his command for the upcoming operation, which read in part:

> To the French and American Soldiers of the Fourth Army. We may be attacked at any moment. . . . Your positions and your armament are formidable. In your breasts beat the brave and strong hearts of free men. None shall look to the rear, none shall yield a step. Each shall have but one thought: to kill aplenty, until they have had their fill. Therefore your General says to you: you will break this assault and it will be a happy day.
>
> Gouraud
> By authority of the Chief of Staff, Pettelat[10]

Time passed slowly as the men awaited the German attack. The monotony was broken only by the dangerous cat-and-mouse game of night patrols moving forward of the original French positions to take German prisoners and gather intelligence information. Firefights between German and Allied patrols stumbling over each other in no-man's-land were increasing in frequency and becoming more vicious and deadly, which French intelligence took to be a sure indication that a German attack was imminent.[11]

During daylight hours, men of the battalions not standing watch on the forward main line were employed in digging and reinforcing trenches, building bombproof shelters, and other duties required to further prepare and improve the rear-area fortifications for the expected German artillery attack. These routine daylight activities were constantly disturbed by above-normal harassing German artillery and mortar shelling with high-explosive and gas loads, and increased flyovers from German reconnaissance and bombing aircraft.[12]

On 14 July, in spite of the expected German attack, the entire French Army took time out to celebrate Bastille Day, France's Independence Day and the nation's greatest holiday. Fourth Army headquarters issued the following message: "The Republic of France presents its compliments to her soldiers in the field, and begs the pleasure and the honor of a glass of wine with them."[13] So that all soldiers of the French Army could share in the toast to the Republic, a bottle of champagne was issued for each four soldiers of all regiments; each two company-grade officers shared a bottle; and the field-grade officers were invited to help themselves to available supplies—meaning they could have all they wanted. International toasts were proposed by all, with the most enthusiastic being raised by units of the French Fourth Army to their commander. Some of Gouraud's soldiers had figured out his plans to defeat the expected German offensive in his sector with minimum exposure of his units to danger.

It was reported that in their toasts that day, many of his soldiers swore that their commanding general would not be disappointed in them when the time came to carry out his orders.[14]

The toasts to Gouraud represented more than recognition of an army commander who used his men effectively. Gouraud was a combat soldier of the first order noted for being at the front and in the trenches with his units. He had been severely wounded at Gallipoli Peninsula in the Dardenelles campaign. His injuries cost the red-bearded general an arm and two broken legs and left him with a permanent limp. His exploits in Algeria had earned him the nickname *le Lion d'Afrique*. For his present actions and exploits his men would call him "the Lion of France." Gouraud's courage and his recognized efforts to utilize tactics to preserve the lives of his men had gained him the great admiration and respect of the men under his command.[15]

The Germans did not celebrate Bastille Day, and their activities at the front line continued as usual. The day before the French celebration, a large intelligence team from one of Gouraud's Fourth Army divisions, commanded by Sgt. Joseph Darnaud, left on patrol at 7:55 PM with orders to penetrate deep into German territory and capture prisoners of the highest rank available. Darnaud's team crossed into no-man's-land undetected, and during the night and into the early morning of 14 July pushed out well beyond the fourth trench line and into German-held ground.[16] There they encountered a large German force and engaged in a fierce and bloody hand-to-hand fight in which the patrol captured approximately two dozen prisoners, including a German major. A quick search of the captured Germans revealed a gas mask case carrying a sheaf of papers that appeared to be of some importance. Back at division headquarters, intelligence officers determined that the papers contained the exact date, times, and sequence of the launching of the expected German drive.[17]

The capture of the German attack plans benefited the French immensely because the captured information revealed that the attack was scheduled for that very night, 14–15 July, five days earlier than Foch had anticipated. Within hours Gouraud had sent orders to all of his regiments to have their battalions still on the forward line fall back to the secondary trench line after dark. The orders warned the units to expect a heavy German artillery bombardment on the forward trenches at ten minutes past midnight and a German infantry attack to begin at 4:15 AM.[18]

At fifteen minutes before midnight every artillery piece in the Allied line, from the Swiss border to the French coast, opened up in a preemptive counter-battery fire. Artillery fire was concentrated on areas where German assault infantry were expected to assemble for the attack. It was a gamble by Foch and a measure of his trust in Gouraud's judgment. Foch knew that if the information found on the German major turned out to be a well-executed hoax, he would have revealed the location of his own concealed massed artillery batteries to the advantage of Ludendorff's counterbattery fire.[19]

At ten minutes after midnight, the German guns opened up en masse as scheduled in support of their attack and the Battle of Champagne-Marne had begun. The artillery duel reached such intensity that for the next seven hours men in the secondary trenches had to shout to be heard. The thunder of guns firing and shells exploding was heard as far away as Paris and caused residents to turn off their gas meters in expectation of an air attack.[20]

On the German side of the front, Crown Prince Wilhelm had climbed an artillery observation tower near Pont Faverger to watch the start of the offensive. He was expressing some concern over the heavy activity of the French artillery, which had just blown up several ammunition dumps within his sight, when the German artillery opened the attack. The massive and devastating French artillery attack caused some doubts to creep into Wilhelm's mind, yet he managed to find a kind of poetry in the vista: "It was an overwhelming scene," he wrote, "the pitch-black sky stabbed by quivering flashes of lightning, bursts of flame, a scene from the inferno, an apocalyptic symphony of destruction."[21]

In front of the 369th Infantry's reserve line, sixteen volunteers pushed themselves hard against the dirt walls and down into the muddy holes of the forward trenches and outposts, waiting for the German barrage to cease and the assault infantry to start its attack. Finally, after five and one-half hours of brutal bombardment, the German heavy artillery lifted its fire and the lighter 77-mm field guns laid down a rolling barrage forward of the French positions.[22]

Although shaken by the intensity of the French artillery attack on their assembly areas, the German assault infantrymen moved forward and crossed no-man's-land behind the rolling barrage. When the rolling barrage was lifted, assault commanders were surprised at the sparse resistance they were experiencing from the French trenches. When the Germans reached the first line of barbed wire in front of the French forward outposts and began cutting through, the camouflage teams triggered the obsolete machine guns, fired off rockets, threw grenades at the Germans, and then ran to the rear and into the original main frontline trenches.[23]

The German infantry cut through the first line of wire, swept past the abandoned outposts, and approached the main frontline trenches. The camouflage teams in the main trenches opened the valves on the poisonous gas canisters, set off remote-controlled mustard gas shells in the dugouts, fired more flares, set off more machine guns, and then made a hasty retreat to the secondary lines. As the forward elements of the German attack troops moved into the French frontline trenches, the massed artillery of the French Fourth Army opened up on them. Casualties from blasts and shrapnel from air-burst high-explosive shells began to soar. When the surviving German infantry scrambled for shelter in the abandoned dugouts and trenches, they encountered the chlorine and mustard gas let loose by the camouflage teams and suffered more casualties.[24]

All the members of the 369th's camouflage team made their way back to the reserve trenches without casualties and joined their companies in preparation for the expected fight with the Germans who managed to break through the trap. Colonel Hayward, recognizing that there was no corps reserve behind him, realized the gravity of the position in which the 369th Infantry found itself: "The first thing I knew all there was between the German Army and Paris on a stretch of front a little more than four miles long was my regiment of Negroes. But it was fair enough at that; all there was between us and Berlin was the German Army."[25]

That night, Lt. Rudolf Binding, a German staff officer who had advanced with the attacking forces, confirmed the effectiveness of Gouraud's maneuver when he wrote in his diary:

> I have lived through the most disheartening day of the whole War, though it was by no means the most dangerous. . . . Our guns bombarded empty trenches; our gas-shells gassed empty artillery positions; only in little folds of the ground, sparsely distributed, lay machine-gun posts, like lice in the seams and folds of a garment, to give the attacking force a warm welcome. . . . We did not see a single dead Frenchman, let alone a captured gun or machine gun, and we had suffered heavy losses.[26]

To Ludendorff's chagrin, the eastern half of his great offensive ground to a halt without achieving any significant success. Gouraud's elastic defense had held; the only ground lost was that planned for in the buffer zone used for the massive artillery barrage on the German troops. Ludendorff's attacks to the west of Rheims, however, had been more successful. His troops were able to penetrate General De Mitry's front, and several assault divisions had crossed the Marne and were eight to ten kilometers beyond Dormans. On General Berthelot's front, where there was no river to cross, Ludendorff's divisions had been able to bisect Mont des Rheims. By nightfall on 15 July, Ludendorff's offensive drive had faltered and stalled. On the morning of 16 July the French defensive crust hardened; at midday, with failure on one front and stalemate on the other, Ludendorff called a halt to the attack.[27] Crown Prince Wilhelm, who had expressed his concerns about the unusually heavy activity of the French artillery just before the German attack was launched, had to report to his father, Kaiser Wilhelm, that the grand attack had failed.[28] Young Leutnant Binding wrote prophetically in his diary: "Since our experiences on July 16th, I know that we are finished."[29]

Gouraud's plan was executed so well that the 369th Infantry's battalions never had to defend their positions. Many of the attacking Germans were killed or wounded long before they could get into rifle, grenade, or bayonet range, and the shocked survivors were forced to lie for hours in the open above the gas-filled forward trenches, exposed to heavy French artillery shelling.[30]

The Germans made minor breakthroughs in several other sectors of the Fourth Army's front, but the few attackers who were even that successful were solidly held at Gouraud's second line. French units began local counterattacks at once on the flanks of these salients to clean them out before the Germans could fortify the reverse side of the few French trenches they had been able to occupy. Gouraud's elastic defense was successful beyond everyone's expectations in the 369th Infantry's sector, and his men's trust in him totally justified.[31]

CHAPTER 14

Marshal Foch Prepares
to Attack

They ran wild simply wild over me,
They're as reckless as reckless can be,
No matter where I'm at, when I take off my hat,
There are little ones, and big ones,
You can pick them off like that,
Oh, how they bite, oh, how they bite all over me,
They make me just as sore as I can be,
But at night when I lay down,
Each little coot will seek a crown,
Oh, how they crawled, how they crawled all over me.

Sgt. J. A. Jamieson, 369th Infantry,
somewhere in the trenches in France, 1918

Marshal Foch had not been idle while General Ludendorff was making his offensive move. Foch had his own plans, which included an immediate offensive to recapture lost ground and straighten his lines as a prelude to a fall offensive intended to finish the war. The French Tenth Army would be his spearhead for this preliminary offensive action, with the point aimed just south of Soissons. The French Sixth, Ninth, and Fifth Armies would attack along their fronts east of the Tenth Army and west of Rheims. General Gouraud's Fourth Army would attack on its front east of Rheims and west of the Argonne Forest.[1]

At 8:00 AM on 15 July, the 369th Infantry received orders to leave the defensive trenches of Gouraud's elastic defense maneuver and march six and one-half kilometers westward to Camp Bravard. There the regiment paused to rest and await further orders. Later that day orders arrived instructing Colonel Hayward to move the regiment nearer the front lines to the vicinity of Minaucourt, west of La Main de Massiges and opposite Butte du Mesnil in the Beauséjour sector.[2]

Just as it reached its destination, the regiment was released from Major General Le Gallais's French 16th Infantry Division and assigned to the French 161st Infantry Division under Major General Lebouc in preparation for a counterattack against a German salient that extended into that division's sector. The regiment immediately moved into the holding trenches, relieved an exhausted French Moroccan regiment, and deployed with the 1st Battalion on the left, the 2d on the right, and the 3d in the center of the line. To the left of the regiment was a veteran French regiment of Chasseurs Alpins; to the right was another veteran French unit, a Moroccan regiment. The 369th Infantry found itself in the fast company of two crack combat-hardened infantry units.[3]

The German artillery fire that accompanied the 369th Infantry's move into position that afternoon was light and sporadic; that would change. For the next three days the regiment found itself under increasingly heavy gas and high-explosive bombardments. Major Little, commanding the 1st Battalion, described the conditions for the troops in the trenches through 16 and 17 July while they waited for orders to attack:

> Hell was at work. Casualties became more frequent. Our trenches were shallow. Now, not only did direct hits do execution, but the shrapnel from air bursts found frequent victims.
>
> Our colored soldiers were tired, and in a sense, hungry. They knew that their only immediate moves were to be forward, and that their only relief from the danger of the moment was to be by the greater danger of assault upon seen enemies.[4]

On 18 July Foch launched the Aisne-Marne offensive to reoccupy abandoned and lost terrain all along the Allied front. On the Fourth Army's front, the French 161st Infantry Division had been ordered to reduce the salient in the Beauséjour and Crochet sectors opposite the German stronghold at Butte du Mesnil. German units in this salient were anticipating a counterattack and were busy digging in, bringing in reinforcements, and preparing to hold what little ground they had gained in their offensive. The French 163d, 215th, and 363d Infantry Regiments of Lebouc's French 161st Infantry Division were to lead the attack. Several battalions of Chasseurs and the 369th Infantry were to remain in reserve and support. The 1st Battalion, 369th Infantry, relieved the French 47th Chasseurs Regiment; the 2d Battalion was positioned to the left of the Tourbe River; and the 3d Battalion was placed in support of the French 163d Infantry Regiment.[5]

During 20 and 21 July the 369th Infantry's battalions continued to push up close behind the French assault regiments and place companies on the line where they were needed to help extricate the Germans from the trenches and

force them back. The officers and men were on constant patrol and reconnaissance assignments, always under heavy high-explosive and gas attacks and
subjected to dangerous sniping by German sharpshooters left behind to harass
the regiment from the rear.[6]

On 21 July the 369th Infantry was relieved and shifted to the Calvaire sector. After two days of hard fighting in the Calvaire section north of Minaucourt the regiment was moved to an area between Butte du Mesnil and La Main
de Massiges, where the battalions were exposed to additional hard combat.
The opposing armies bickered back and forth over the area for the next four
weeks, fighting in extremely difficult terrain and weather. Casualties within the
regiment continued to mount as small but savage German attacks continued
during daylight hours across a front of more than one thousand meters. At
night, numerous large enemy patrols trying to penetrate the wire had to be
fought off. At the same time, the regiment was required by division headquarters to send out its own patrols into no-man's-land to probe for information,
putting a further strain on manpower resources.[7]

As the attack gained momentum, the 369th Infantry and the other regiments of the French 161st Infantry Division began to advance so rapidly that
they came across large quantities of rifles, helmets, bayonets, gas masks, packs,
blankets, entrenching tools, lanterns, and stockpiles of ammunition abandoned
by the fleeing Germans. Of major importance were excellent maps that revealed artillery, machine-gun, and rifle-fire patterns used by the Germans in
defending their position.[8]

The heaviest gas attacks thus far experienced by the regiment occurred
during this period in an area of operations containing numerous low-lying
marshes in which gas collected, then rose in visible clouds to be spread again
across the front by the wind. Working and fighting while wearing gas masks
was demoralizing for everyone, and many of the inexperienced men did not
even recognize what gases were being used. Some of those who had been exposed without their gas masks crawled into captured dugouts or tunnels and
lay down, believing they would die from the choking and nausea. Officers and
noncommissioned officers had to take off their masks and demonstrate that the
gas in use was not fatal in order to get the men out of the trenches and back into
the fight.[9]

By 6 August Foch had straightened his lines between Soissons and Rheims.
German casualties were heavy, though not ruinous, due in the main to an
orderly and skillfully executed withdrawal of the assault divisions. The initiative had passed to Foch, and with morale sagging on the German home front,
Ludendorff recognized that his hope of crushing the Allies before the Americans could bring their forces fully into place would not be realized. The second
half of Ludendorff's operation, a cherished attack against the British, had to be

scrapped. Ludendorff would later call 8 August 1918 "the Black Day of the German Army."[10]

On the early morning of 18 August, a German raiding party entered the lines in front of the 369th Infantry with the usual orders to take prisoners for interrogation. They located and attacked an outpost with rifle fire and then went into the dugout to fight hand-to-hand with trench knives and clubs. The party captured Lt. A. M. Jones and four enlisted men of the regiment and started back to their lines through an abandoned communications trench.[11]

Ahead of the returning Germans and near that communications trench, Sgt. William (Bill) Butler of Company L and two comrades were manning a remote listening post. In the first faint light of dawn, Butler caught sight of the patrol and its prisoners working their way toward his position. Butler waited until the patrol was within a few yards of him, then shouted for the lieutenant and the four men to drop to the ground and opened fire with his Chauchat light machine gun. He killed four Germans, then went forward and captured those who were not able to get away, among them a wounded lieutenant who later died. Butler left his second in command in charge of the listening post, and with the German captives and the five Americans in tow, worked his way back to regimental lines to report to his combat group commander with his prizes.[12] A German report captured at a later date described Butler's actions as "an enemy group in overwhelming numbers" and claimed that due to the superior size of the rescue party, seven German enlisted men and one officer failed to return from the patrol.[13] For his valor and courage Butler was awarded the Distinguished Service Cross and the Croix de Guerre.[14]

At midnight on 25 August the regiment received orders to move to an assembly point behind the trench lines at Somme-Bionne. After the battalions reached the assigned coordinates, they loaded up on 150 or so canvas-topped French Army trucks, the famed camions, driven by Senegalese troops. Hayward had received no instructions in his orders beyond the assembly point and had no idea what their destination was to be. The convoy moved out into the night and proceeded south through the rolling French countryside. At 3:00 AM the next morning, the trucks halted at Courtisols, ten kilometers to the east of Châlons, where the regiment was billeted for the rest of the night.[15]

The next morning, Hayward received open orders to take his men by foot to Camp Saint-Ouen, near Dompret, for extended rest, refitting, and training. After marching to the south on 28–30 August, the regiment arrived at their much-anticipated destination and billeted in what some of the officers described as the best camp they had occupied thus far in France. For the first time in more than 130 days, no battalion of the regiment was on the line or under enemy fire.[16]

Immediately, division began sending administrative, equipping, and training support to the regiment in anticipation of the Americans' part in the big push that Foch planned to execute in the near future. It seemed to the men of the regiment that every available asset in the local French military system was being brought to bear to promote the morale and efficiency of the unit. The efforts of the French were gratefully accepted, and everyone settled into the comfort of a much-needed rest period.[17] Hayward commented on the treatment of the regiment to his law partner in New York: "The French generals, from Gen. Gouraud down, say that we did our work as well as the veteran French infantry regiments on either side of us. . . . You should see my bullies now. All clean, de-loused, new uniforms, spick and span and happy, and how they can drill and manoeuvre."[18]

The delousing Hayward mentioned in his letter was a great relief to the men. During the heavy fighting of the previous five weeks the troops had experienced a real taste of the French *totos*, referred to by the American troops as "seam squirrels" or "cooties."[19] Sgt. J. A. Jamieson best described the experience: "It seemed as though when you killed one a whole regiment came after you, and they selected no other time than when you were drowsy and sleepy."[20]

Lice were not the only pests the men of the regiment had to deal with in the trenches. Large black rats ran everywhere and gnawed into everything. After a time the men became somewhat accustomed to the constant scurrying noises at night. The ingenuity of the American soldier in finding new ways to entertain himself rose to the occasion in a pastime that involved killing rats with grenades and keeping score of the count. Sometimes the sport got out of hand, as when Pvt. Lionel Rogers let a grenade slip out of his hand and as a result landed in the hospital, fortunately with only minor injuries.[21]

On the afternoon of 7 September a lone French motorcycle courier, covered with dust and splattered with mud, roared up and skidded to a stop in front of regimental headquarters to deliver urgent orders from Lebouc. As luck would have it, the regiment's rest period was being cut short.[22] The 369th Infantry packed up that afternoon and marched out of the camp early the next morning to proceed north on foot, arriving that night at Vitry-le-François. Then, in the "hurry-up-and-wait" complex common to all armies, the officers and men of the regiment "sat on their heels" and waited for further orders.[23]

The next evening, a convoy of the now-familiar rough-riding camions arrived for transport and the regiment motored farther north, to dismount in the middle of the night at Croix-en-Champagne. The next day, 10 September, the regiment conducted a long and trying forced march to camps near Somme-Bionne, the exact spot from which they had started for their rest area nearly two weeks before. The following day was spent issuing ammunition and other supplies and preparing to move to the front.[24]

On the evening of 11 September the regiment moved up into the trenches at a point where the French 215th Infantry Regiment needed relief. The French commander turned over the Beauséjour sector, located just to the west of Calvaire and one and one-half kilometers south of Butte du Mesnil and near Vilquin, to the 369th Infantry and pulled his men out of the line to lick their wounds and catch their breath.[25]

Immediately, the regiment received word from division headquarters to expect a projector attack on 12 or 13 September. The projector attack, one of many ruses employed by both sides, was to become a favorite tactic of the Germans until the end of the war. Although almost always effective to some extent, the projector attack seemed to succeed best against Allied units who were fresh to the front and still unfamiliar with the various tricks used in combat. This particular method of attack began with German aircraft appearing above the target area and performing aerobatics, with the intention of drawing curious troops out of the dugouts and trenches to watch.[26] A German observation aircraft standing off and out of the battle area would determine when enough men had gathered in the open to justify an attack and would then signal artillery batteries to deliver a massive gas bombardment. Following that attack, a concentrated high-explosives bombardment, usually lasting about an hour, would be delivered on the Allied trenches. After the artillery bombardment, a massed German infantry attack would be launched against the dazed survivors in the hope of catching them before they could recover enough to organize and repel the assault.[27]

On 12 September several German aircraft appeared over the lines of the 369th Infantry's sector and began performing rolls and loops. At that time the 1st Battalion was on the line, with the 2d and 3d Battalions in support. A few minutes after the appearance of the aircraft, German artillery and heavy mortars opened up on the trench line and over the next hour and twenty minutes dumped a heavy gas barrage and then more than nine thousand rounds of high-explosives shells on the 369th Infantry's positions. When the German guns ceased firing, seven infantry regiments went over the top to attack the lines of the 1st Battalion.[28]

When the assaulting German troops approached the wire, they found themselves caught in heavy interlocking fire from the 2d and 3d Battalions' machine-gun companies, which had been moved onto the line, and by the 1st Battalion's light and heavy machine guns. The assault stalled in no-man's-land, and none of the attacking German soldiers was able to reach the parapets of the 369th Infantry's forward trenches.[29]

During the daylight hours of 13 and 14 September, the officers and men of the 369th Infantry's battalions manned the trenches and outposts and repelled numerous localized, yet fierce, heavy attacks. Nor could they rest at night. The requirements of placing deep patrols into no-man's-land to penetrate the German lines and bring back prisoners and information put a further strain on the officers and men. Finally, on 15 September, the regiment received welcome relief by a French Fourragère regiment. Within this five-day period in the Beauséjour sector the 369th Infantry experienced the heaviest fighting and the severest casualty rates it had thus far seen in the war.[30]

The exhausted regiment at last marched away from the line, retracing its steps south until it reached the towns of Somme Tourbe and Somme Bionne, where the officers and men would try to finish their abbreviated rest period and undergo eight days of training in open warfare.[31] The men knew this rest period was only a short respite; the training could only be in preparation for a greater battle: Foch's fall offensive.

CHAPTER 15

The First Stages of the Fall Offensive

What a sight met our eyes as we advanced. The dead were everywhere and the wounded suffered in the churned up fields.

André Simonet, Marchel de Logis, French Army,
attached to the 371st Infantry

Units of the Allied armies began repositioning along the entire Western Front in early September 1918 (see map 4). Marshal Foch was preparing his forces, reinforced by General Pershing's AEF, to bring the war to an end with a gigantic fall offensive.[1] The main attacks were to begin in late September after the reduction of the Saint-Mihiel salient to the south of Verdun. General Pershing's First Army, consisting of twenty U.S. divisions, was ordered to make this preparatory attack beginning on 12 September. After reducing the salient, the First Army was to shift the bulk of its combat formations some ninety-five kilometers east to the Argonne Forest to join in the main effort with the French and British forces. The Americans, though faced with heavy and aggressive defense, finished reducing the salient by 16 September. The process cost the U.S. Army seven thousand casualties.[2]

With the Saint-Mihiel salient reduced, Foch began focusing on the next step in his plan, which involved two major and two minor elements. One major attack was to consist of a combined French and American assault to be made in the Meuse-Argonne sector aimed at capturing Charleville-Mézières and gaining control of the rail communications systems located there. The other major attack would be a British assault between Perrone and Lens. In the minor attacks, a Franco-British force was to make an assault in the Perrone–La Fere sector while an Anglo-Belgian force thrust into Flanders.[3]

The first attack, scheduled for 26 September, was to be executed by Pershing's AEF and French General Maistre and his Army Group Centre in the Meuse-Argonne sector. On 27 September General Haig was to attack into Flanders with his British army to overrun the Hindenburg Line. On 28 September King Albert was to take his Anglo-Belgian force up against the Ypres-Armentières sector in Flanders.[4]

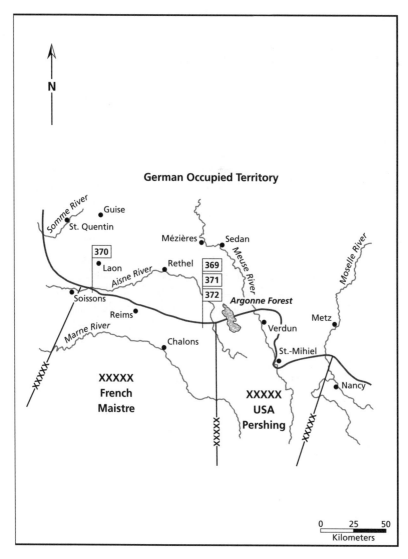

Map 4. Locations of the 93d Division Regiments at the Start of the Fall Offensive, September 1918

As September ground on toward mid-month, it had to be obvious to even the most casual observer—and most certainly to any German spy standing around after dark along one of the many dozens of main roads leading to the Allied side of the front—that a major battle was soon to come.[5] Each evening at dusk, Allied infantry units disgorged from temporary billets, formed up in columns, and struggled forward. The foot-weary soldiers constantly found themselves being pushed off the roads by a heavy traffic of war machines and materials. Trucks by the hundreds, horse-drawn batteries of French 75s, and tractors pulling heavy guns ground toward the front. Machine-gun carts, cavalry troops, an occasional tank unit, ambulances, command cars, and various other types of mobile equipment jammed the roads and threw up clouds of dust that choked the infantrymen slogging along the roadsides.[6]

The blacked-out columns of the French, British, Belgian, and American armies stumbled along into the dark night, halting and starting and halting again, but always moving toward the front. Lost units searched for the correct diverting road, short-tempered military police worked to untangle traffic snarls at crossroads, equipment breakdowns were pushed off the roadway to be later recovered and repaired. Couriers on motorcycles skidding and dodging wildly in and out of the traffic added further chaos to the already overwhelming confusion.[7] Then, as the first light of dawn approached, the villages and towns along the route seemed to swallow up the masses of men; the machines of war left the roads and disappeared into farm buildings or camouflaged positions in nearby woods. By daybreak the white chalk roads stretching toward the front were deserted and appeared deceptively peaceful.[8]

In the weeks just prior to mid-September, regiment-sized units all along General Gouraud's Fourth Army front had been rotated to the rear to be trained and equipped for open warfare in anticipation of the breakout. All of these units had either returned to their divisions or were among those pushing along the roads to the front. Within the French IX Corps sector of the French Fourth Army, the French 2d Moroccan Division and the French 161st Infantry Division, which included the 369th Infantry, had been deployed on the line for some time. To the right of the French IX Corps stood the French XXXVIII Corps, and to the left, the French II Corps.[9]

According to General Gouraud's plans for his French IX Corps, the French 157th Infantry Division, which included the 371st and 372d Infantry Regiments, would soon move up to strengthen the corps for the attack.[10] The French IX Corps was to attack along the eastern slope of the Champagne Plateau, a chalky, hilly region cut west to east by two streams: the River Dormoise, running just south of the city of Dormoise, and the Alin (Avègres), running between Ardéuil and Montfauxelles. The resulting valleys and intervening ridges formed natural defensive obstacles of which the Germans had taken full advantage. Massive wire entanglements, machine-gun and artillery emplacements, fortified dugouts, and trenches saturated the area. Along the rivers and to the west of the main axis of advance of the IX Corps lay low, marshy areas that severely impeded the advance of any attacking force on foot, much less any truck or tank traffic.[11]

The first and main German defenses in the area that the two divisions containing the 369th, 371st, and 372d Infantry Regiments would attack lay on a line running west-southwest to east-northeast a few hundred meters south of a road west out of Cernay-en-Dormois that passed through the summit of Butte du Mesnil. These lines, on a plateau called the Maison de Champagne Upland, were the best organized of the German defenses in the French Fourth Army's area and were the first obstacle the IX Corps would be required to penetrate.[12]

Behind the main German defenses, two lines of heavy fortifications had been constructed on the northern face and ridge of the Dormoise River valley in an area called the Gratreuil Upland. The first, on a small promontory between the Dormoise River and a small tributary to the north, looked down into the Dormoise River valley and would control any attempts made by the Allied forces to cross the river. The second line, on the main ridge itself, consisted of a rise called Bellevue Signal Ridge and the summit, Hill 188, which the Germans had turned into a major fortress with a continuous line of trenches, tunnels, and deep dugouts dispersed throughout the area.[13] In back of the second line and beyond the Alin River on the ridge known as the Marvaux Upland, German defenses were not as continuous or as deep as they were in the southernmost defenses. Instead, small villages had been fortified with machine-gun and light artillery pieces; house-to-house fighting would be required to drive out the defenders.[14]

As of early September, the 371st, 372d, and French 333d Infantry Regiments, all assigned to the French 157th Infantry Division under the XVII Corps, were still engaged in combat operations along the front in Subsector Verrières in the Verdun area of the Meuse-Argonne region. Allied plans called for divisions of the newly formed U.S. First Army to replace all of the French units in the Meuse-Argonne region by mid-September. In early September regiments of the French 157th Infantry Division received orders to move first to the rear areas to receive open-warfare training and then on to the Champagne region to join Gouraud's Fourth Army as part of General Garnier-Duplessix's IX Corps.[15]

During the night of 7–8 September, under cover of heavy fog and light rain, the 372d Infantry was relieved on the line by the 129th Infantry, 33d Division, U.S. Army, and was able to pull back without drawing German artillery fire. The regiment moved to a rest area near Boise-de-Brecourt and Bois-de-Pierre, about ten kilometers south of Hill 310 and near the village of Rampont. Billets were crude, but there were adequate barracks with cots and running water, and the men enjoyed some comfort while training in gas and open-warfare techniques.[16]

Some 250 camions showed up in the regimental area of the 372d Infantry at about 7:00 PM on 13 September, and the officers and men climbed aboard to endure a tiring nineteen-hour ride south to the vicinity of Brienne-le-Château (Haute Marne). The regiment received additional training there, and on 16 September boarded a train bound for Vitry-le-François. From Vitry-le-François the regiment moved in stages to its destination near the towns of Hans, a few kilometers northwest of Somme-Bionne.[17]

At the same time the 372d Infantry was moving out of Subsector 304 on 7–8 September, the 371st Infantry was relieved on the line by the 313th Infantry, 79th Division, U.S. Army. The regiment marched from the lines to a rear area near Boise-de-Brecourt and Bois-de-Pierre at Helitz–l'Eveque to rest and receive additional training. Colonel Miles had gone to Chaumont to arrange for rations and other supplies before the orders to move arrived and was surprised to find his regiment gone when he returned.[18]

On the evening of 14 September the 371st Infantry boarded camions and started the trip to the west, moving along the same route the 372d Infantry had taken. During more days of marching, trucking, and occasional pauses for more training, the regiment wound its way along the network of roads behind French lines, finally reaching Hans near Somme-Bionne on 23 September, just before the arrival of the 372d Infantry. After both regiments had settled into their billets, an order came down from higher headquarters for the men to get all the rest possible within the next forty-eight hours.[19]

The 369th Infantry of the French 161st Infantry Division had been relieved on the line on 15 September by a French Fourragèere regiment, and moved south to the vicinity of Somme-Tourbe and Somme-Bionne with orders to rest and undergo eight days of open-warfare training. Although no one from higher command said so, the training was obviously in preparation for the anticipated Allied offensive.[20]

By 24 September three of the 93d Division's regiments—the 369th, 371st, and 372d Infantries—were located in and around the neighboring villages of Somme-Tourbe, Somme-Bionne, and Hans, resting and training in preparation for moving forward into the Champagne Front as a part of the French IX Corps under Gouraud's Fourth Army.[21] During this time the officers and men of the regiments stripped down to the bare essentials for battle; all excess items were stored in warehouses in the area. Each man carried extra canteens, extra ammunition, reserve rations, and one blanket along with his helmet, rifle, and gas mask.[22]

As the men prepared for battle, they were keenly aware of the activity along the roads leading past their billeting areas and were quick to notice when traffic reached saturation on 24–25 September as men, equipment, and supplies shuffled toward the front. The tremendous activity was a signal to anyone, friend or foe, that a great battle was about to be fought.[23]

While waiting to be committed to the upcoming battle, the men of the three regiments of the 93d Division found some diversion in watching as various types of huge artillery guns were positioned nearby. The monster artillery pieces were being prepared to send their shells over and beyond the front lines and into the German rear marshaling areas and supply routes. The most fascinating of these behemoths were the 14-inch naval guns mounted on railroad flatcars and towed about behind the front lines by locomotives. The crews of mixed French and African artillerymen delighted in showing off their knowledge of gunnery to the awed Americans and impressing them with the size and weight of the shells and the gun's thirty-two-kilometer range.[24]

On the afternoon of 25 September the Fourth Army was placed on alert, and all who were to participate in the attack were ordered to report to their units. The men of the three regiments of the 93d Division gathered together and settled in to await the order to advance to the front line.[25]

The initial objective of Gouraud's Fourth Army was the capture of the railroad yards and complex at Mézières and the railroad tracks extending east and west behind the German main lines. On the right flank of the Fourth Army was the American First Army's I Corps commanded by Lt. Gen. Hunter Liggett. Its objective was to capture the rail complex at Sedan, about twenty-five kilometers east of Mézières.[26]

On 24 September Brigadier General Goybet, the commander of the French 157th Infantry Division, issued the following orders and instructions to his unit commanders (translated from the French):

A breaking and exploitation battle will be engaged in on the CHAMPAGNE FRONT. This Corps, including the 2d Moroccan Division, 161st D.I., and 157th D.I. will take part in it. The 2d Moroccan D.I. (to the left), the 161st (to the right) have a breaking mission. The 157th D.I. in A.C. Reserve has in principle an exploitation mission—nevertheless it can receive during the action a quite different mission. The 9th Corps is framed on the right by the 38th Corps and to the left by the 2d Corps.

Successive objectives [maps supplied to units showing these objectives not reproduced here]:

Execution of the attack by the rupture divisions.

The attack will be made up to the second objective included under protection of a rolling barrage. Before attacking a new objective, rolling barrage will be stopped so that assaulting units may be put in order. . . .

Beyond the 2nd objective, the attack will progress supported by the accompanying artillery. It is no longer a question of time, each division will progress for itself.

The attack on the 3rd objective will take place at an hour fixed by the command. It will do its best to reach the brown line in order to have sufficient advance in front of the 2nd objective. . . .
Command posts at the beginning of the attack:
157th Div. P.C. Henry
2d Moroccan Div. P.C. Balon
161 Div. Minaucourt
I.D. 157th Somme-Bionne (Town Hall—"Marie")[27]

At dusk on 25 September the officers and men of the 369th Infantry marched from their rest and training areas at Somme-Tourbe and Somme-Bionne, working their way through the massive traffic congestion on the roads to the north. They arrived at prepared positions behind the front lines to the east of Minaucourt just before 10:00 PM.[28]

The 371st and 372d Infantry Regiments and their sister French regiment, the 333d, forming Goybet's French 157th Infantry Division and designated as the XI Corps reserve and exploiting force, would remain in their billeting areas until the attack had begun. Once the attack had been launched they would then move up behind and follow the French 2d Moroccan Infantry Division and French 161st Infantry Division after these divisions had penetrated the first objective—the line of trenches and fortification at and just behind the German front line.[29]

At 11:00 PM on 25 September, the entire artillery assets of the French Fourth Army opened up with a barrage that lasted almost six and one-half hours and expended more ammunition than was used on both sides during the entire U.S. Civil War. Capt. Chester D. Heywood, 371st Infantry, described the shelling from his vantage point:

> Our billets were on a ridge that overlooked the Champagne to the north and the Argonne Forest to the east. At the first crack of the guns we were all out of our blankets and watching the show. The noise was terrific. Trench mortars and lighter guns were between us and the enemy, with the heavies behind us. The flashes from the batteries made an almost continuous line of fire along the front. . . . Shells from the rear sounded like freight trains over us. Hour after hour the din continued.[30]

André Simonet, a veteran French officer and interpreter-instructor attached to the 371st Infantry who was with Heywood at the time of the artillery attack, later commented: "That night an artillery bombardment began the like of which I have never heard. The thunder and roar of the massed artillery shook the earth and the sky was alight with the flashes of the guns. It was won-drous—it was insanity and the fever of it gripped us all."[31]

At 5:00 AM on 26 September, the heavy guns ceased their preparation shelling and the French 75-mm batteries opened up with a rolling barrage. At 5:30 AM the French 2d Moroccan and the French 161st Divisions along with the rest of the French Fourth Army assault divisions left their trenches and ad-vanced behind the rolling barrage through heavy fog and mist. As the troops advanced, they found an enemy stunned by the artillery bombardment and German dead and wounded lying all over the battlefield.[32]

Similar army-sized attacks, echeloned at twenty-four-hour intervals, were to be launched along the entire Allied front from the Swiss border to the Bel-gian coastline. The Fourth Army's assault was the beginning phase of the last and greatest Allied offensive action of the war.[33]

CHAPTER 16

The Attack on
Bellevue Signal Ridge

Corporal Stowers' conspicuous gallantry, extraordinary heroism and
supreme devotion to his men were well above and beyond the call of duty,
follow the finest traditions of military service and reflect the utmost
credit on him and the United States Army.

Medal of Honor citation for
Cpl. Freddie Stowers

As Marshal Foch's fall offensive launched into being in the morning hours of
26 September 1918, the 369th Infantry, with its 1st Battalion forward as
the division's ready reserve, stood in general reserve for General Modelon's
French 161st Infantry Division. The French 157th Infantry Division, containing the 371st Infantry and 372d Infantry, would follow the French 161st In-
fantry Division in support. Leading the attack, the French 161st Infantry Division was aligned as follows: The French 163d Infantry Regiment was on the
left front, in contact with the French 2d Moroccan Infantry Division on its left
flank and with the 3d Battalion, 369th Infantry, in support. The French 363d
Infantry Regiment was on the right front, in contact with the French 74th
Infantry Division on its right flank and with the 2d Battalion, 369th Infantry, in
support (see map 5).[1]

As the attacking regiments moved forward early that morning, the 1st
Battalion, 369th Infantry, was instructed to stay in contact with the French
2d Moroccan Infantry Division's reserve regiment and to follow one to two
kilometers behind the French 161st Infantry Division's attacking regiments.
Colonel Hayward's instructions for the 369th Infantry were that two battalions operating in support roles were to be prepared to move forward and advance through the two assault regiments on the division attack line to exploit
breakthroughs as they occurred.[2]

The French 161st Infantry Division forced its attack on the outer and first
German defense line along a line between Ville-sur-Tourbe and Hurlus. The
assault battalions found little resistance, but at the second line the advance of
the assault regiments ground to a halt as the Germans mounted a fierce and

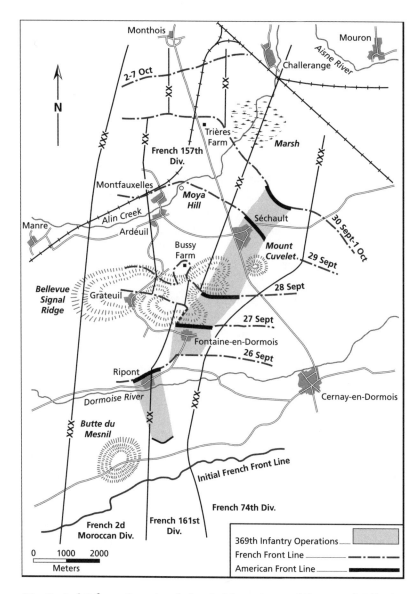

Map 5. 369th Infantry Operations during the Meuse-Argonne (Champagne) Offensive, 26 September to 1 October 1918

determined defense.[3] Later that day the French 161st Infantry Division managed to force its way through the second German defense line and again pushed slowly through ever-increasing resistance toward its first objective: the village of Ripont on the north bank of the Dormoise River. As the division advanced on its objective, the 369th Infantry received orders to come on the line and fill a gap just northeast of Butte du Mesnil between the French 161st Infantry Division and the French 2d Moroccan Infantry Division on its left. The two forward regiments of the French 161st Infantry Division had been forced to contract their fronts in the attack, and the French 74th Infantry Division was required to mount a heavy attack on fortified positions to the right of its front.[4]

Major Spencer's 3d Battalion moved up to fill the gap, established liaison with the French 2d Moroccan Division on its left and the French 163d Infantry Regiment on its right, and entered the line of attack a few hundred yards to the right front of Butte du Mesnil. The battalion then fought its way over open terrain to the marshy bottomlands of the Dormoise River. Under severe German machine-gun, mortar, and artillery fire, the lead companies forced a crossing just south of Ripont. After heavy street fighting in the village, the 3d Battalion succeeded in overcoming the defenders, in the process capturing several artillery pieces and machine guns and rounding up a number of German prisoners.[5]

At the end of the day, the 369th Infantry, whose 3d Battalion had been in contact with the enemy most of the afternoon, had advanced a total of about four thousand meters, with two thousand meters in piecemeal support and the rest in direct contact with German forces. The companies of the 3d Battalion had suffered heavy losses at the river crossing, in maneuvering in the marshy ground, and in capturing the town. Several officers and men had been killed, and many more had been wounded, including Spencer, who was struck by enemy fire on six separate occasions while personally leading the attack.[6]

An expected and critical barrier to the 3d Battalion's advance during the day was the marshy ground at the Dormoise River, which forced the platoons of the attacking companies into machine-gun fire-zones established by the German defenders. A platoon of Company K tried to ford the swampy area and got caught in the open in the marsh; many were wounded and unable to make their way out. Cpl. Elmer Earl, an infantryman, went into the marsh to pull the wounded to dry ground and give them first-aid treatment, then carried many of them to safety under direct and heavy German machine-gun fire. Earl was awarded the Distinguished Service Cross for his valor.[7]

Serious as it was, the day was not without its lighter moments. Pvt. Elmer McCowin of Company K, who was awarded a Distinguished Service Cross for his actions later in the day, related some of his earlier experiences:

> On September 26 the Captain asked me to carry dispatches. The Germans pumped machine gun bullets at me all the way. But I made the trip and back safely. Then I was sent out again. As I started with the message

the Captain yelled to bring him back a can of coffee. He was joking, but I didn't know it at the time.

Being a foot messenger, I had some time ducking those German bullets. Those bullets seemed very sociable, but I didn't care to meet up with them, so I kept right on traveling on high gear. None touched my skin though some skinned pretty close.

On the way back it seemed the whole war was turned on me. One bullet passed through my trousers and it made me hop, step and jump pretty lively. I saw a shell hole six feet deep. Take it from me, I dented another six feet when I plunged into it hard. In my fist I held the Captain's can of coffee.

When I climbed out of the shell hole and started running again, a bullet clipped a hole in the can and the coffee started to spill. But I turned around, stopped a second, looked the Kaiser in the face, and held up the can of coffee with my finger plugging up the hole to show the Germans they were fooled. Just then another bullet hit the can and another finger had to act as stopgap.

It must have been good luck that saved my life, because bullets were picking at my clothes and so many hit the can that at the end all my fingers were hugging it to keep the coffee in. I jumped into shell holes, wriggled along the ground, and got back safely. And what do you think? When I got back into our own trenches I stumbled and spilled the coffee![8]

Lt. George Miller, the battalion adjutant, confirmed McCowin's story: "When that soldier came back with the coffee his clothes were riddled with bullets. Yet, half an hour later he went back into No-Man's-land and brought back a number of wounded until he was badly gassed. Even then he refused to go to the rear and went out again for a wounded soldier. All this under fire. That's the reason he got the D.S.C."[9]

During the night of 26–27 September Modelon ordered a displacement of the 369th Infantry. The 3d Battalion, in contact on the line, shifted its front one thousand meters to the right, placing it about five hundred meters south of Fontaine-en-Dormoise and astride the road leading north into that village. The next morning the tired and depleted 3d Battalion attacked again against heavy German ground and artillery fire and strong defensive positions to capture Fontaine-en-Dormoise. After clearing the town of defenders, the battalion launched another attack north beyond the village, where the men began to encounter machine-gun and mortar fire coming from their left from the heavily fortified German positions on Bellevue Signal Ridge and its summit, Hill 188.[10]

Hill 188, the topmost point of Bellevue Signal Ridge, was a strong defensive position. A beehive of trenches and fortifications contained many machine-gun nests, some in concrete bunkers and pillboxes and all protected by heavy barbed-wire entanglements. The advance of the 3d Battalion slowed as the men came up against more hardened German defenses. The men gained respite as night began to fall and the battalion could stop its advance. They dug in between one hundred and two hundred meters forward of Fontaine-en-Dormoise at the lower eastern foot of Bellevue Signal Ridge. During the night, Hayward and the regimental headquarters moved into Fontaine-en-Dormoise and Captain Cobb's 2d Battalion moved up to relieve the 3d Battalion.[11]

At daybreak on 28 September the 2d Battalion, 369th Infantry, with a Moroccan battalion on each flank, attacked the fortified German lines. French artillery support was either lacking or largely ineffective, and the battalion experienced hard fighting while attempting to attack uphill in a dismal overcast and drizzling rain. As the battalion moved forward, it had to cut through jungles of barbed-wire entanglements and dig German defenders out of well-hidden bunkers and concrete emplacements. The 2d Battalion had soon pushed beyond the range of what little effective French artillery support there was, yet it was still able to advance about one thousand meters more to a point just to the south of the upper eastern end of Bellevue Signal Ridge before digging in for the night.[12]

While the French 161st Infantry Division was engaged in taking its objective on the lower eastern end of Bellevue Signal Ridge on 26 September, the French 157th Infantry Division was still in its positions around Somme-Bionne awaiting orders to move to the attack. Later that day, the French IX Corps commander ordered the division to move up just behind the lines and prepare to move forward to exploit gains made in the attack by the two leading divisions, the 2d Moroccan Infantry Division to the left and the French 161st Infantry Division on the right of the French IX Corps axis of advance. During the night of 26–27 September the regiments moved into positions just to the rear of the trenches of the original French front line, dug in, and waited (see map 6).[13]

At 1:00 PM on 27 September, the French 157th Infantry Division moved forward in a column of regiments with the 371st Infantry leading, the 372d Infantry in the center, and the French 333d Infantry following. The line of march was along the division's axis of advance, Butte du Mesnil–Ripont–Bussy Farm–Les Petit Rosières, and was to continue until contact was made with the enemy. On contact, the 371st Infantry and 372d Infantry were to move to the attack, with the 372d Infantry on the right flank and the 371st Infantry on the left (see maps 6 and 7). The Laure Battalion of the French 333d Infantry Regiment was to hold itself in support of the attacking regiments, and the remainder of the French 333d Infantry was held in division reserve.[14]

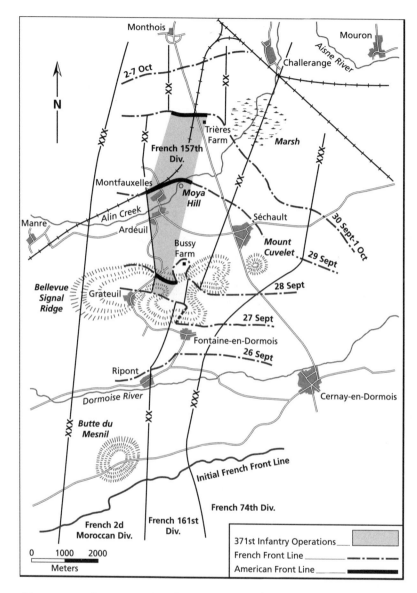

Map 6. 371st Infantry Operations during the Meuse-Argonne (Champagne) Offensive,
26 September to 1 October 1918

During the late afternoon of 27 September the French 157th Infantry Division's infantry commander, Col. T. C. Quillet, issued orders to implement the IX Corps commander's plan to execute a flanking maneuver. The 371st and 372d Infantry Regiments would be involved in a coordinated attack with the

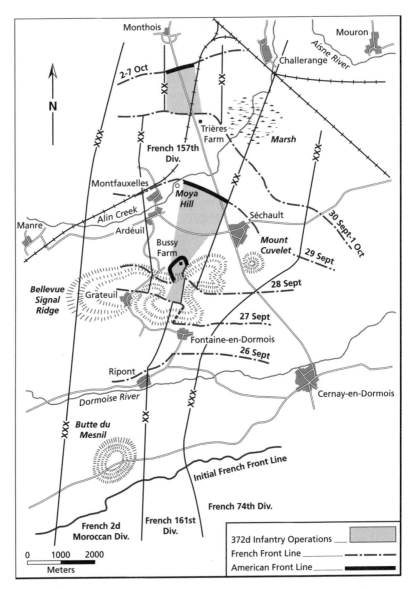

Map 7. 372d Infantry Operations during the Meuse-Argonne (Champagne) Offensive,
26 September to 7 October 1918

369th Infantry designed to drive the German defenders from the main summit of Bellevue Signal Ridge and Hill 188.[15]

At about 5:00 PM on 27 September, while still moving forward to make contact with the enemy, the 371st Infantry and 372d Infantry received orders that their mission had changed. They were to fill another gap that had developed between the French 2d Moroccan Infantry Division and the French 161st Infantry Division. Under dense fog and light drizzle, the regiments began to advance against the hill. The 372d Infantry moved up onto the center of the southern crest of Bellevue Signal Ridge to form the right flank of the division and made contact with the French 163d Infantry Regiment located between it and the 369th Infantry. The 371st Infantry came up on the left of the 372d Infantry to form the left flank and made contact with the right-flank regiment of the 2d Moroccan Infantry Division. Both regiments then dug in for the night.[16]

Maj. Joseph Pate's 2d Battalion, 371st Infantry, was charged with making the initial assault on Hill 188 on the morning of 28 September. Early in the night of 27–28 September, several patrols from the 2d Battalion attempted without success to gain information about the reported gap in the lines. At about 1:00 AM Pate went forward on a reconnaissance of his own and ended up in the command post of a French battalion commander of the adjoining French 163d Infantry Regiment of the French 161st Infantry Division.[17] The French battalion commander informed Pate that although Hill 188 had been strongly defended, the Germans appeared to be evacuating their positions along the entire ridge; there should be little opposition to taking the hill. At about 5:45 AM a German noncommissioned officer brought before Pate reported that he and thirty-five men had been left behind to defend a portion of the hill and they wished to surrender because they did not care to risk their lives on a lost cause. These two events led Pate and Colonel Miles to believe that taking Hill 188 would be an easier task than originally expected.[18]

At 6:45 AM on September 28, under cover of a dense fog, Pate's 1st Battalion jumped off from the south crest of Bellevue Signal Ridge in an attack across a front of five hundred meters on the left of the Ripont–Bussy Farm–les Petit Rosières axis, with the objective being the left half of the defenses on Hill 188. At about the same time, the 3d Battalion of the 372d Infantry opened a similar assault on the right of the division axis with the main objective being the right side of the defenses on Hill 188. As they advanced, both regiments began receiving heavy German artillery fire of both high-explosive and poison gas shells. To add to the chaos, French artillery shells started falling into the assault companies, forcing them to stop and take cover. Signal flares launched by the shelled units finally convinced the French gunners to lengthen their fire, and the companies again moved forward.[19]

Initially, direct German resistance from the heavily fortified defenses was light, although German artillery fire remained heavy as the assault companies of the 1st Battalion, 371st Infantry, continued to advance to the crest of Bellevue Signal Ridge. Captain Wharton's Company C had just penetrated the massive barbed-wire entanglements in front of the German fortifications on Hill 188 when the Germans ceased fire and crawled up on the forward trench parapet with their hands in the air. The platoon leaders—Lts. Carlos G. Harris, Samuel R. Bryson, and James G. Ramsey—believing that the Germans were surrendering, ordered their platoons to move forward to take prisoners. The officers and men had closed to within about one hundred meters of the German trenches when whistles sounded and the Germans turned and jumped back into their defensive positions, and the entire hill came alive with automatic weapons fire. The assault companies of the 1st Battalion and some of the 3d Battalion were caught in intense interlocking bands of heavy machine-gun fire and were under heavy mortar fire as well. The devastating hail of lead and steel seriously wounded Lieutenants Ramsey and Bryson and almost annihilated Company C.[20]

Companies B and D were also caught in the German ruse with resulting heavy casualties, but the survivors were able to drop back, take defensive positions, and reorganize. At about 11:00 AM the reorganized companies moved forward to get into position for a final assault on the German positions on Hill 188. While reconnoitering to determine the extent of the German fortifications, Lt. James Boswell, commanding D Company, was killed by a sniper. The executive officer, Lt. Marcus B. Boulware, took command, moved the company up, and in concert with B Company enveloped the German machine-gun and mortar positions. The two companies then began to drive the German gun crews out of their positions with rifle and automatic weapons fire directed on their flanks. Where the Germans chose to stand their ground, the men of the two companies went in with grim determination and drove them out in close combat with grenades, bayonets, and knives.[21] After the battle, Pate described this phase of the attack on Hill 188 as "extremely gruesome as our men could not be restrained from wreaking their vengeance upon the enemy who had so shamefully entrapped their comrades earlier that morning."[22]

Pvt. James P. McKinney was a bit more casual in his description of what happened in the German trenches: "Most of the Huns quit as soon as we got them. Even the ones that had been on the machine guns yelled for us to spare them. I guess in the excitement some of them fared poorly."[23] Pate's 1st Battalion finally succeeded in taking the main fortification on Hill 188, and in doing so captured seven machine guns, five trench mortars, large quantities of rifles, and three antitank guns.[24]

The desperate situation brought out qualities of leadership and heroism in some of the men. Cpl. Freddie Stowers, a squad leader in Company C, realized that all of his officers had fallen in the German ruse on Hill 188 and went forward to assist in reorganizing the survivors of his platoon. As he moved up, fire from several enemy machine-gun positions slashed across the battlefield, striking Stowers. Disregarding his injuries and unaware that he was mortally wounded, Stowers took command of the men he could find and led them forward through the heavy fire to assault and capture the trenches and machine-gun positions to his front. Shortly afterward, as Stowers was preparing defensive positions to fight off a counterattack, he collapsed; he later died of his wounds.[25] Stowers was recommended for the Congressional Medal of Honor by his commanding officer, but the recommendation was lost—and remained so for seventy years. The recommendation was found in army records in 1987, and in 1988, President George Bush presented the Congressional Medal of Honor to sisters of Stowers in a ceremony at the White House.[26]

Cpl. Sandy E. Jones was performing his duties in the rear as a company clerk when he received word that his company was pinned down, trapped by the Germans' deception on Hill 188. Jones rushed forward to the battle area and, under heavy enemy machine-gun fire, gathered up the remnants of two platoons, reorganized them, and moved forward to continue the attack and capture the trenches to his front. Jones received the first of thirteen Distinguished Service Crosses awarded to officers and men of the 371st Infantry within the next six days.[27]

Also in that action, Pvt. Burton Holmes of Pendleton, South Carolina, was engaging the enemy with his Chauchat light machine gun when he was hit by enemy fire that badly wounded him and damaged his weapon. Still under heavy artillery and machine-gun fire, Holmes worked his way back to his company area, found another light machine gun, and went back to the front lines. While again carrying the fight to the enemy, Holmes was struck a second time by enemy fire and killed. He was posthumously awarded the Distinguished Service Cross.[28]

Reduction of the remaining German trenches on Hill 188 by the 371st Infantry, and of most of the remainder of the Bellevue Signal Ridge defenses by the 372d Infantry and 369th Infantry, was completed by late afternoon of 28 September. The three regiments worked through the night digging and preparing positions to defend against an expected counterattack.[29] As mentioned previously, the men of the 369th Infantry placed their defensive night positions at the upper eastern side of Bellevue Signal Ridge, which placed them facing a small portion of the entrenched German defenders still situated on a spur of the ridge. A French regiment separated the 369th Infantry from the 1st Battalion of the 372d Infantry, which had advanced down the north slope of the ridge where they had dug in for the night. The 1st Battalion of the 371st Infantry advanced past Hill 188 and across Bellevue Signal Ridge to dig in just forward of the north summit. There it joined up with the 1st Battalion of the 372d Infantry on its right flank and the French 2d Moroccan Infantry Division on its left flank.[30]

As the last light faded, a fine mist interspersed with light rain did nothing to hide the dismal scene. The area the regiments were hastily preparing to defend had been fought over so hard and shelled so heavily that very little shelter was left intact other than a few abandoned German artillery positions with camouflaged overheads. The majority of the exhausted men had to be content with stretching captured shelter-tent halves or their own blankets over mud- and water-filled German trenches for protection against the cold drizzle, which continued throughout the night.[31]

As battle reports filtered into regimental and then division headquarters, it became evident that all of the assault battalions of the three American regiments engaged in the attack on Hill 188 and Bellevue Signal Ridge had taken heavy losses. Pate's 1st Battalion of the 371st Infantry had suffered the most, yet he observed that "the heavy losses suffered by our battalion on the 28th of September were by no means the only damage wrought by the defenders of Hill 188. Troops from either the 2d Moroccan Division or 161st Division, or both, attacked the position on the 27th of September and left scores of their dead upon the field."[32]

Later that night, Pate went on another personal reconnaissance mission, something he was becoming well known for, and discovered that the Germans had evacuated the Bussy Farm ruins. On being notified that the farm was abandoned, Miles ordered Maj. Tobe C. Cope's 3d Battalion to move forward through the lines of the badly mauled 1st Battalion to occupy the area to the left of the Bussy Farm ruins. This action, completed by 7:00 AM, placed the battalion in the axis of advance of the 372d Infantry and pushed a small but potent salient into the German defenses.[33]

On the morning of 29 September, with the 2d Battalion in the lead, the 369th Infantry launched an attack across the upper eastern tip of Bellevue Signal Ridge and in further hard fighting cleared out the remaining German defenders. The regiment continued the fight across the open ground atop the ridge and passed to the left of Mount Cuvelet, which had been taken by the French 363d Infantry Regiment. During the day Major Little's 1st Battalion moved up to pass through the 2d Battalion, and at about 2:45 PM launched an attack to capture the village of Séchault.[34]

In the process of capturing Séchault, Little's battalion discovered and relieved two companies of the 372d Infantry that had become separated from their battalion. The two lost companies had advanced through and into the rear of the German lines and had spent the night dug in near Séchault. The two lost companies helped the battalions of the 369th Infantry to mop up Séchault and then moved west to rejoin their regiment, which was dug in on a line that extended from Moya Mill on the left and tied in just west of Séchault with the 369th Infantry. Later that day, the 1st and 2d Battalions of the 369th

Infantry dug in on a perimeter extending around the northeastern outskirts of the village.[35]

On 28 September, as the 372d Infantry approached its objective on the line extending from Moya Mill to Séchault, 1st Lt. William W. Hames, in charge of the 37-mm trench-gun section, skillfully and effectively accomplished his support mission. When all of his guns were knocked out of action, he joined one of the infantry platoons in the assault and, with the aid of two men, captured a machine gun and three prisoners. Hames was severely gassed but continued on in the assault until the next day, when he collapsed from the effects of the gassing. For his courage and initiative Hames was awarded the Distinguished Service Cross.[36] On that same day the 372d Infantry lost a popular and promising young officer when recently promoted Capt. Alan F. Waite was killed by a German artillery shell while acting as regimental liaison officer and aide-de-camp to the French 157th Infantry Division.[37]

At 10:00 AM on 29 September, in accordance with French 157th Infantry Division orders, the 371st Infantry launched another attack from its positions near Bussy Farm along the axis Bussy Farm–Ardéuil–Montfauxelles–Trières Farm toward Monthois. Cope's 3d Battalion led the attack through scattered German artillery shelling, encountering intense machine-gun fire from well-hidden positions around farms and houses. The battalion first captured Ardéuil, then Moya Mill, and finally Montfauxelles with its important railroad yard and shops.[38]

During the attack, Captain Heywood's Company K, at the left flank of the battalion, came under heavy machine-gun fire from German positions located on a low hill in the sector of the French 333d Infantry Regiment. Heywood's company attacked the positions, cleared out the machine guns, and captured thirty-five prisoners including three officers, one 77-mm field gun with ammunition, and several machine guns. Because the regiment had advanced so rapidly, it was unable to make contact with the regiments on its flanks, and Miles halted the advancing companies with orders to establish front lines for the night a few hundred meters north of Montfauxelles and Moya Mill.[39]

The battle tactics had shifted now from fighting the strongly entrenched defenses on Bellevue Signal Ridge to open-terrain warfare. The men of the 93d Division began to experience the disadvantages of the inaccurate and clumsy French Lebel rifle, and many bemoaned the loss of their long-range and accurate Springfield rifles. Nevertheless, at times the Lebel did prove to be effective. At about 10:00 AM on 29 September, a German plane appeared over the battlefield and proceeded to pass close overhead and strafe Companies I and K, 3d Battalion, 371st Infantry. On the plane's second pass, the men of both companies fired their rifles en masse at the aircraft and sent it crashing to the ground in flames. During the battle, units of the 371st Infantry brought down three airplanes with rifle fire, becoming the only U.S. regiment in the war to accomplish such a remarkable feat.[40]

Early on the morning of 30 September the 371st Infantry attacked again against an enemy fighting an orderly and stubborn rearguard action supported by well-placed machine guns and accurate artillery. The regimental order of attack was with the 3d Battalion in advance, the 2d Battalion in close support, and the heavily depleted 1st Battalion in reserve. As the assault companies pushed on toward Trières Farm, they outran their French artillery support while being hammered by German artillery using high-explosive and poison gas shells.[41] The 3d Battalion continued on across the open terrain, digging out machine-gun nests and snipers located in trenches, abandoned gun emplacements, and houses. The 2d Battalion, following in close support, was beginning to suffer heavy casualties from German artillery shells that were passing over the 3d Battalion and falling into the 2d Battalion's zone.[42]

On that day, Pvt. Junius Diggs of Company G, 371st Infantry, whose home was in Chesterfield, South Carolina, became the most decorated private soldier of the four regiments of the 93d Division. After his company was forced to make a temporary withdrawal due to a violent German machine-gun and artillery response to its attack, Diggs went forward under the heavy hail of shell and machine-gun fire to rescue wounded comrades left on the field. Diggs continued to go back into danger for the rest of the day until he had recovered every wounded individual.[43] For his actions he received the Distinguished Service Cross; the Croix de Guerre with Palm; and the French Medaille Militaire, an award reserved for generals commanding armies and enlisted men who especially distinguish themselves by acts of valor.[44]

In mid-afternoon on 30 September, the 3d Battalion, 371st Infantry, had reached a point just beyond Trières Farm near the junction of the railroad and the Monthois-to-Séchault road. The three depleted companies were consolidated into one and, with remnants of the French 333d Infantry Regiment, which was operating on the battalion's left, established a hasty and very thin defense line.[45]

It was in a railroad cut near this junction that 2d Lt. Robert A. Gilmer of Anderson, South Carolina, went forward under fierce machine-gun fire to find the best position for his platoon. As Gilmer exposed himself to the enemy fire to reconnoiter the area, he was struck by machine-gun fire and killed. Gilmer was posthumously awarded the Distinguished Service Cross.[46]

The 3d Battalion, 371st Infantry, which had entered the action with twenty-one officers, was down to one captain and six lieutenants. Company commander Lt. Herbert B. Morris later commented on the condition of the battalion: "The allied army that afternoon to me was a sadly shattered G Company with only

[Lt.] Spencer [wounded] and our little bunch to help me fight the Central Powers."[47] Welcome orders came that night from Miles to Morris and the other company commanders on the line that battalions of the 372d Infantry were to move up into their positions early the next morning and take over the sector. The 371st Infantry was finally going to stand down for a much-needed rest and the opportunity to recover and bury its dead and care for its wounded.[48]

CHAPTER 17

The Push beyond
Bellevue Signal Ridge

I did very little. During this fight with several others, I carried dispatches
to the front line trenches from headquarters. They decorated me, I sup-
pose, because I was the only one lucky enough to escape being knocked
off.

Pvt. Benjamin Butler, 372d Infantry

The first stages of Marshal Foch's attack met with great success all across
the Western Front but exacted a heavy toll on the fighting units. By the
evening of 29 September, the 1st and 2d Battalions of the 369th Infantry were
so decimated that Major Little consolidated them into one battalion. He placed
himself in command and made Captain Clark, commander of the 2d Battalion,
second in command, and then ordered a brief rest period.[1]

The rest was brief indeed. Early on the morning of 30 September the
French 161st Infantry Division headquarters directed a division attack to begin
at 7:00 AM after an artillery preparation scheduled for first light. The consolidated battalion of the 369th Infantry was designated to lead the regiment, with
the 3d Battalion following in reserve. The attack was to be echeloned, with the
French 163d Infantry Regiment, on the left of the 369th Infantry, in the lead.
The 369th Infantry was to start its movement when the French 163d Infantry
had gone forward three hundred meters. The French 363d Infantry Regiment,
on the right of the 369th, would start its attack when the 369th Infantry had
advanced three hundred meters.[2]

At 8:23 AM Little ordered his consolidated battalion to advance. As the men
of the companies left their shell holes and dugouts, they immediately began taking heavy casualties from well-positioned and well-hidden German machine-
gun nests. The battalion spent the whole morning maneuvering to get at the
German positions, but the machine-gun nests were finally flanked and destroyed; by noon the consolidated battalion was again moving forward. At
about 2:00 PM the battalion had reached the southern edge of the woods near
Les Rosiers Fermé and again encountered heavy German machine-gun and
sniper fire from positions in the woods. After several attempts to break through

the German line failed, Little withdrew the battalions three hundred meters to the south and called for artillery support to reduce the German defenses.[3]

On the previous afternoon, 1st Lt. George S. Robb of D Company had been leading his platoon in an attack against a German machine-gun emplacement in a brick house on the edge of Séchault when he was struck in the left side by a machine-gun bullet. Robb applied first-aid bandages to his wound and continued with his duties. His company commander, Lt. George F. Seibel, learned of his condition and ordered him to report to the battalion aid station for treatment. Forty-five minutes later Robb was back at the head of his platoon, and all through the remainder of that afternoon he led his men in the continuing attack. That night, in spite of his painful injury, he looked after his men, inspected his lines, saw that defensive positions were dug, and set up forward outposts.[4]

On the morning of 30 September, during the attack launched by the consolidated battalion, Robb was again wounded, this time by shell fragments. He did not seek medical aid for the second set of wounds, but remained with his platoon and continued on with the attack. Later that day, at a temporary company command post located in a shell hole on the battlefield, splinters and fragments from an exploding German shell hit Robb and at the same time killed Seibel, Lt. Ernest A. McNish, and several enlisted men.[5] Disregarding his additional wounds, Robb took command of the company and continued the attack north of Séchault, directing the clearing out of German machine-gun nests and sniper posts. Robb then pushed on to advance his company one-half mile beyond Séchault, far forward of any other elements of his battalion, where, late that same afternoon, he had his men dig defensive positions in preparation for a counterattack by the Germans.[6] Robb then reported by messenger to Little that he could not go on, was reporting to an aid station, and was turning his command over to his first sergeant as no other officers remained to assume command of the company. When he reported to the aid station to have his wounds treated, Robb found that the grip of his service revolver had been shot off and his helmet was sporting a bullet hole.[7]

The next day, while Robb was confined to the battalion hospital for treatment of his wounds, a German gas shell exploded just outside the hospital bunker's door. With both of his hands, his arms, and his body bound in bandages, Robb could not put on his gas mask. Major Little, who was in the hospital visiting, was able to get Robb's gas mask on for him, but not before Robb had suffered a severe gassing. Fortunately, the gas was not of a deadly variety and Robb recovered without serious aftereffects.[8]

For his conduct during those two days 1st Lt. George S. Robb was awarded the Congressional Medal of Honor. His citation, General Order 16, War Department, 1919, reads, in part: "His example of bravery and fortitude and his eagerness to continue with his mission despite severe wounds set before the enlisted men of his command a most wonderful standard of morale and self-sacrifice."[9]

At about 3:00 PM on 30 September, the French 161st Infantry Division's regiments had reached a line running from the southwest corner of Bois de la Malmaison to Les Petits Rosiers. Further advance on the left was held up by the flooded Avègres River (Alin Creek), and to move around the marsh would require entering the operational zone of the French 157th Infantry Division.[10]

As the regiments settled in after reaching their objectives, Little assessed his personnel and found that he had available for duty about 100 men and three officers in the 1st Battalion. The 2d Battalion commander, Captain Clark, was able to muster about 300 men and nine or ten officers. Captain L'Esperance, commanding the 3d Battalion, reported that he had 137 men and seven officers left to answer roll call. At 4:35 PM Little dispatched a message to Hayward reporting his strength and stating that he felt that no further attempt should be made to go through the woods facing the battalions without either tank support or effective heavy artillery fire to reduce concrete pillboxes and other fortifications. In closing the message he wrote, "I believe that every man will obey orders to go into those woods if orders are given; but, under present condition, they will all stay there—and the 15th N.Y. will be a memory."[11]

Shortly after Little sent his message he received a message from Colonel Hayward that had crossed it en route:

Sept. 30/18, 16:15 o'clock

Major Little—

The Artillery fire you asked for will be given. After its completion, continue your advance as before.

Colonel Hayward
Lt. Col. W. A. Pickering[12]

The French artillery support that Little received amounted to about half a dozen shots. Nevertheless, on receiving Hayward's orders, Little sent scouts forward and was preparing his companies to attack the heavily fortified woods when a messenger hurried up with a note from regimental headquarters marked "Urgent."

30 Sept. 18, 17 h 30

To C. O. 1st Batta. 369 R.I.U.S

Latest orders from the I.D. is to the effect that the 363rd will relieve us and pass through your lines tonight.

> Sit tight and hold on until the relief comes.
>
> > By order of Colonel Hayward
> > R. Whittlesey, 1st Lt. Acting Adjutant[13]

Little later found out that Hayward had been advising French 161st Infantry Division Headquarters during the day that the regiment might not be able to continue its mission due to its heavy losses and near exhaustion.[14]

At about 1:00 AM on 1 October, elements of the French 363d Infantry Regiment moved into the line to relieve the 369th Infantry. At 6:00 AM the French artillery delivered a heavy bombardment on the woods in front of the line, and shortly after 8:00 AM the French 363d Infantry Regiment moved out to capture the woods and then take Challerange. The 369th Infantry remained in place for part of the day for a much-needed rest and food after a thirty-hour fast. That afternoon the tattered and depleted battalions of the regiment moved back to the southern slope of Signal Ridge and settled into bivouac.[15]

The 369th Infantry was hardly recognizable as such. Since the beginning of the offensive on 26 September the regiment had suffered heavy casualties from machine-gun fire, constant artillery high-explosive and gas bombardment, and aircraft bombing and strafing. The regiment had fought its way through almost nine kilometers of the most heavily fortified and best-defended German trench and barbed-wire systems in the sector. They had captured large quantities of prisoners, arms, and equipment while forcing the Germans to abandon their bunkers and machine-gun nests and retreat to the rear.[16] With the battalions critically reduced in strength and everyone nearing exhaustion, to their credit, the men were moving forward to attack when relief orders arrived. At that moment, even in its severely diminished state, the 369th Infantry held more than one-third of the French 161st Infantry Division's total frontage.[17]

To the left of the 369th Infantry and in the operations zone of the French 157th Infantry Division, the 372d Infantry by 29 September had pushed forward against severe resistance to a line running just north of Montfauxelles, Moya Mill, and Séchault. That evening a battalion of the French 333d Infantry Regiment entered the lines and relieved the regiment, and it retired to just south of Bussy Farm. Colonel Tupes spent the next day reorganizing the 1st and 3d Battalions, which had incurred heavy losses in officers and men while on the line, into a provisional battalion which he then placed in reserve. At 5:00 AM on 1 October the regiment entered the lines just north of Trières Farm with the 2d Battalion in contact, relieved the 371st Infantry, and immediately began reconnaissance patrols to its front.[18]

At 7:00 AM that same day, the French 157th Infantry Division headquarters issued warning orders for an attack toward Monthois to begin when the French 2d Moroccan Infantry Division was ready, but in any event to be launched by 2 October. The intent of the attack was for the Moroccan divison to capture the heights of Croix-des-Soudans, located to the left of the French 157th Infantry Division. When the Moroccan division had control of the heights, rockets would signal the French artillery to begin a rolling barrage, and then the French 157th Infantry Division would mount its attack to take Monthois and Challerange.[19]

During the day on 2 October the French 120th Infantry Division relieved the French 2d Moroccan Infantry Division and assumed that division's mission of assisting in taking Monthois by capturing the heights of Croix-des-Soudans.[20] The town of Monthois was a major rail center and a large supply depot for the German Army. Although the Germans were demoralized from the intensity and persistence of the Allied forces' attacks, they were intent on removing all critical supplies from the town before it could be captured. Extensive fortifications and gun emplacements had been hastily thrown up to hold the town against the Allied advance until the area could be cleared of essential war materials.[21]

The French 120th Infantry Division attacked at 11:00 AM on 2 October but did not gain its assigned objective of clearing the high ground north of Croix-des-Soudans. French IX Corps Headquarters, however, believed a rocket signal seen in the direction of the French 120th Infantry Division indicated that the high ground had been captured and ordered the French 157th Infantry Division to begin its attack. The provisional battalion of the 372d Infantry, flanked by battalions of the French 333d Infantry Regiment, attacked at 1:50 PM behind a rolling barrage of French artillery and against heavy and accurate German gunfire. The regiments were within eight hundred meters of Monthois by the end of the day, even though the French 120th Infantry Division still had not completely cleared the plateau to the southwest of Monthois.[22]

Capt. Edward M. Robison was severely wounded while leading his company forward in the attack. In spite of his wounds he remained with his men for two days through heavy enemy shell and machine-gun fire, encouraging and inspiring them to follow him. Robison continued on until he collapsed from loss of blood. He was awarded the Distinguished Service Cross.[23]

Sgt. William Creigler, who had come to the regiment with the 1st Separate Company, Maryland National Guard, found that all of the officers of his company had been wounded and were unable to continue leading the attack. Creigler took command and led the company in completing its assigned mission. He was awarded the Croix de Guerre for his gallantry and persistence in continuing the mission of his company. In August 1921, when the 1st Separate Company was reorganized within the Maryland National Guard, Creigler would gain further prominence when he was appointed to the rank of captain.[24]

On 3 October the French 157th Infantry Division was ordered to hold its position while the French 120th Infantry Division again attempted to take the plateau in the vicinity of Croix-de-Saingly. Orders remained in effect that after that objective had been gained, the French 157th Infantry Division was to continue its attack and capture Monthois. But the French 120th Infantry Division was again unsuccessful, and the French 157th Infantry Division had to sit for another day and hold its lines.[25] Further attacks by the French 120th Infantry Division against the plateau area and by other units all along the front on 4 October failed again because of stubborn defense by the Germans. As the attack by the French 157th Infantry Division was keyed on the success of the French 120th Division, the 372d Infantry continued to hold tight in its positions through 5 October.[26]

Early on that same day, the Germans proved that they were still dangerous opponents by first delivering a well-directed artillery barrage and then launching a counterattack against the French 157th Infantry Division's front, with the main thrust aimed at the 2d Battalion, 372d Infantry. The attack was quickly repulsed, but the 2d Battalion stayed in its positions as ordered and did not counterattack. No attacks were ordered for 6 October, and that night the French 125th Infantry Division relieved the French 157th Infantry Division. The 372d Infantry was relieved in its defensive positions by the French 70th Infantry Regiment and, on the morning of 7 October, moved out of the lines and marched back to Minaucourt for a short rest period.[27]

Just before moving out of the lines, the 372d Infantry incurred a great loss when Lt. Urbane F. Bass, Medical Corps, was killed while attending the wounded at a forward aid station that was under heavy German shell fire. Bass, from Fredericksburg, Virginia, had received his medical degree from Shaw University in 1906. He volunteered to serve in the U.S. forces and completed his officer training at the Fort Des Moines, Iowa, training facility for black officers. Bass had gone forward to the line near Monthois so that he could provide immediate assistance to the wounded. A shell that exploded in the aid station severed both of his legs at the thighs, and he died within minutes from shock and loss of blood. Bass was posthumously awarded the Distinguished Service Cross.[28]

On 8 October Colonel Tupes received communiqué 5508 from Colonel Quillet, commander of the French 157th Division. The message (translated) read:

> The Colonel, Commanding the I. D., had recommended your regiment for a citation in the orders of the French Army worded as follows:
>
> "Gave proof, during its first engagement, of the finest qualities of bravery and daring which are the virtues of assaulting troops.
>
> "Under the orders Colonel Tupes dashed with superb gallantry and admirable scorn of danger to the assault of a position continuously

defended by the enemy, taking it by storm under an exceptionally violent machine-gun fire and very serious losses. They made numerous prisoners, captured cannon, machine guns, and important war material."[29]

The French were not the only ones giving accolades and awards to their foreign brothers-in-arms.[30] 2d Lt. Georges Wichart, Infantry, French Army, attached to the 372d Infantry, was awarded the Distinguished Service Cross for his actions from 27 September to 7 October 1918. His citation read:

> During the attack on Monthois he voluntarily undertook the most hazardous of missions, fearlessly traversing ground swept by machine-gun fire and severe bombardment to secure liaison between neighboring French units and to reconnoiter our first-line positions. His reports were invaluable. On the night of Oct. 2 he led a battalion to its position of attack and personally reconnoitered the line under intense machine-gun and artillery fire, furnishing a splendid example of coolness and utter disregard of danger to the men of the battalion.[31]

The three regiments of the 93d Infantry Division serving with the French IX Corps in the Champagne region during Marshal Foch's fall offensive were ordered removed from the line for rest, reorganization, and refitting. During the period these regiments were being employed as shock troops and were penetrating the main German defensive lines, there were many individual acts of courage and heroism. A few of them are mentioned previously. The French IX Corps and the French 157th Infantry Division recognized the great efforts made by the three American regiments and sent praise and congratulations.[32] The efforts and fortitude of the three American regiments employed in this action and in this sector can perhaps best be measured when one considers that the maximum time a U.S. infantry regiment could be expected to carry out its mission in an assault of this nature before becoming exhausted and requiring relief was estimated at three days. These three regiments fought a fierce, successful battle against a dedicated and well-fortified enemy for up to a total of nine days in action.[33]

The performance and dedication to service of the medical detachments serving with units on the field of battle are often overlooked, yet it is they who must deal with the carnage wreaked by modern weapons; and when the battle is over, their work still must go on.[34] Lt. P. E. Deckard, commander of the medical detachment of the 3d Battalion, 371st Infantry, wrote about his experiences during the hard-fought days and nights at Bellevue Signal Ridge and Ardéuil:

Our Medical Detachment had its hardest task of the war in the Champagne offensive. For a few days and nights, while our regiment was engaged in the most severe fighting of its part of that drive, we of the Medical Detachment worked, to the point of exhaustion at times, on battle injuries of all descriptions suffered not only by men of our regiment but also by men from many adjoining organizations who reached our battalion aid stations in the confusion of the battlefield. It was heartrending to have brought to us for surgical treatment such large numbers of the officers and men with whom we had lived so long, from our first acquaintance in the regiment, back in South Carolina, to these eventful and terrible days in France. Long before the battle we had learned to know many of them as comrades and pals and many of them we now saw for the last time on this side of the Great Divide. One must salute these men in sincere tribute.[35]

Deckard did not mention that Sgt. Lee R. McClelland, Medical Detachment, 371st Infantry, from Asheville, North Carolina, was tending the wounded near Ardéuil on 30 September under continuing heavy artillery fire when a shell fragment struck his leg, severely wounding him. McClelland did not report his painful injury and continued attending to the wounded personnel under his care until his unit could be relieved. McClelland received the Distinguished Service Cross for his valor and commitment to his duties.[36]

CHAPTER 18

The 370th Attacks at
Canal de l'Oise–l'Aisne

Did you ever hear a bullet whiz,
Or dodge a hand grenade?
Have you watched long lines of trenches dug
By doughboys with a spade?
Have you seen the landscape lighted up
At midnight by a shell?
Have you seen a hillside blazing forth
Like a furnace room in Hell?

Have you stayed all night in a ruined town
With a rafter for a bed?
With horses stomping underneath
In the morning when they are fed?
Have you heard the crump-crump whistle?
Do you know the dud shell's grunt?
Have you played rat in a dugout?
Then you have surely been to the front.

"Over There," Lt. Blaine G. Alston,
370th Infantry, somewhere in France

While its three sister regiments were preparing to engage the Germans in the Champagne region, the 370th Infantry, along with the two other regiments of the French 59th Infantry Division, was moving on line to launch its attack in the Soissons sector. At 5:00 AM on 16 September, after spending the night in Saint-Bandry, the battalions of the regiment formed up and marched to the village of Tartiers. On reaching the ruined village at dusk, the men found shelter and cover in caves, wrecked buildings, and bomb shelters. They slept easier that night after receiving orders from Major General Vincendon that the 370th Infantry had been designated as the division's support regiment, which meant more rest and, for the moment, little exposure to combat.[1]

During the night of 16–17 September the designated assault battalions of the French 59th Infantry Division—the French 232d Infantry Regiment under Lieutenant Colonel Lugand and the French 325th Infantry Regiment under Lieutenant Colonel Michel—moved into position on the plateau southeast of Vauxaillon to relieve the battered French 66th Infantry Division.[2] The French 59th Infantry Division's assigned front line extended from the eastern edge of the Bois de Mortier at the Ailette River south across the river plain. From there the line ran up the escarpment slope south of Mont de Singes and then farther south along the ridge to the division boundary just to the east of Moisy-Fermé. Lugand's French 232d Infantry Regiment was located on the left division front and tied into the French 31st Infantry Division at the Ailette River. Michel's French 325th Infantry Regiment formed the right flank of the division front along the ridge facing Mont de Singes. In addition to relieving a regiment of the French 66th Infantry Division, Michel's regiment also took over part of the line of the badly mauled French 17th Infantry Division.[3]

On the following night the division's forward elements worked hard to extend their lines forward along the l'Oise–l'Aisne Canal. They also relieved and took over the entire front of the French 17th Infantry Division. In the changeover the French 59th Infantry Division had also assumed the immediate operational mission of the two relieved divisions: to attack and to capture Mont des Singes and the heavily wooded areas to the east of Moisy-Fermé, and then to advance along a northeasterly axis to the l'Oise–l'Aisne Canal.[4]

As the assault regiments were getting situated on 17 September, the 370th Infantry was ordered to move forward to be in a better position to support the planned division attack. On the march toward the front, four companies of Lieutenant Colonel Duncan's 2d Battalion were ordered detached and were rushed off to join the French assault battalions.[5] Captain Patton's 3d Battalion arrived at Antioche-Fermé and settled in for the night, and the remainder of Duncan's 2d Battalion stopped at Mont Touley. Major Stokes marched his 1st Battalion on to the vicinity of Les Tueries and billeted within the protection of several caves in the area. These units, minus the four detached companies, were designated the division reserve.[6]

The four detached companies of Duncan's 2d Battalion marched on into the night to try to join up with the two French assault regiments, which were scheduled to make a morning attack on the German lines along the fronts of the relieved French 66th and 17th Infantry Divisions. When the companies arrived at the frontline trenches, Companies F and G were split off and sent to the French 232d Infantry Regiment on the floodplain while Companies I and L were attached to the French 325th Infantry Regiment on the ridge along the division's right front.[7]

On the morning of 18 September, with the four detached companies assimilated into the French assault regiments, the planned attack was launched. All through the rest of the day, attempts by the two French assault regiments and the four companies of the 370th Infantry to advance on their objectives met with stubborn resistance from well-entrenched and fortified German units positioned on the forward edge of the plateau of Mont des Singes. Fierce close-in fighting between French and German units continued through 19 September and into the next day with little noticeable change in the lines.[8]

As the attack progressed on through 19 September, PFC Nathaniel C. White was killed in action while performing his duties as a message runner for Company F, struck down while making his way between command posts through heavy artillery and machine-gun fire. As was mentioned earlier, message running was considered to be one of the most hazardous of assignments at the front lines. For his courage and sacrifice White was posthumously awarded the Distinguished Service Cross.[9]

During the continued fighting on 20 September, Sgt. Mathew Jenkins of Company F saw a member of his platoon get hit while he was moving well forward of the company line. As intense enemy machine-gun fire cut through the air and around his head, Jenkins ran forward of his own lines and, jumping from shell hole to shell hole to avoid being hit, managed to reach the wounded man and drag him back to safety through the same gunfire and shell holes.[10]

Jenkins found further opportunity for distinguished conduct in combat the next morning when he received orders to take a detachment of thirty-two men and cross through the lines to join up with a French force located in concealed positions in no-man's-land. The combined force was to attack and capture a hardened German defensive position, a tunnel known locally as the Hindenburg Cave, which was part of a set of strongly fortified structures extending across the front of the division's sector.[11]

As Jenkins was moving his force forward to meet the French unit, heavy German artillery fire began falling on his small command, killing three of his men. When he was finally able to reach the French unit, he found that the detachment's commanding officer had been killed. On reporting the loss of the officer to the French commander of the sector, he was ordered to take command of the attack force and proceed with the mission.[12]

Jenkins made his plans to capture the tunnel and launched his attack at 9:00 AM. After a short but hot firefight, Jenkins and his combined French and American force routed the German defenders and captured the cave. While the small force was consolidating its capture, a German force moved in behind them and cut them off from their supporting French company.[13] Jenkins quickly reorganized his force for defensive operations and began fighting off a series of strong

German attacks. After several fierce fights with the attacking Germans, Jenkins's command ran out of ammunition. The resourceful Jenkins dispatched several of his men to search the tunnel and German positions for abandoned weapons. The search turned up seventeen German machine guns and ample supplies of ammunition left behind by their crews as they retreated from the cave. Jenkins had the men set up the German machine guns along hastily established defense lines, and after some quick experimentation to determine how to operate the weapons the men turned them on their former owners.[14]

Jenkins and his small French-American force held their positions for more than thirty-six hours, without resupply of food or ammunition, until a French regiment that had just come up to replace the French 59th Infantry Division's assault battalions realized that the cave was being held by friendly forces, fought through the German lines, and rescued the group.[15] On the evening of 22 September Jenkins marched out of the cave with twenty-three of his own men and the remnants of the attached French force. His exploits during those four days earned him the Croix de Guerre and the Distinguished Service Cross.[16]

While Jenkins and his men were attacking and defending the Hindenburg Cave, the French 59th Infantry Division had received orders for the assault battalions to cease their attacks and move into defensive positions. At that time the four detached companies of the 370th Infantry were released from their French regiments and sent to rejoin the 2d Battalion.[17]

On the night of 22–23 September, the entire 370th Infantry was ordered on the line to take over a full sector. Major Stokes's 1st Battalion relieved the French Battalion Garnier on the line along the road between Champ Vailly and La Folie–l'Ecluse near the l'Oise–l'Aisne Canal and Guilleminet Fermé. Captain Patton's 3d Battalion went into reserve near Tincille-Fermé, about fourteen hundred meters southwest of Antioche-Fermé; and Duncan's 2d Battalion, in support capacity, located itself in the vicinity of Les Tueries, about seventeen hundred meters west of Vauxaillon. At the same time, and to achieve better command and control of the regiment's front, Colonel Roberts moved the 370th Infantry command post up to Antioche-Fermé.[18]

On the morning of 24 September Pvt. Charlie T. Monroe of Headquarters Company found that the commander of his Stokes mortar platoon was out of action. Monroe took charge of the guns and began directing fire while under attack by a heavy German artillery barrage. The German shells threw up so much dirt that the guns were sometimes buried; Monroe even found himself buried at one point and had to dig out after a large shell exploded near his gun emplacement. He continued to bring the guns back into action each time they were knocked out and to direct fire on the German positions. For his coolness and valor under fire Monroe was awarded the Distinguished Service Cross.[19]

By midday on 24 September the 370th Infantry had taken control of the entire left subsector of the French 59th Infantry Division. The right boundary of the subsector was a line from Champ Vailly to a point three hundred meters west of where the road from Pinon to Brancourt crossed the l'Oise–l'Aisne Canal. The left boundary followed the canal from the bend west of Courson west to the Pinon road and canal crossing. The French 325th Infantry Regiment of the 59th Infantry Division was to the right, and the French 31st Infantry Division, French XVI Corps, was on the left. These movements were part of Marshal Foch's preparations for the fall offensive, which would involve the entire French front (see map 8).[20]

As the men of Stokes's 1st Battalion settled into their trenches and outpost positions on the line to await further orders, they found themselves subjected to constant artillery attack with both high-explosive and gas shells. The 2d Battalion, which came up on the night of 27–28 September to relieve the 1st Battalion, suffered the same harsh treatment plus heavy and continuous mortar attacks and machine-gun fire directed against them from fortified points in the Bois de Mortier, a densely wooded area north across the canal and in front and to the left of the battalion line.[21]

At about 1:00 AM on 28 September, French intelligence reports came down to regimental headquarters indicating a withdrawal by the German units in front of the 370th Infantry's sector. Intelligence officers predicted that the Germans would fall back to defensive positions at the l'Oise–l'Aisne Canal and the Bois de Mortier during the night of 27–28 September. This movement was later determined to be part of a general withdrawal of German units facing the French 59th Infantry Division approved by the army group of the German crown prince. The move was brought on by the need for reinforcements in the Champagne and Meuse-Argonne areas, where the French Fourth Army and the American First Army had launched general attacks. Also, from a tactical point, the local German commander wanted to avoid further losses in holding an extended salient running along the ridge of Mont des Singes, a distance of about four kilometers and containing the village of Laffaux.[22]

On the night of 27–28 September, as Patton's 2d Battalion was relieving Stokes's 1st Battalion, both units were pummeled with constant and accurate German artillery, mortar, and machine-gun fire laid on to cover the withdrawal of the German infantry units in the line. In the midst of the relief, the French 59th Infantry Division issued orders to the 370th Infantry and ultimately to the 2d Battalion to launch an attack at dawn on 28 September to pursue the withdrawing Germans and push them across and beyond the canal. The relief was completed just in time for the attack to begin, and at daybreak the 2d Battalion went over the top to find that the Germans in front of it were executing a well-organized fighting withdrawal.[23]

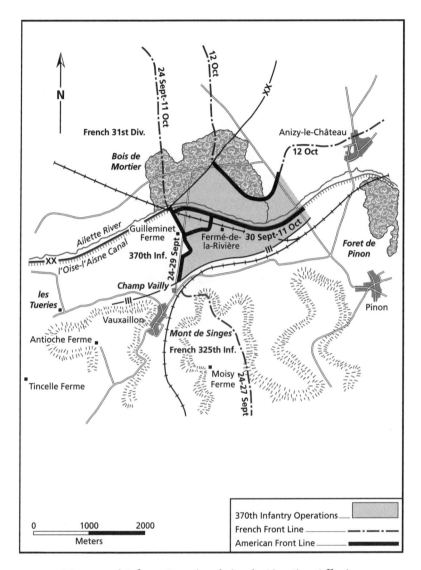

*Map 8. 370th Infantry Operations during the Oise-Aisne Offensive,
24 September to 12 October 1918*

The 2d Battalion immediately encountered heavy German resistance on its right flank and was unable to advance in that area. The battalion's left flank was successful in taking a stand of woods west of Fermé-de-la-Rivière, and by noon the battalion held a position facing the farm and extending north along the canal.[24]

German forces were observed to be conducting a general withdrawal in an orderly fashion from the salient in the Laffaux area, and shortly after noon the French 59th Infantry Division headquarters issued orders for a division attack with three regiments on the line, with the 370th Infantry on the left. The center and right-flank regiments of the French 59th Infantry Division were to pivot on the right flank of the 370th Infantry and then attack northeasterly on a line through Pinon–Ouvrage Pierre, Ouvrage Jacques, and the canal from the bend east of Fermé-de-la-Rivière to l'Ecluse. The 370th Infantry was tasked with protecting the division from German counterattacks coming from the wooded areas northwest of Anizy-le-Château while the pivot maneuver was being executed. Once the maneuver was completed, the regiment was to advance on line with the other two regiments.[25]

During the afternoon of 28 September the French 59th Infantry Division's right-flank regiments captured Pinon, the defensive strong points of Ouvrage Pierre and Ouvrage Jacques, as well as Mont des Singes, thus eliminating the Laffaux salient. The Germans hotly contested the area as they continued their orderly fighting withdrawal toward their defensive positions across the l'Oise–l'Aisne Canal.[26]

At 5:20 PM French 59th Infantry Division headquarters ordered the attack to continue throughout the night, with the objective being to reach the south bank of the canal by daybreak. The 370th Infantry was to take and occupy a portion of the sector from l'Ecluse east to the Pinon-to-Brancourt road.[27]

The fighting continued through 29 September as the Germans fiercely resisted giving up territory in their withdrawal, and only small gains were made. As the battalions of the 370th Infantry gained portions of the canal, they sent patrols into the Bois de Mortier, only to be pushed back by heavy machine-gun fire.[28] The battle continued into 30 September, with the French regiments on the right flank gaining enough ground to capture a line of fortifications in the Bois de Pinon and the sawmill west of the Anizy railway station. The 3d Battalion, 370th Infantry, moved into position along the railroad track south of the canal to relieve the 2d Battalion, although Company F remained to occupy a portion of the canal and the woods west of Fermé-de-la-Rivière. Shortly after midday, the 3d Battalion, with Company F attached, attacked and captured the farm and the rest of the canal extending from the left division boundary to the Pinon-to-Brancourt road.[29]

Although the 370th Infantry contributed significantly to the success of the attacks in the sector, problems in command performance at the company and battalion levels continued to haunt the regiment. This time a complaint came from a General Rondeau, who was in temporary command of the French 59th Infantry Division while General Vincendon was on leave. In a letter to AEF

Headquarters signed "Le General Rondeau," the French commander wrote a scathing indictment stating that

> barring the Colonel, Regular officer (white) of the American Army, all units, battalions, companies and sections are commanded by black officers of pronounced inefficiency.... [D]uring the day of the 28th, the officers of a battalion, including the chief of the battalion himself, at three different times made erroneous reports as to the situation of their units, all these officers being foregathered at the P.C. of the Chief of Battalion instead of being at their Post.... [T]he men are strong and full of enthusiasm, only asking to march behind a chief who will command them.[30]

It is not clear which battalion Rondeau was criticizing, but since the 2d Battalion was engaged in relieving the 1st Battalion during the early hours of 28 September and was then involved in the attack that took place just after the relief was completed, most likely Captain Patton and his 2d Battalion were the focus of the general's complaint.[31]

Responding to Rondeau's criticism, Pershing sent a member of his general staff, Maj. L. R. Fredendall, to investigate the complaint. Fredendall arrived at the headquarters of the 370th Infantry Division on 5 October. In his subsequent report Fredendall wrote:

> I . . . found the men cheerful and their morale good.... [T]he Germans were only forty yards away on the other side of the canal.... [T]he men were exchanging fire with the Germans from shallow trenches and rifle pits.... [E]veryone was cheerful and the men all said "Good Morning" to me.
>
> At no time did I see any signs of panic or demoralization. Four hundred men of the regiment are missing. I do not believe they have run away. They are simply lost and will be found scattered among French units.[32]

Fredendall did appear to confirm Rondeau's comment about the officers' behavior at the front: "About the other officers whom I saw: I am constrained to say that most of them were too fond of their dugouts."[33]

One of the more damning items in Fredendall's report had to do with the military education of the officers: "The thing which struck me most was the colossal ignorance of the officers. Few could read a map and none, with but one exception, could give me his location on a map."[34] The officers' inability to read maps may have been the cause of Rondeau's caustic letter. Fredendall's report further states that "a certain battalion was ordered to take a certain farm. They did take a farm and reported that they had taken the one that they had been ordered to take. It happened that they had not taken the right farm, however, and our allies on going forward to occupy the 'captured' farm were, I gather, somewhat chagrined to be received by the Germans."[35] The French Army's employment of the regiment in manual labor rather than in training exercises when the men were not on the line, criticized by Captain Marvin in his report the previous June, was coming back to haunt the 370th Infantry.[36]

Major Fredendall's assessment of the officer corps of the 370th Regiment was not quite as negative as General Rondeau's, although he did recommend that "this regiment be taken away from the French; that with the exception of four or five colored officers . . . all the officers be replaced by white officers; that it be trained for two weeks thereafter. It will be a good regiment as the men only require to be intelligently led."[37]

Some question exists regarding Rondeau's firsthand knowledge of the performance of the officers and men of the regiment inasmuch as he had taken temporary command of the division on 6 October. In other words, Rondeau was not in command on 30 September, the day his letter referred to, although he may have been present in the division. In any event, Vincendon, when he returned to duty in December, expressed extreme pleasure with the performance of the regiment, and in particular with Duncan, Patton, and Capt. John T. Prout. Whether the praise was given as a conciliatory gesture in the flood of emotions at the end of the war or was truly sincere is impossible to determine.[38]

However serious Rondeau's displeasure with the officers of the 370th Infantry, and however accurate his criticism, he was not disposed to do anything about it on his own. Foch's fall offensive was about to begin, and the regiment could not be released for further training because every available unit, regardless of its condition, was needed on the line.[39]

Roberts continued his command with the two white officers he had brought with him plus Prout, who was added later to command a battalion, and most of the black officers already assigned to the regiment when he took command. As it turned out, the regiment was able to perform its mission with the officers present at the time of Fredendall's report. Although many may have lacked appropriate military training through no fault of their own, the conduct of the majority of the officers proved that they were not lacking in courage and initiative.[40] Numerous examples attest to that.

For example, on 28 September 2d Lt. Rufus B. Jackson of Chicago, Illinois, in command of the Stokes mortar section of his company, had received orders to fire on German machine-gun nests that were preventing his company from continuing the attack. Jackson was not furnished with exact locations of the machine-gun nests and could not deliver fire as ordered. His solution to the problem was to crawl forward into exposed positions and, while being targeted by heavy German machine-gun and artillery fire, locate and plot the machine-gun nests. Jackson then crawled back along the same hazardous route to return to his mortars and directed accurate fire to destroy the German machine guns. For that action Jackson received the Distinguished Service Cross.[41]

On that same day, Lt. William Warfield was maneuvering his platoon forward of the lines when his unit became separated from his company. The Germans discovered Warfield's platoon trapped between the lines and began harassing it with machine-gun fire, which caused several casualties. Without help, Warfield charged one of the closest machine-gun nests, overran it, and killed the gun crew. He scooped up the machine gun and carried it back to his platoon, and in the process was severely wounded. In spite of his wounds, Warfield continued to command his platoon until they worked their way back to their own lines to rejoin the company. For his actions Warfield was awarded the Distinguished Service Cross.[42]

On 30 September, the date mentioned in General Rondeau's letter of complaint, two companies of Patton's 2d Battalion were ordered into a support role and were relieved by Duncan's 3d Battalion. Duncan had been issued orders to make an immediate frontal attack across open ground to take Fermé-de-la-Rivière and the railroad line south of the canal.[43] A similar attack the previous day had failed. Capt. William B. Crawford from Denison, Texas, had just been placed in command of Company L when he was tasked with leading the attack. Crawford, wanting to ensure success, went forward and personally led the advance element of his company through a scathing machine-gun and artillery barrage, for which he received the Distinguished Service Cross.[44]

One of many examples of what the men could and would do under fire while under the leadership of their officers occurred on 28 September when Pvt. James Fuquay, a light machine gunner from Company H, had his weapon jam at a critical point in the attack. Fuquay coolly disassembled his light machine gun, corrected the stoppage, and reassembled the weapon while heavy machine-gun, mortar, and artillery fire tried to dislodge him from his position.[45] Fuquay was severely wounded in the left arm as he was repairing his weapon, yet he refused treatment, put his weapon back into action, and continued to fire on the enemy. Finally, after heavy loss of blood from his wounds and while still at his post trying to operate his weapon, he lost consciousness. Fuquay was awarded the Distinguished Service Cross.[46]

In another incident on that day, Sgt. Norman Henry of Chicago received a Distinguished Service Cross for his actions while leading his squad of the machine-gun company in an attack under heavy German machine-gun, rifle, and artillery fire. Henry observed that one of his guns, critical to the attack,

was out of action and moved to what proved to be an exposed position to assist
in repairing it. While making the repairs he came under direct and constant
machine-gun and rifle fire. After the gun was functional and Henry had led his
squad on to capture its objective, he went forward and again braved heavy
enemy machine-gun fire to assist the only surviving officer in his company in
assembling the scattered squads to prepare defensive positions.[47]

On 5 October at Fermé-de-la-Rivière, Supply Sgt. Lester Fossie of Company M, who hailed from Metropolis, Illinois, observed a messenger fall in the
open between the lines after being wounded by a German sniper. Fossie crossed
the open area under heavy fire from machine guns and snipers and brought
the wounded messenger to Company M headquarters for treatment. Fossie
received the Distinguished Service Cross for his valor.[48]

These and subsequent actions of the enlisted men proved the one positive
point on which Rondeau and Fredendall agreed: the high morale and courage
of the men. It seems unlikely that many of these men could have performed
such acts of valor without at least some level of appropriate leadership and
example of conduct from their officers.[49]

The survival rate of the officers and men wounded in action depended on the
quick and professional application of aid by the medical detachments assigned
to the battalions. Capt. Spencer C. Dickerson headed up the 1st Battalion's medical team, Lt. James F. Lawson headed the 2d Battalion's medical team, and Lt.
Claudius Ballard led the 3d Battalion's medical team.[50]

Lieutenant Ballard was severely wounded while engaged in treating his
charges at a forward aid station. He refused to leave his post and continued to
provide medical care in spite of his own injuries. During the heaviest fighting
around Guilleminet Fermé and Fermé-de-la-Rivière, Lt. Park Tancil, a dental
surgeon, was required to take charge of one of the forward aid stations and render aid while under severe artillery fire containing both high-explosives and gas
shells. Maj. James R. White, the regimental surgeon, continued to make the
rounds of the aid stations in the lines and to render aid when and where needed.
For their steadfast commitment to rendering medical aid under extreme conditions, all of these medical officers were awarded the Croix de Guerre. Several
enlisted men of the medical detachment also received the Croix de Guerre, and
Pvt. Alfred Williamson received both the Croix de Guerre and the Distinguished Service Cross.[51]

The battle along the l'Oise–l'Aisne Canal continued on through 4 October, and
the regiment was able to accomplish all of its assigned objectives in spite of
heavy German artillery fire containing high-explosive and poison gas shells,
and harassing machine-gun, mortar, and rifle fire. After the captured areas were
mopped up, the officers and men of the regiment dug in to hold their gains and

prepare for the next attack. Patrols and small sorties crossed the canal through 12 October to harass and capture prisoners for interrogation and to attempt to establish crossings.[52]

The initial objective of pushing the front to the Canal de l'Oise–l'Aisne had been achieved, and after completing mopping-up operations in its sector, the 370th Infantry consolidated its positions, regrouped, replenished its ammunition and supplies, and prepared to attack across the canal.[53]

CHAPTER 19

The 370th in Pursuit

The 370th R.I.U.S. . . . , fired by a noble ardor, got at times even beyond the objectives given them by the higher command; they have always wished to be in the front line, for the place of honor is the leading rank.

Major General Vincendon,
commanding the French 59th Infantry Division

The German Army units facing the French 59th Infantry Division had accomplished their immediate goal and achieved a moderately successful evacuation of the Laffaux salient to the Ailette River and the l'Oise–l'Aisne Canal, which afforded a natural line of defense. The French right-flank regiments, fighting against a stubborn rearguard action, finally pushed the Germans across the canal and river on 3 October. In the 370th Infantry's subsector, along the division's left flank, the German defenders fiercely contested an area south of the canal containing a set of locks. After all of the men and materials had been evacuated, the last of the German rear guard crossed the two waterways and dug in their heels on the north side, prepared to resist any further advances.[1]

From 4 to 12 October all three battalions of the 370th Infantry fought along the canal and river trying to dislodge the German defenders. When they were not engaged as shock troops in frontline assaults on various enemy fortifications or in support roles, they conducted patrols and small raids beyond the trench lines and into German-held territory both during daylight hours and at night.[2]

One of several unusual incidents during this period occurred on 4 October, when a group of volunteers from Company F, 2d Battalion, penetrated the German lines in a daring attempt to determine whether German forces were still occupying the Bois de Mortier. Company F's commander, Capt. Chester Sanders, led the patrol. A graduate of the Des Moines Officer Training Camp, Sanders was, from all reports, totally fearless in combat. Sanders took his patrol across the canal and the Ailette River, penetrated deep into the Bois de Mortier, and was one hundred meters behind the suspected German emplacements when the group was discovered and fired on from all directions by several enemy machine guns in heavily fortified positions. Unable to return by its original route, the patrol probed the German lines for weaknesses until it found a route out and fought its way back to the French lines, without major casualties. Sanders reported to his battalion commander the obvious: the woods were not only still manned, but quite heavily so. For his leadership and daring Sanders received the Croix de Guerre; the patrol members received special commendations from the French.[3]

This was not the only incident in which Sanders demonstrated his fearlessness under fire and his ability to invoke unwavering loyalty from his men. About a dozen hidden German machine guns in Sanders's sector were raising havoc with French and American movements along a road serving as a line of communication. Sanders and twenty volunteers from his company ran across the road, which was under direct German observation, to draw fire from the enemy machine guns to pinpoint their positions. Sanders and his men were fortunate because the Germans suspected that French or American troops were in the underbrush along the roadside waiting to make a surprise attack and directed their machine-gun fire there instead of at Sanders and his men. Several were slightly wounded in the action, and the French, who were understandably astonished at the Americans' brass, decorated three of the men. The machine guns were attacked and destroyed by French artillery fire.[4]

An example of the type of operations the 370th Infantry conducted during this time was an attack on German lines on 7 October by three raiding parties, again from Sanders's Company F. After a violent five-minute artillery bombardment, the attack was launched against the fortifications at the locks in the triangle formed by the railroad tracks, the l'Oise–l'Aisne Canal, and the Vauxaillon Road. One of the raiding parties captured the German trenches along the canal after a brutal grenade and hand-to-hand fight that resulted in excessive casualties.[5] The Germans launched several savage counterattacks with overwhelming forces. The severe losses the raiding party had sustained left it with insufficient manpower to hold its newly gained position, and it was forced to retreat back to French lines. Before leaving the captured German positions, however, the men destroyed a significant amount of enemy equipment and gathered a large quantity of intelligence material.[6]

Sergeant Suesbury described just how hotly contested the line along the canal was during an action involving his machine-gun section on the night of 11–12 October:

It was October 12 when the third section of the Machine gun Company took its position in a shell hole just a few yards from the Hun position.

This was necessary because under cover of darkness, the Huns would cross the Dam and take a position on the Loin Le Ferré railroad, which at this point was elevated to the height of twenty-five feet—such a position was dangerous for us.

On this particular evening—the darkest evening we ever saw in France—the Dutchmen with luck that favored them succeeded in passing my point of resistance which extended from the right wall of a torn white building to the left as far as I could fire. Here they placed a machine gun which I numbered seven, the other six advanced within twenty-five yards of my emplacement and opened a slow, searching fire trying to locate our machine gun.

Just about this time [my] loader and myself had been relieved of watch and we were trying to take as much sleep as possible. We had not gone to sleep when we heard our machine gun reply to the Hun fire. The fight was a hot one, six against one. Just about three minutes later some one was calling me, telling me the gun was jammed. I jumped up without helmet, ran to the position and proceeded to fix the gun. One of the boys gave me his helmet as my head was above the shallow trench and shrapnel was falling everywhere. I cleaned the gun under fire, and I want to tell you that it is not a coward's job in the middle of a fight, when there are six to one against you and you have to stop and repair your gun, but this was done and another box of ammunition substituted; the one we were using contained bad stuff. The entire crew came to the gun and worked like demons and we gave those Huns hell. The rapid firing gun that supported us was ordered to "burn the gun up" in order to draw the fire to him so should luck favor us we would have a chance to catch a flash from a Hun gun, which we did a few minutes later.

I saw the flash, turned the gun in that direction, took sight, and opened hell-fire on him. From right to left we swept a deadly accurate fire, until silence indicated the result to us. Gun number seven had opened fire on us, his range was a little too high to effect [sic] us. One of the Germans tried to advance to our position; he was stopped by an infantryman. Another attempt was made to reach us, with my gun in the right position, another rattle of the gun, another Hun was gone. At this moment a flare went up; from this flare I could see another gun and before he could change his range I had mine elevated just six inches above the railroad track. With this advantage again I opened fire and the crew fought until the last man was killed. This ended the German's seven guns which were a constant menace to our position. Please remember this was one American Machine gun and crew against seven German.

Next morning we received orders to go "Over the Top" at 9:00 AM All prepared, and with a yell the advance began. We went over in genuine Yankee fashion. There was no resistance—we found seven German guns and crews lying about the field.[7]

The orders received on 12 October by Suesbury's gun crew and the entire 370th Infantry directed a division attack against the German lines along the Ailette River. The 1st Battalion was ordered to cross the canal and river to clear the Bois de Mortier of the German troops and fortifications that Sanders had earlier discovered and then to move forward to capture Penancourt. The 3d Battalion was attached to Lieutenant Colonel Lugand's French 232d Infantry Regiment, and the 2d Battalion was assigned as the French 59th Infantry Division reserve, leaving the 1st Battalion as the 370th Infantry's lone assault force.[8]

The attack was launched at 11:00 AM, and after a hard fight the 1st Battalion captured the Bois de Mortier and pushed on to take Penancourt before sundown. The battalion dug in where it was and awoke the following morning to find the Germans engaged in a general withdrawal to the northeast. The 1st Battalion moved forward and dogged the heels of the fleeing German troops all through the day until it reached a point to the west of Molinchart and dug in for the night.[9] Meanwhile, the 3d Battalion, attached to the French 232d Infantry Regiment, pursued the retreating enemy along the Anizy-le-Château–Cessières–Bois de Oiry line, reaching the woods at dusk on 13 October, where it halted and dug in.[10]

During the night of 13–14 October the French 31st Division passed through and relieved the French 59th Infantry Division. The division was withdrawn for rest and reequipping, with the 370th Infantry being sent to the Saint-Gobain Forest area. Rather than resting, however, the men of the regiment spent ten days working on road maintenance in the area and two days repairing or replacing equipment in preparation for moving back into the line. The ten days of manual labor would seem to demonstrate that in spite of General Rondeau's complaint pointing up the urgent need for additional training, none was to be afforded the officers and men of the regiment. Neither the French 59th Infantry Division commander nor AEF Headquarters undertook steps to provide further training for the regiment.[11] While the regiment was performing road maintenance, Major Stokes was relieved of command of the 1st Battalion and assigned as an administrative officer in regimental supply. Capt. John T. Prout was appointed to command the battalion.[12]

On 27 October the French Third Army relieved the French Tenth Army and the French 59th Infantry Division was assigned to relieve the French 127th

Infantry Division on the front line in an area just northeast of Laon. On 30 October command of the sector passed to the French 59th Infantry Division, and the 370th Infantry received orders to join in the attack to capture the line along the Serre River and to pursue and maintain contact in the event of an expected German withdrawal.[13]

The 2d and 3d Battalions proceeded by foot from Cessières to the front on 27 October; the 2d Battalion moved into the line to man support positions around Grandlup and the 3d Battalion moved into reserve at Manneaux Farm. Two days later the 1st Battalion moved to Grandlup to join the 2d Battalion, and the familiar pattern of sustained combat operations against the German lines began again. The officers and men of the regiment participated in night patrols well forward of their lines, searching out and attacking enemy outposts while at the same time their own outposts were fighting off attacks from enemy patrols. Both types of actions resulted in numerous small but deadly machine-gun, bayonet, and grenade fights.[14]

Day and night, the regiment remained under constant and severe artillery shelling. Although casualties were light, Company A suffered a tragic loss in the vicinity of Chantrud Farm when an artillery shell exploded in a group gathered at the company mess kitchen, killing thirty-five men and wounding about fifty. Company A consequently had to be removed from the front line until it could be reorganized and built back into a functional and effective unit.[15]

On the night of 4–5 November, the Germans began another withdrawal. The following morning the 1st Battalion took up pursuit in support of Battalion Michel of the French 325th Infantry Regiment and moved along the Brazicourt-Rapière–Hill 150 axis (near Saint-Pierremont) on the right side of the division's front. That evening the 1st Battalion was ordered to enter the line and take up positions on the heights overlooking the town of Saint-Pierremont (see map 9).[16]

The next morning Company C, commanded by Capt. James H. Smith, was ordered to attack from a point just outside Saint-Pierremont and capture the town. The company was to then execute a crossing of the Serre River to capture and take up positions along a railroad track that ran parallel to the river. Although the company encountered heavy resistance, they took the town on schedule and began crossing the river. After a hard struggle under heavy machine-gun fire, Company C succeeded in making the crossing and then attacked and seized a section of the railroad track at the river, in the process taking three artillery pieces and several machine guns. For this action Company C was awarded the Croix de Guerre as a unit citation.[17]

The 1st Battalion continued the advance, passing through the Bois du Val Saint-Pierre, where Company C captured a German field artillery battery. The battalion advanced to the River Le Brune and dug in for the night on low hills

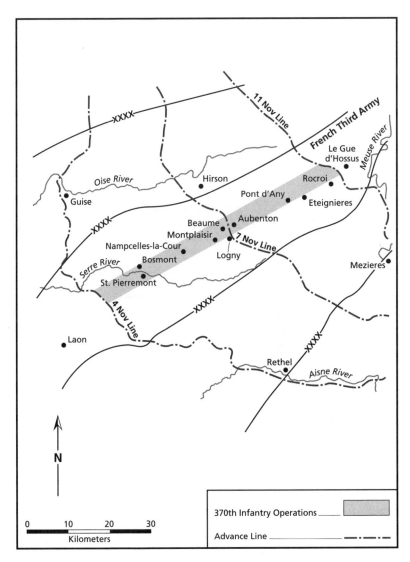

Map 9. 370th Infantry Operations during the Oise-Aisne Offensive,
4–11 November 1918

south of the river and east of the town of Nampcelles-la-Cour.[18] Meanwhile, on 5 November, the 3d Battalion moved forward in a general support role, passing through Bosmont and Montplaisir, spending the nights of 5 and 6 November in foxholes dug in open fields and conducting mopping-up operations during the daylight hours.

On 7 November the advance continued at 6:00 AM with the entire French

59th Infantry Division moving on toward the railroad tracks at Aubenton, where heavy resistance was encountered. The tracks on the eastern division boundary were captured at nightfall, but the line tapered away to the south, leaving Aubenton and Logny in German control. The division line was finally set for the night south and north of Hurtebise and east of Beaume. The 1st Battalion, following in support, saw little action that day and spent the night at Montplaisir behind the lines.[19]

On the morning of 8 November the 3d Battalion relieved the 1st Battalion, and the 2d Battalion moved into the line east of Beaume along the railroad line. Again stiff resistance was encountered, a heavy fight ensued, and little ground was gained.[20] As the 2d Battalion moved on Beaume, Pvt. Tom Powell of Hawkinsville, Georgia, and Company H was killed in action while carrying messages through heavy machine-gun and mortar fire. Powell was posthumously awarded the Distinguished Service Cross.[21]

It was in the same action that PFC Alfred Williamson, a medic mentioned earlier, earned his Distinguished Service Cross. While assigned to duty in the first-aid station of his company, Williamson volunteered to accompany the attacking troops to be available to render medical aid when needed. On the line, Williamson constantly exposed himself to enemy fire while giving medical aid to wounded comrades. For his courage under fire Williamson was awarded the Distinguished Service Medal.[22]

In the afternoon of 8 November, Company M, under the command of Lt. Osceola A. Brown, received orders to move up to support a French company making an attack on Logny, a strongly fortified village under German control located on the right division boundary. The company moved forward and was directed by regimental headquarters to deliver covering fire as the French company moved up to attack the town. The French company had reached its attack position and briefly engaged the German defenders when a combination of devastating artillery and machine-gun fire was directed against it. The French company commander reported that he could not continue and that he was breaking off the attack and withdrawing his company.[23]

Brown had simultaneously moved his company through the same artillery and machine-gun fire into position behind the French as ordered and was laying down covering fire for the attack when he was informed that the French unit had withdrawn. After evaluating the situation Brown concluded that it was better to move his company forward and attack than to move rearward through the heavy German artillery and machine-gun fire they had encountered in moving to their present position. Brown ordered his platoons forward and attacked the original French objective. After overcoming several surprised defending machine-gunners and entrenched riflemen, who had observed the French unit withdraw, Brown went on to capture the town. For that action

Brown and several others were awarded the Croix de Guerre.[24] There must have been an embarrassing moment at the French 59th Infantry Division headquarters when the report arrived that Company M, the support unit, had captured the objective after the French assault unit had retreated.[25]

Later in the day on 8 November, the 2d Battalion was ordered to clear out and capture enemy positions along the Hirson-to-Aubenton railroad track and on the heights of Aubenton. After heavy fighting and many losses the battalion accomplished its mission at about nightfall. Unfortunately, the French division on the left did not advance as ordered, claiming strong resistance on its front, and the 2d Battalion found itself about two kilometers forward of the connecting French lines with an exposed left flank. The German defenders quickly sensed the weakness and attacked into the gap with enfilading machine-gun fire. Three men and two officers of the regiment were killed and thirty-five men were wounded before the gap could be closed.[26]

While the 2d Battalion was engaged in its attack on 8 November, Sgt. Ralph Gibson of Chicago earned the Distinguished Service Cross for three separate acts of bravery. He began the day by setting an example of courage for his men and others nearby by calmly leading his platoon across an open field swept by enemy machine-gun, rifle, and artillery fire to reach, attack, and capture his objective. Later that same day Gibson was placed in charge of reconnaissance patrols on two occasions and each time was ordered to find several enemy machine-gun positions believed to be located in the line of advance of his company. He took each of his patrols out under heavy enemy artillery fire and by exposing himself to fire from German machine guns was able to return with accurate numbers and locations of the German positions facing his company.[27]

By nightfall the French 59th Infantry Division had captured the railroad line but little else. The 3d Battalion was charged with protecting the right flank of the division extending back from Logny, while the 1st Battalion was on the line along the railroad east of Aubenton.[28] On the morning of 9 November the French 59th Infantry Division commander ordered a general attack across the division's front that turned out to coincide with the German units executing another rapid withdrawal. As the battalions moved forward, they found the defensive positions immediately in front of them abandoned. The battalions pursued the retreating Germans in advance-guard formation and met with little resistance before reaching the objective of the Maubert-Fontaine–to–Hirson railroad tracks. That night the 3d Battalion moved up to hold the right side of the line at Pont d'Any.[29]

An administrative transfer of command occurred on the morning of 10 November, with the French 59th Infantry Division reassigned to the French XVI Corps. With that change the forward regiments, which included the 3d Battalion, moved out on new orders in advance-guard formation and pursued the fleeing Germans toward the Taillette–Cul des Sarts line. The 3d Battalion was north of Eteignières and moving along well in pursuit when it came under heavy German artillery fire and was pinned down for most of the afternoon.[30] Toward evening, the hostile artillery fire decreased and the 3d Battalion and the other forward elements of the French 59th Infantry Division reached a line along the eastern and northern edges of the Bois des Hingues and were able to settle in for the night. On the morning of 11 November, while rumors of a possible cease-fire circulated through the division, the 3d Battalion and the other forward elements of the division picked up their pursuit of the retreating German Army. Their initial objective was Resinowez, but as the morning wore on, orders changed the objective to Le Gue d'Hossus, Belgium. Later in the morning official word was received that an armistice would go into effect at 11:00 AM and all pursuit should stop at that time. The forward elements of the division continued on and occupied the objective, which included the capture of an enemy combat train of about fifty trucks. This act, which occurred a few minutes before 11:00 AM, would be the last significant accomplishment of the regiment.[31] All units ceased pursuit at the stroke of eleven on 11 November, stood down in position, and, amid sporadic celebrations, awaited further orders.[32]

In the fall 1918 offensive, which ran from 15 September through 11 November, the 370th Infantry fought hard and well against an enemy who was aggressive both in the attack and in his fighting withdrawal. Although figures vary, the cost to the regiment for remaining in contact with the enemy for most of that period was approximately 560 officers and men wounded and 105 killed in action or dead of wounds.[33]

CHAPTER 20

Final Days on the Vosges Front

Not a few of the prisoners taken by the regiment declared that the Germans were in positive fear of the Negroes, who, they complained, would never quit even under heavy fire.

Lt. Jerome Meyer, 732d Infantry

The Vosges Mountain Range, composed of rugged hills and low mountains, steep valleys and ravines, thick forests, and wide rivers, lay at the eastern end of the Western Front near the Swiss border (see map 10). For military commanders this terrain has always been a maneuvering nightmare, and neither the Allies nor the Germans had any desire to contest ground the other presently occupied.[1] In fact, there had been no serious challenges for territory in the region since the very beginning of the war when the French Army advanced into Germany and then was pushed back to the main trench line it occupied thereafter. Over time the sector had evolved into a rest area for combat-weary units because it had a moderate level of frontline activity acceptable to both sides.[2]

The 370th Infantry entered the war at the Vosges Front, and the 369th, 371st, and 372d Infantry Regiments were destined to finish out the war there. The officers and men of the American regiments found the front a strange contrast to their recent extreme combat experiences in the battle areas to the west. The most evident and immediately noticeable difference was that the villages in the Vosges Front were unofficially off-limits to shelling on both sides of the line, and civilians went about their everyday lives in a normal fashion, seemingly oblivious to the war.[3] Another obvious difference was that the native population in the Vosges had a higher standard of living and a stronger work ethic than did their western neighbors. Houses were better constructed and built of more substantial materials; shops and stores were larger, better kept, and contained a greater variety of wares; and some of the homes and businesses were illuminated with electricity. Streets were clean, roads were paved, yards and surroundings of houses were neat and orderly, and factories and farms were in full production.[4]

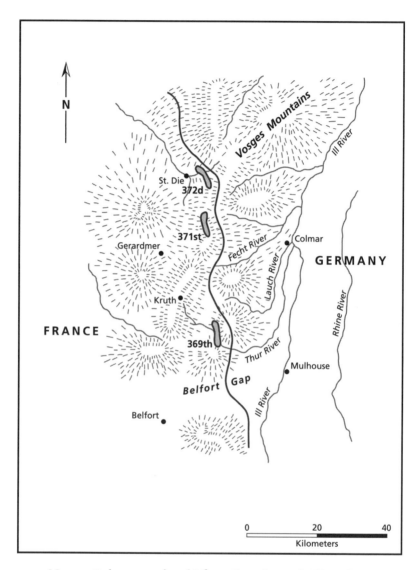

Map 10. 369th, 371st, and 372d Infantry Operations on the Vosges Front,
13 October to 11 November 1918

Conditions on the front line were equally unusual. In contrast to the continuous trench lines of the western areas of combat, the forward units were located in outpost positions totally surrounded by wire entanglements. At night the outposts were closed in and isolated from direct contact with friendly units until daylight. During the day, contact patrols worked between the line and the outposts to keep in touch with the men manning the forward positions.

Reconnaissance patrols were sent out in the usual manner with the intent of capturing prisoners for interrogation purposes and to maintain a presence in the line, but there were fewer of them and they operated with less intensity and seemingly less purpose, since general attacks were unheard of in the region.[5]

The occasional German patrols probing the lines did force the Allied troops to maintain some vigilance, but most of the time it seemed a halfhearted effort. German patrols had made a practice of creeping in behind the outposts at night and hiding along a path or trail to wait for daylight in order to capture a single man or small group on its way to or from an outpost. After pouncing on and subduing the unfortunate man or men, the German patrol would continue hiding until dark and then escort their unfortunate prisoners across to their own lines for interrogation.[6] Occasional incidents caused a temporary flurry of activity and increased vigilance, but for the most part the area remained far calmer than the western area of the front.

One such incident occurred just prior to the arrival of the three American regiments. A French officer carrying critical documents and somewhat careless in honoring his responsibilities was captured while moving alone within a few hundred meters of German positions. The capture caused an uproar within the French command over security in the area.[7] Just at the time the three regiments reached their new posts and were settling in, orders went out that no personnel other than those on escort duty, on reconnaissance patrol, manning combat group outposts, or other essential functions could move forward of an established security line. Men were required to move in groups of no less than two when just behind the line, and officers in the same areas were to be accompanied by at least two armed enlisted men. Officers working beyond the security line began the unofficial habit of carrying their sidearm in hand and ready for use when inspecting positions.[8]

The exhausted Americans were quick to discover and enjoy the better living conditions on the Vosges Front. Abandoned houses were available for temporary billets when the men were at the line but not on duty in an outpost, and the dense woods meant that fires could be lit when the men were out of view of German positions. The men were surprised to find that the Germans shelled the area only twice a day, and always at the same time, allowing everyone to take shelter well beforehand and ride out the bombardment in safety and comfort.[9]

Best of all was the time when the battalions were moved into reserve and occupied positions and billets in the towns and villages in back of the line. Living quarters there were quite comfortable, and food, sweets, and tobacco were plentiful and relatively cheap in the shops.[10] One commodity was much too available to some of the American troops, it seems, and consequently, General Goybet published order 1663/2, dated 15 October 1918, for the two American regiments of his French 157th Infantry Division:

The following is published for the information of all concerned. . . . The General commanding the 157th Division prescribes formally that the entrance of inns and the sale of wines or spirits are strictly forbidden to the American colored troops of the division at all times and all hours and in the whole sector. It is the same for the Military Cooperatives.[11]

Apparently the men were compensating for the months spent eating barley sugar instead of drinking the daily ration of wine that was given to the French soldiers.[12] There was some concern among the men of the three regiments that the high command felt that black troops could not be trusted to handle alcoholic spirits. And in fact, the restrictions probably stemmed from the drunkenness and mischief that had occurred when the units first came under French control and some of the men consumed all of their daily wine issue at one sitting. In any event, the men officially went without alcoholic beverages, although it is well known that any soldier worth his salt can find a way to get alcohol, particularly in France.[13]

One disadvantage came along with the many advantages of being stationed in a relatively quiet area of the front: the assignment to the machine-gun companies of the heavy machine gun known as the St. Etienne. Easily identified by its heavy cast brass receiver, this weapon was a classic example of change for the sake of change. The gun was a redesign of the reliable 1914 Hotchkiss machine gun made by officers of the French arsenal at Saint-Etienne. Their creation was a machine gun with a propensity to jam at critical moments in a firefight. Because of its unreliability and its limitation in continuous fire (because it used strip-fed rather than belt-fed ammunition), the gun had been removed from more active fronts and reassigned to units in the quiet Vosges region.[14]

The 369th Infantry Moves to the Vosges

The battered and reduced 369th Infantry withdrew from the front lines in the Argonne region on 30 September and for the next four days settled into a bivouac on the southern slope of Signal Ridge, where the officers immediately began an extensive reorganization. Heads were counted and search parties sent into the battle area to recover those killed in action. In the process, Lt. Charles S. Dean of Morristown, New Jersey, was found to be missing along with most of his platoon from the machine-gun company of the 2d Battalion. On 1 October search parties found Dean's body and those of his platoon lying together, all facing toward the enemy trenches. During the night of 27 September Dean had taken his unit forward into no-man's-land to lend fire support to Major Cobb's battalion, which was being cut to pieces by German machine-gun and rifle fire. Dean and his men had advanced to a spot where they had to cut through enemy wire when the German defenders apparently heard their wire cutters and opened up a murderous fire with registered heavy machine guns, killing every man in the unit.[15]

Dr. Willis H. Keenan, Medical Corps, was another casualty. Keenan had moved his surgical team into an abandoned house in Séchault and set up operations during the assault from 26 to 30 September. Four days after the regiment was relieved, and after treating hundreds of casualties and saving many lives and limbs, Keenan collapsed from mental and physical exhaustion and was ordered evacuated to the rear. Keenan remained under hospital care for seven months before returning to normal life and his profession as a doctor. For his sacrifice and his unusual courage and devotion to duty Keenan received the Distinguished Service Cross.[16]

On the evening of 6 October the entire French 161st Infantry Division was relieved from further offensive action and passed into corps reserve. The 369th Infantry marched through most of the night to go into bivouac at Minaucourt, the place from which it had launched its venture into the Allied offensive a dozen days earlier.[17] The men continued to rest until they were loaded onto camions on 8 October and sent south to billets in and around the village of Arrigny about twenty kilometers southwest of Vitry-le-François. The regiment's official rehabilitation began there, and continued rest and good food brought a marked improvement in the men's morale and strength.[18] On the afternoon of 13 October the 1st Battalion marched to the town of Chavanges, where, in the middle of the night, they boarded railway cars and started a long train ride to the south and east, bound for places as yet unknown to anyone in the regiment.[19] The train traveled on through the night, and at about 10:00 AM the following morning arrived at the outskirts of the city of Belfort in upper eastern France not far from the Swiss and pre-1914 German borders. After detraining, the 1st Battalion marched to Roope and then rode by camions to the Thur River valley in the Vosges Mountains. Major Little later described the ride into the mountains:

> Our day's journey was one of real delight. The sun shone brightly, the atmosphere was clear. Our motors climbed over perfect roads, ranges of mountains from 4500 to 6000 feet of altitude. . . . From the summits we enjoyed magnificent views of the Alps on one hand, the Vosges on the other, and between, lay a great, comparatively flat, country leading to the Rhine, with the Black Forest beyond.[20]

The 1st Battalion was one to two days ahead of the rest of the regiment and was directed to billet at Bitschwiller. The remainder of the regiment arrived to find billets at Saint-Amarin, Moosch, Willers, and Thann, a line of villages that included Bitschwiller and extended about eight kilometers along the banks of the Thur.[21]

The exhilaration Little felt on his ride through the mountains was somewhat dampened when he arrived to learn that no plans had been made to feed his battalion—or the regiment—and that the local French command had no surplus commissary supplies. Colonel Gastinel, the French officer supporting the regiment, relieved the situation by borrowing sufficient food from several French regiments located in the area. Given this poor start, perhaps it was not surprising that food rations remained substandard in quantity and quality until after the armistice.[22]

The 1st Battalion moved up on line into Secteur Collardelle of Sous Secteur A, Secteur de la Thur, on 17 October to relieve the French 1st Infantry Regiment. All three battalions would serve in the trenches while in the Vosges Front, and the men enjoyed the relaxed combat situation so different from their recent experiences in the chalk hills and valleys of the Champagne region. From that day until the armistice on 11 November, the men thrived on the relatively quiet front and the rest and relaxation available when they were out of the line.[23]

The only serious action in the sector occurred on 28 October while the 1st Battalion was on the line. At about 5:00 AM the Germans opened an unusual and intense artillery barrage and sprayed the forward posts with heavy machine-gun fire for about an hour and a half. Heavy fog in the valley and along the line prevented the men in the outposts from seeing whether or not enemy troop movements were occurring, although one post spotted two German soldiers approaching the wire. French counterbattery artillery did not fire to suppress the German artillery barrage, but the regiment's heavy machine guns answered the German machine-gun fire. Unfortunately, all but one of the St. Etienne machine guns malfunctioned and the crews had to resort to throwing grenades into the wire in front of their positions to prevent infiltrations under cover of the fog.[24]

The short action eventually ground to a halt, but one officer and two men were killed and nine men were wounded. The officer, Lt. Elmer E. Bucher, was mortally wounded as he was moving in the open between his two assigned outposts trying to coordinate fire into the German lines. He was posthumously awarded the Croix de Guerre.[25]

Other than the twice daily ritual shelling, the 369th saw minimal further action on the lines during its stay in the Vosges area. Several officers of the regiment were sent to the rear to attend various service schools conducted by the

French Army, and the men were allowed to rest and recuperate in the rear areas of the regiment. Then, on 11 November at 11:00 AM, the anxiously awaited orders arrived for all of the officers and men on the line to stand down for the armistice.[26]

The 371st Infantry Moves to the Vosges

In the early morning darkness of 1 October, amid the crash and roar of French artillery fire and German counterbattery fire, the 371st Infantry pulled off the line and out of combat to a temporary reserve position along an old railroad track north of Ardéuil and Montfauxelles. The regiment would remain in these positions in corps reserve.[27]

On 7 October the regiment was ordered into army reserve, and, by battalions, the officers and men—tired, dirty, and lacking much of their equipment, which was lost in days of close combat—moved out of the combat zone late that afternoon; after a tiring march they reached their destination of Auve. The march was particularly hard on the many men who were suffering from foot problems caused by days of being wet and having no chance to dry their feet or change their boots.[28]

At Auve, while the officers and men rested, reorganized, and reequipped, the regiment received Order 255 from Ninth Army headquarters, dated 7 October 1918:

> The 157th and 161st Divisions and the 2nd Moroccan Divisions are leaving the Army Corps.
>
> The Commanding General [of] the 9th Army Corps presents his earnest and his most hearty congratulations for the glorious success they have achieved through their wonderful spirit and indomitable tenacity. The General bows to the brave American regiments who have wonderfully and hardily competed with their French comrades.
>
> This is not the place to give an enumeration of the splendid deeds which have marked each of the days of our victorious progress. They have to be found written in the conquered soil, materialized through the trophies captured from the enemy and engraved in the heart of your chief who bows deeply and salutes the troops.
>
> General Garnier-Duplessix, Commanding the 9th A.C.[29]

On 8 October General Goybet, commanding the 157th Infantry Division, of which the 371st and 372d Infantry Regiments were still a part, published General Order 234 describing in detail the division's exploits:

I am proud to forward you herewith the thanks and congratulations of General Garnier-Duplessix and I want at the same time, dear friends, of all ranks American and French, to tell you as your leader and as a soldier, from the bottom of my heart how grateful I am to you all for the glory you acquired for our splendid 157th Division.

I have the utmost confidence in you all; you have stood up to it beyond all my expectations. In these nine hard days of battle you have pushed ahead for eight kilometers, through powerful enemy organizations, captured close to 600 prisoners, taken 15 guns, light and heavy, 20 Infantry Mortars, close to 150 Machine Guns and a very important supply of Engineer material and Artillery ammunition, and brought down by rifle fire 3 Aeroplanes.

The Red Hand, emblem of this Division, is now in truth a blood reeking hand. It grappled the Boche at the throat and made him yell for mercy. Our glorious comrades who died are well avenged.[30]

On the day following receipt of General Goybet's order, the infantry commander of the 157th Division, Colonel Quillet, issued an order proposing that the 371st Infantry be awarded the Croix de Guerre unit citation.[31]

Somewhat rested and recuperated, the regiment assembled on 11 October and marched to Valmy to entrain for the town of Corcieux. Four sections of trains totaling fifty cars carried all of the officers, men, baggage, animals, basic ammunition load, and three days of rations.[32] While they enjoyed a leisurely journey through the French countryside, the officers and men anticipated their first real rest after six months in the trenches and participating in the last major offensive of the war. When the train sections arrived in Corcieux, the men off-loaded themselves and their equipment and settled into quarters for the night. The next morning the regiment found out that no rest period was in store for them just yet. The following day they boarded camions and were trucked to Habeaurupt and Rudlin-Luschbach in the Vosges Mountains in the Alsace-Lorraine region not far from the 369th Infantry's position. There the regiment took over a frontline sector, relieving a French regiment.[33] As had the 369th Infantry, the regiment found the area to be quiet and relatively undisturbed by war. The officers and men rotated in and out of frontline outpost duty, did occasional patrolling, and were able to get much-needed rest when in rear areas in reserve.[34]

One of the strong-points under the control of the regiment was on the Tête des Faux, which was so close to the German lines that grenades were often exchanged, although nothing more serious developed as both sides wished to keep the situation low key. One morning around the first of November, several German grenades dropped into the regiment's positions but did not explode. Examination of the grenades revealed that the detonators had been removed, and tied to each was a piece of paper with German propaganda messages printed on it. The papers, obviously written by someone who had lived for a long period in the United States and understood the local dialects, were immediately forwarded to headquarters. One read:

> Never Say Die!
>   Don't die till you have to!
>   What Business Have You to Die for France, for Alsace-Lorraine, or for England, in France?
>   Isn't it better anyhow to live than to die, no matter for how "glorious" a cause?
>   Isn't it better to live and come back to the old folks at home, than to rot in the shell holes and trenches of France?[35]

The message went on for several pages of commentary disparaging the French, the British, the U.S. government, and the military command in general and ended with: "Wake up and stop the war. You can if you want to. Your government does not mean to stop the war for years to come, and the years are going to be long and dreary. You better come over while the going is good."[36]

The troops who read the messages paid no heed. They had all been in combat against the Germans, had defeated them, and knew that the war was about to end. In fact, rumors that an armistice was imminent were running rampant throughout the units in the area.[37]

Small offensive actions continued to be planned and executed within the operations areas of the three regiments of the 93d Division present on the Vosges Front even as late as 10–11 November. A raid planned for the 2d Battalion, for example, was to consist of three groups with orders to capture prisoners in and along the Germans' outpost line facing the battalion's lines. The groups were to be led by Lts. John B. Given, B. K. Sikes, and W. A. Thorne. This action was ordered while instructions were being sent down from division headquarters to prepare to advance across no-man's-land to either occupy the German positions as soon as the armistice went into effect or to pursue the retreating German forces. Although the orders for the raid were very detailed, there is no indication that it was ever executed as it was obviously overtaken by the event of the armistice.[38]

The 372d Infantry Follows the 371st

On 7 October, after being engaged for ten days in the Champagne region, the 372d Infantry was ordered out of the line and moved back to the village of Minaucourt for a much-needed and relatively quiet night's sleep. The next day the regiment marched to Hans and Somme-Bionne for three days of rest, reorganization, and reequipping.[39]

The first activity for every regiment brought out of the line for any length of time was to bathe and be deloused, and the 372d Infantry was no different. The men were sent in small groups to the bath and delousing station, where they removed their clothes, wrapped them in bundles, and turned them over to the clothing delousing section. They then enjoyed the luxury of hot-water showers—the first in months—after which they were drenched in a louse-killing chemical that appeared to be similar to vinegar. After that, they went through the shower again to rinse off the chemicals.[40]

While the men were enjoying the showers, their clothing bundles were placed in large steam chambers and treated for thirty minutes to kill all live lice and any eggs hidden in the clothing. Handlers removed the clothing bundles from the steam chambers, sorted them, found identification tags, and called out the names or serial numbers of the owners, who picked up their bundles of clothing and dressed. There was quite a bit of joking as the men put on their uniforms to find them completely wrinkled from the steam treatment.[41]

Someone at 372d Infantry headquarters failed to do the appropriate planning. The newly deloused men's packs and equipment were not deloused, and the packs and personal belongings they recovered were in most cases still contaminated with lice. In a few days the men had to go through the delousing process again.[42]

On the morning of 12 October the unit received orders to load onto train sections and prepare to move to the Vosges Mountains to join up with the 371st Infantry and the French 157th Division headquarters. The loading was completed before dawn on 13 October as faint explosions accompanied by the flashing lights of artillery fire against the north night sky reminded the officers and men of the ordeal they had just come through.[43]

The trains arrived the next morning at a debarkation point in the Vosges Mountains, and the regiment off-loaded its equipment and marched nineteen kilometers to the village of Saint-Leonard. Quarters were arranged, and the men settled in to what they thought would be a long stay, only to find, as had the 371st Infantry, that the next day they would march farther into the mountains to relieve a French regiment in a sector near Ban-de-Laveline. This village would serve as regimental headquarters and was connected to the line and to other nearby villages by camouflaged roads.[44]

The 1st and 3d Battalions moved into position over the camouflaged roads under the cover of rain and fog, and relieved the French battalions on the line without incident on 16 October. The next day, the rain and fog lifted before the 2d Battalion and the machine-gun company had finished moving into their areas. They were observed through gaps in the camouflage over the roads and suffered several casualties from German artillery fire.[45]

Life on the line and in the billeting areas was much the same for the 372d as that experienced by the 369th and 371st Infantry Regiments. Action was limited on both sides until the night of 10 November, when a heavy raiding party was sent into the German lines to capture prisoners. The party ran into a larger party of Germans out on a raid themselves, and one officer and twenty-two men of the regiment ended up prisoners of the Germans. The Americans suffered only a short imprisonment, as they were all released within a few days after the armistice went into effect.[46]

So it was that three of the regiments of the 93d Division, decimated and battle-weary, wound down their participation in the war in relative comfort and safety, anxiously awaiting the end of hostilities.[47]

CHAPTER 21

Armistice

We stood up and we didn't say a word,
It felt just like when you have dropped your pack
After a hike, and straightened out your back
And seem just twice as light as any bird.

We stood up straight and, God! but it was good!
When you have crouched like that for months, to stand
Straight up and look right out toward No-Man's-Land
And feel the way you never thought you could.

If you had listened then I guess you'd heard
A sort of sigh from everybody there,
But all we did was stand and stare and stare,
Just stare and stand and never say a word.

"November Eleventh," Pvt. Hilmar R. Baukhage,
371st Infantry Regiment

Rumors of an armistice and its projected date had been circulating through the Allied armies since early November 1918, and many men had begun to ignore them. On the morning of 11 November, as the actual cease-fire time approached, heavy explosions and constant machine-gun fire erupted from the German lines along the Vosges Front. Machine gunners turned their weapons against embankments and expended all of their ammunition, and grenadiers pulled pins and threw all of their grenades over the side of their emplacements.[1] On the Allied side, the French artillery started expending ammunition as well, and the combined activity led some Allied officers to believe that a full-scale attack by the Germans was under way.[2]

At 11:00 AM a series of signal rockets burst high over the front lines, and German troops came running out onto the parapets of their emplacements in groups. Captain Heywood observed that the Germans were "yelling, dancing, throwing their little round hats in the air and acting like crazy men."[3] A few

German troops came across no-man's-land looking for American soldiers in hopes of bartering for food and tobacco. As the war was not yet officially over and only a cease-fire was in effect, many of the Germans found themselves detained temporarily as prisoners of war. In view of the shortages the German troops were suffering, they were likely better off as prisoners of the Allies.[4]

By 12 November hordes of Germans, soldiers and civilians, had begun to approach the positions of the three regiments of the 93d Division asking to be received as visiting guests. The Allied commanders were concerned that spontaneous conflicts might result in gunfire and break the cease-fire, and orders were issued and conveyed to both sides of the line that visiting would not be permitted. The American troops were sent into their positions with instructions to move visitors back across the lines at bayonet point. In spite of these measures, German visitors continued to cross the lines, and some Americans were invited to visit the Germans in their trenches and billeting areas. Fortunately for everyone, no incidents occurred that resulted in gunfire, indicating perhaps a greater desire for peace and harmony on both sides among the ranks than commanders realized.[5]

Another class of visitors growing daily in numbers comprised released Allied prisoners of war, released interned civilians, and refugees wanting to return to their homes or to report to the proper authority. The Germans were more than glad to rid themselves of the responsibility of holding and feeding prisoners of war, but the mass of people coming into the Allied lines became overwhelming. Somehow they all had to be cared for, processed, and issued passes permitting them to travel into the interior.[6] Although there was plenty of food for the visitors, the regiments had no excess clothing supplies to issue against the November chill of the Vosges Mountains. It was imperative that all of the people entering the area be processed quickly through collection stations and moved to the rear where they could be better cared for, and every effort was made to do so.[7]

Within a few days after the armistice the three infantry regiments received orders to begin packing and to be prepared to move forward across the lines to occupy areas that were presently in German hands.[8] On 17 November at 4:30 AM, the men of the 369th Infantry went over the front of their dugouts in Secteur Collardelle, but this time they met no machine-gun or artillery fire coming from the German side. The regiment passed through deserted German dugouts and went on for several kilometers before billeting for the night. The next morning the regiment pressed on toward the village of Ensisheim, where General Lebouc, the commander of the French 161st Division, was to review all of the regiments under his command.[9]

Ensisheim had not been evacuated as were the towns nearer the front on the German side, and the inhabitants gave the regiments of the French 161st

Division a gala reception. Flags fluttered on houses, and pictures of President Woodrow Wilson appeared in the windows. Banners strung across the streets welcomed the French and American soldiers with: *"Vive la Republique!"* "Greetings to Our Deliverers," and "God Bless President Wilson!" All were welcome sights for the battle-weary officers and men of the 369th Infantry.[10]

The entire French 161st Infantry Division marched in regimental order through downtown Ensisheim and past a reviewing stand set in front of a church on the main plaza. French officers' method of reviewing the troops is quite different from the manner of American generals, as Major Little noted:

> The French General, in acknowledging a salute would smile cordially; and, if he happened to be personally acquainted with the officer who was passing, he would call to him a greeting. Thus, as the 1st Battalion passed, General Lebouc shouted "Ah—Little—I am glad to see you— you are looking well—it is a beautiful day!" And to a number of our company or platoon commanders, he called out compliments upon the fine marching of the men.[11]

On completion of the review, the regiment marched on for fifteen to twenty more kilometers to settle into billets at Blodelsheim, Fessenheim, Balgau, and Nambsheim. On 20 November the regiment was ordered to send patrols to secure the Rhine approaches.[12]

On 22 November the following letter arrived at 369th Infantry headquarters:

22 November 1918

Le Colonel Hayward
Cdt. le 369e Regt. d'Infte, U.S.

My Dear Colonel:

I am greatly pleased with your thoughtful attention. You have collected the water of the Rhine in your hand and you have placed the Black Watch along the river.

It is ours from now on but no Frenchman ignores that it is to the Americans that we owe this conquest. Therefore, you will permit me not to accept the personal compliments you paid, except with the following reserve. I shall never forget that the opportunity has been given me, in the course of this war, to have under my command an American regiment which, with little previous training, has fought with extreme bravery, and which since the last combat has applied itself to such regular and steady work that as far as attitude and military discipline are concerned, this American regiment can compare with any of my French regiments.

Therefore, it is to yourself, Colonel, to Lt. Colonel Pickering and to your battalion commanders that must be addressed all congratulations. And it is for this reason that I make it a point to reward officially the 369th R.I.U.S. with a collective citation in the orders of my Division.

When the citation is approved, I shall have great joy in decorating your flag and in kissing you in front of your Regiment. And that day we shall not only drink water from the Rhine, we shall drink Champagne, and it will be a beautiful day for your General Commanding the Division.

Believe, my dear Colonel, in my sentiments of affectionate comradeship.

Lebouc[13]

And so in the early afternoon on 13 December 1918, near the city of Mulhouse, the officers and men of the French 161st Division formed a rectangle almost one thousand meters in length and five hundred meters across the ends. All members of services assigned to the division were present, as were the three primary branches—infantry, cavalry, and artillery—and all troops were facing inward.[14]

A corps of bugles sounded a flourish, and all commands, responding to the calls of their individual leaders, came to attention. At the western end of the formation, a dozen horsemen approached and entered the rectangle. In the lead, astride a white horse and clad in a dress uniform of crimson trousers, horizon blue greatcoat, and high-crowned red hat with gold bands of oak leaves, rode General Lebouc.[15] The commander rode to his right and stopped to face the formed ranks of the 369th Infantry. In front of the formation and facing the general stood Colonel Hayward, Colonel Pickering, and Major Little, the only officer remaining of the three battalion commanders who served at Bellevue Signal Ridge and Séchault.[16] Lebouc dismounted in front of the assembled officers, read the citation, pinned to the colors of the regiment a Croix de Guerre, and then, true to his word, kissed not only Hayward, but Pickering and Little as well.[17]

The 371st Infantry

Shortly after the armistice, orders came down from French 157th Infantry Division headquarters to all of the regiments under its command to discontinue preparing defensive works. Further, they were to gather all war materials not being used, such as excess ammunition, engineering materials, and anti-gas materials, and deposit those items in designated dumps. Orders also directed the regiments to request from visiting German officials any information they might have on minefields in front of the division's frontline positions.[18]

Just before midnight on 13 November, the 371st Infantry received orders to pack up and prepare to advance into German-held territory. That next morning the battalions began marching north toward the German border, but then received new orders to proceed back into France. The reverse march continued until 18 November, when the regiment arrived at the towns of Bruyères and Laval, where it remained for the next two months.[19]

Both towns were largely untouched by the war and provided excellent quarters for officers and men. The return to a peacetime atmosphere was an emotional letdown for men accustomed to the strain and pace of combat, and headquarters quickly devised activities to fill their days. Formation drills and various sports games were instituted, but still time dragged, and in the words of Captain Heywood: "The 'when do we go home' fever was in everyone's blood."[20] As the troops had become lax in such things as proper wearing of the uniform, saluting, and policing of areas while in the front lines, these matters became the primary focus of enforcement by officers and noncommissioned officers as the regiment readjusted to the different world of garrison duty.[21]

On 21 November sad news arrived at regimental headquarters: Maj. Tobe C. Cope of the 3d Battalion was dead.[22] Cope, who had risen from sergeant, Regular Army, to command an infantry battalion in combat, had died of wounds received in the face which at the time had seemed negligible but later developed into gangrene. Cope would posthumously receive the Distinguished Service Cross for his valor and sacrifice.[23]

At Thanksgiving and then again at Christmas, AEF Headquarters made an effort to provide all American troops throughout France with special provisions for the holidays—all troops except the regiments of the 93d Division attached to the French Army; no such provisions were provided for them. The units used their own nonappropriated funds to purchase special foods and other items to celebrate the holidays. Heywood was bitter about the oversight: "We, as part of the French Army, did not rate anything. We did the best we could for the men with our own funds."[24]

The YMCA did not forget the regiments, however, and provided gifts of chocolate cake and candy, cigarettes, and chewing gum to all of the officers and men.[25] Heywood gave the YMCA's efforts to serve and provide comfort for the men well-deserved praise:

> They were the only one of all the American welfare units who came near us. During the occupation of defensive sectors they packed cigarettes and such other things as they had for the comfort of our men all the way up to the front lines. In the Champagne Offensive they followed the attack and

during the assault of the 1st Battalion on Hill 188, September 28, 1918, one of the colored Y.M.C.A. men, Hugh O. Cook, worked in the aid station with the gassed and wounded cases until he became gassed himself and had to be evacuated.[26]

On 2 December a memo was distributed concerning a proposed memorial to be purchased with funds collected from the officers and men and placed on Hill 188. Also to be obtained was a regimental memorial medal.[27] Funds for the monument and the medal were raised, and the monument now stands on Bellevue Signal Ridge. The medals were struck in bronze and contained the regimental emblem in relief on one side with the names and dates of the battles in which the regiment participated in France. The reverse side, also in relief, featured a soldier of the regiment in the act of charging the enemy; below him was a cotton field with men picking cotton next to a typical southern cabin; and on the right was a palmetto tree, the symbol of South Carolina. The regimental motto scrolled across the cotton field: "Dulce et Decorum est Pro Patria Mori."[28]

The monument was completed and placed after the regiment had gone back to the United States. Gen. G. A. I. Dumont, the French military attaché, reported its exact location: "The monument is located 600 meters northwest of Bussy Farm, 1 kilometer slightly to the southeast of Ardéuil and 2 kilometers northeast of Gratreuil."[29] The medals arrived in the United States after the regiment had demobilized, and although the officers made every attempt to locate all the members of the unit, many could not be found and did not receive their hard-earned memento of their experiences in France.[30]

On 16 December Brig. Gen. Mariano Goybet, commander of the French 157th Infantry Division, personally decorated the men who had been nominated for the Croix de Guerre with Palm and the Legion of Honor. Other awards of the Croix de Guerre could not be made in the time allowed because of the overwhelming number of officers and men who had earned them. The awards were made to the officers and men of the 371st Infantry at Quartiers Barbazan at Bruyères starting at 10:30 AM in a ceremony conducted in front of the entire 371st Infantry.[31]

On 17 December the 371st Infantry and 372d Infantry received General Order 265 from Goybet's headquarters, which read in part:

On the 12th of December 1918 the 371st and 372nd R.I.U.S. were returned to the American command. . . .

. . . The 157th D.I. will never forget the irresistible and heroic rush of the colored American regiments up the "Côte dis Observatoires" and into the "Plaine de Monthois." The most formidable defences, the strongest machine gun nests, the most crushing artillery barrages were unable to stop them. These superior troops have overcome everything with a supreme disdain of death, and thanks to their courageous sacrifice, the Red (Bloody) Hand Division, for nine days of hard fighting always maintained the front rank in the 4th Army's victorious advance.[32]

On 20 December headquarters of the French 157th Infantry Division issued Order 248 to its regiments, which dissolved the division.[33]

During the time that the 371st and 372d Infantry Regiments were part of the French 157th Infantry Division, all the men had worn the division insignia, the outline of a red hand sewn on the right uniform sleeve at the shoulder just below the seam.[34] Several stories account for the origin of the name "Red Hand" and the wearing of the patch. The most plausible explanation seems to be that the division had been involved in an action during the later part of May 1918 in which French and British divisions were in a general retreat. The general then commanding the French 157th Infantry Division saw an opportunity to attack and seized the moment, surprising the Germans and stalling their assault against the division's front. The French 157th Infantry Division continued to advance without artillery support and captured large numbers of German prisoners and materials. During that action the division lost one-half of its officers and men. The name "Red Hand Division" and the wearing of the patch commemorated that bloody event.[35] The French 157th Infantry Division was recovering from this action when the two regiments of the 93d Division joined it. As what was left of the three regiments of the division was only enough to make up one complete French regiment, the 371st and 372d Infantry Regiments were assigned to complete the division.[36]

Although the two regiments asked to have the red hand insignia adopted as the 93d Division's shoulder patch, AEF Headquarters rejected the request. Rumors circulated in the regiments that some officers in the higher command believed the symbol of a bloody hand was too gruesome. Instead, a circular black patch with a sky blue French Adrian helmet in profile was later adopted.[37]

The 372d Infantry

The officers and men of the 372d Infantry celebrated the armistice with the French civilians and soldiers in the villages in their sector. The regimental band was called out, and the rest of the day was spent in singing, marching, and speech making. The mayor of the major village in the sector ordered the electric generating plant put into service and all of the light bulbs replaced in the streetlights so that the celebrations could continue into the night.[38]

During the next few days the regiment's outposts watched the Germans busily removing all war materials from the lines and blowing up mines and ammunition dumps that could not be moved in time to avoid being taken by the Allies. So many mines and ammunition dumps were exploded during the three days following the armistice that the villages on the Allied side and the regimental area were enveloped in a pall of smoke.[39]

At 5:00 AM on 17 November, the 372d Infantry departed the front lines, and after a hard march of some forty-eight kilometers arrived between 9:30 and 10:30 PM at the village of Granges-sur-Vologne, close to the village of Bruyères, where the 371st Infantry was billeted. It was one of the most difficult marches the regiment ever made, and many men dropped out from fatigue and had to be recovered by wagons.[40] Granges-sur-Vologne was a larger village than most in the area and provided ample and comfortable billeting for officers and men. The inhabitants were cordial and provided whatever they could for the comfort of the members of the regiment.[41]

Thanksgiving was a gloomy day in Granges-sur-Vologne, as it was for all of the regiments of the 93d Division. On 17 December the 372d Infantry joined the 371st Infantry and paraded for General Goybet, and while the villagers gathered and watched, stood formation as those nominated received the Croix de Guerre with Palm and the Medaille Militaire. As each medal was pinned in place, Goybet, in his typical manner, made a short speech commending the recipient for his valor and courage. When the regiment returned to Granges-sur-Vologne and was dismissed, many of the villagers approached the men who had received awards and asked how they had come to be decorated. It was reported that some rather wild tales came to light.[42]

Christmas, like Thanksgiving, was a quiet and somber celebration. The French villagers did not exchange gifts or have a big dinner as was typical in America, and the only activity of the day was a solemn service at the local church. The men gathered on Christmas night, and with the band and a few officers passed through the streets serenading the villagers with Christmas carols and folk songs from home until dawn.[43] The holidays were not completely bleak; packages of all kinds arrived from home both before and after Christmas—the contents, of course, shared by all.[44]

On 30 December a belated Christmas gift of much greater proportions arrived. Orders were received directing all battalions to pack and be prepared to depart for the coast on New Year's Day. Everyone in the regiment packed in somewhat reckless haste for fear that not being ready might delay their movement, and on the morning of 1 January 1919 the regiment marched to Lavelin-devant-Bruyères to entrain for Le Mans and the first leg of the trip home.[45] The men's enthusiasm was only slightly dampened by the rain that fell during the entire journey and having to ride in the tiny, crowded French military boxcars.

The 372d Infantry arrived in Le Mans on 3 January and marched through deep mud and slush to the forwarding camp, where the officers and men endured eight further miserable days living in tents and fighting the cool, wet weather. Another delousing was performed on the regiment on 10 January, and the next day everyone entrained for the port of Brest.[46]

The 370th Infantry

The 370th Infantry captured its final objective of the war, the village of Le Gue d'Hossus, Belgium, just before 11:00 AM on 11 November and then stood down from action.[47] On 12 November the 3d Battalion, which was supporting a French regiment in contact with the retreating Germans at the time of the armistice, was ordered to move back to Auge with the rest of the regiment. After several days of rest and reorganizing, the entire regiment was ordered to Verneuil-sur-Serre and Froidmont-Cohartille.[48] At these stations the 370th Infantry found that, unlike its sister regiments of the 93d Infantry Division, it could not escape the ever-present urge of the French 59th Infantry Division commander to put the men to work as laborers repairing roads and other communications facilities. The men labored at these menial and miserable tasks until the regiment passed from French command, then entrained for Soissons on 12 December.[49]

At Soissons, the regiment marked time while performing duties more in keeping with a combat regiment by drilling, training, and engaging in sports, as did the other regiments of the 93d Division. And also like the other regiments of the 93d Division, the officers and men waited anxiously for orders sending them to the coast and aboard ships bound for the United States of America.[50]

CHAPTER 22

Homeward Bound

And so it will be in this city's memory, archives and in the folk lore or the descendants of the men who made up its straight, smartly stepping ranks . . . [t]hat [the fact that] this 369th Regiment, with the exception of its eighty-nine white officers, was composed entirely of negroes, made no difference in the shouts and flag waving and handshakes that were bestowed upon it.

New York World, 18 February 1919

The four regiments of the 93d Division made their separate ways home early in 1919.

The 369th Infantry

On 31 December 1918 and 1–2 January 1919, the battalions of the 369th Infantry Regiment boarded trains in the Vosges Front area and started across France for the U.S. debarkation processing camp at Le Mans. There the regiment was deloused and reequipped, and shipping manifests were made up for the men and their supplies. The time spent at Le Mans was for the most part boring, but the men remained in high spirits in anticipation of going home.[1]

The regiment entrained at Le Mans on 10 January for the trip to the port city of Brest, to arrive on the evening of the next day. Within minutes of their arrival the men of the regiment, now returned to control of the U.S. Army, found themselves embroiled in a racially motivated incident.[2] As a section of the train pulled into the station, a private of the regiment stepped down from a coach and went to find the nearest latrine. When he attempted to return to his coach, he realized that he was lost and approached two military policemen to ask directions. One of the military policemen found fault with the manner in which the private addressed him and struck a hard blow to the private's head with a nightstick. Several members of the regiment standing in the area saw the incident and moved in on the military policemen, intending to work them over. Captain MacClinton, one of the regiment's officers, pushed through the crowd, held back the angry men, and ordered them to disperse.[3]

A captain of military police then came on the scene and made insolent remarks to MacClinton, who was quick to take umbrage. MacClinton was about to do to the MP captain what he had just stopped his men from doing to the policemen when Major Little arrived, intervened, and demanded to know what was going on. The captain of military police turned his insolence on Little and got an immediate dressing down for it. The MP captain then, in a most respectful manner, let it slip to Little that he had been warned by his superiors about the arrival of a black regiment. The statement as recounted by Little was that "our '. . .' were feeling their oats a bit and that instructions had been given to 'take it out of them quickly, just as soon as they arrived, so as not to have any trouble later on.'"[4]

This was the beginning of a campaign of systematic harassment that continued for the entire three weeks that the regiment remained in the Pontanezen Barracks at Brest. The officers and men were able to weather it without any major incidents, even though the military police saved their worst for the black soldiers.[5] Military police are not the best-liked and most-respected branch of the U.S. Army, as a soldier of the 369th Infantry, whose identity is unknown, noted in his journal:

> Deloused and detailed night and day and it seems as if we at last have struck something worse than the Germans and many were taken sick as a result of the conditions under which we were compelled to live and work. The word "attention" comes into its own at this camp, being very strictly enforced by the front-dodging M.P.'s, the pampered pets of the war—Feb. 1/9.[6]

At long last the officers and men of the regiment were ordered to board their ships for home. The battalions formed up and marched from the barracks to the docks under orders of total silence to avoid further incidents with military police. Headquarters, Headquarters Company, and the 1st Battalion boarded the SS *Stockholm* on 31 January; the 2d Battalion boarded the SS *Regina,* and the 3d Battalion, the SS *Le France* on 1 February.[7]

The trip across the Atlantic Ocean was smooth and uneventful. The 3d Battalion reached New York on 9 February, and the rest of the regiment arrived on 12 February. Mayor James J. Hylan of New York City and his Committee of Citizens met the ships at the docks with a hearty welcome that helped to erase the bad memories of the days at Pontanezen Barracks.[8] After the rousing welcome and celebration with families and friends at the docks, the battalions boarded nearby trains bound for Camp Upton at Yaphank, New York, to begin demobilization.[9]

It may be recalled that the 369th Infantry Regiment had been refused their request to march in the parade of the regiments of the 42d (Rainbow) Division with the rejoinder that "black was not one of the colors of the rainbow." At that time, Colonel Hayward promised the men that the regiment *would* march through New York City on its return from France, and would march alone.[10] Hayward was true to his word. On 17 February 1919 the entire regiment assembled in full dress with Brodie steel helmets, Springfield rifles, and greatcoats and marched in platoon column through 35th Street to Madison Avenue, then down Madison Avenue to 23d Street to form up for the parade. There the regiment shifted into the standard French parade formation of a company phalanx, a solid mass of men in a thirty-five-foot square. In this formation sergeants march two paces in front of platoons, lieutenants march on a line in front of the sergeants, and the company commander marches five paces in front of the line of lieutenants.[11]

At 11:00 AM sharp the regiment stepped off, with Hayward and the regimental staff in front of the national and regimental colors, and Lieutenant Europe and his now famous military marching band just behind the colors. The formation proceeded west through 23d Street to 5th Avenue, turned north to march under the Victory Arch at 25th Street, and on to 110th Street. There they turned west to Lenox Avenue and marched through Harlem amid cheers and shouts of greetings from family, friends, neighbors, and proud citizens of the black community.[12] The 15th New York Infantry Regiment had returned home.[13]

The 371st Infantry

On 10 January 1919 the 371st Infantry left Le Mans for Brest on American-made trains with roomy and comfortable cars. They arrived to find that a gigantic camp had sprung up around the location of the old Pontanezen Barracks. The battalions went into quarters in tents at first, and then later, as other units departed, moved into warmer and drier wooden barracks.[14]

There was an air of frantic urgency in the camp beyond what might be expected of men excited about returning home. To their surprise and consternation, instead of enjoying a well-earned rest, the officers and men of the regiment, along with all of the other units encamped at Pontanezen Barracks, found themselves working day after day and night after night. Through mud, rain, and cold the men moved equipment and supplies on the dock, built duckboards for the camp, and cleaned up dumps full of salvaged equipment.[15]

The men later learned that reports of abysmal living conditions at Brest had made their way back to the United States, and a special congressional committee was being sent to investigate the camp. General Pershing had assigned the well-known and respected Gen. Smedley Butler, U.S. Marine Corps, to get the camp and docks cleaned up, and if getting the job done meant delaying up to fifty thousand men from shipping home, so be it. The regiment never learned whether the congressional committee found the camp in good order.[16]

On 26 January the 371st Infantry marched into Brest, where Vice Admiral Moreau of the French Navy decorated the unit colors with the Croix de Guerre and all officer and enlisted candidates with the French Legion of Honor, the Medaille Militaire, and the Croix de Guerre with Bronze Palm. Before awarding the unit citations, Vice Admiral Moreau read the following orders to the regiment from General Headquarters, French Armies of the East (translated from the French):

> The 371st R.I.U.S. . . . has shown, during its first engagement the very best qualities of bravery and audacity which are characteristic of shock troops. Under command of Colonel Miles, it launched itself with a superb spirit and admirable disregard of danger at the assault of a position stubbornly defended by the enemy. It took it by terrific fighting under an exceptionally violent machine-gun fire. It then continued its progression in spite of the fire of enemy artillery and its cruel losses, taking numerous prisoners, securing cannon, machine guns and important material.
>
> Pétain, Marshal of France[17]

On 1 February the 371st Infantry marched to the docks in denim work uniforms, joined the 372d Infantry, and to the music of the two regimental bands coaled up the gigantic transport SS *Leviathan*. The job was done in record time after a rumor raced through the ranks that once the coaling was completed, the regiments would board and sail for home.[18] And indeed, on 3 February both regiments marched back to the docks, in step with martial music played by their bands, and boarded the *Leviathan,* which proved its name by carrying 11,795 souls bound for home.[19]

The vessel traveled by the southern route and arrived in Hoboken, New Jersey, on 11 February. The next morning, lighters carried the men to docks up the North River to entrain for Camp Upton, New York, where, on 17 February, the 371st Infantry was broken up and the officers and men sent on to different camps and stations in South Carolina to be discharged.[20] On 28 February Colonel Miles published General Order 3, his farewell to the regiment. The last paragraph read:

> The regimental commander in taking leave of you wishes to thank you for the uniform loyalty and faithfulness of your service and for the hero-

ism and disregard of personal loss and suffering under the supreme test of battle. It will always remain a source of greatest pride to the regimental commander that he organized and commanded you.

P. L. Miles, Colonel, 371st Infantry, Commanding[21]

After that the 371st Infantry simply faded into history. There was no fanfare of bands playing and crowds cheering, as the other regiments of the 93d Division enjoyed on their arrival home. The 371st was a National Army regiment composed almost entirely of draftees, reserve officers, and National Guard officers, and it was completely disbanded. The other regiments of the division, being National Guard in origin, returned to their home states and cities, where most continued as military organizations within their communities.[22]

The 372d Infantry

On 11 January 1919 the officers and men of the 372d Infantry marched from their billets at Le Mans and boarded comfortable American-made trains for the trip to the coast. They detrained the next day at Brest, marched the long road up to the Pontanezen Barracks, and settled into tents to await orders to board a ship for home. Like the 371st Infantry, the 372d found itself in a sea of mud and slush and committed to hard labor cleaning up the camp for the impending visit of the congressional committee.[23] Pershing made a personal inspection and declared the camp unsatisfactory and unsanitary, and the cleaning and scrubbing started all over again.[24]

Finally, after eleven days, the regiment moved into wooden barracks that contained cots, making life a bit easier. Unfortunately, many of the quarters were infested with lice, and in the middle of everything else the whole regiment had to go through delousing again.[25]

On 24 January the regiment paraded at the Cours Dajot, overlooking the Port of Commerce at Brest, where thousands of civilians, soldiers, and sailors gathered to observe the award of a unit citation.[26] As the regimental band played "Keep the Home Fires Burning" and several patriotic selections, Vice Admiral Moreau pinned the Croix de Guerre with Palm on the regimental colors. Captain Walsh, the regimental adjutant, was also decorated.[27]

Moreau then addressed the officers and men of the regiment, praising their gallantry:

The regiment . . . gave proof during its first engagement of the finest qualities of bravery and daring, which are the virtues of assaulting troops. Under the orders of Colonel Tupes the troops dashed, with superb gallantry and admirable scorn of danger, to the assault of a position continually defended by the enemy, taking it by storm, under an exceptionally violent machine-gun fire.[28]

After the award ceremony the regiment went back to Brest and continued the cleaning and construction work in the camp until 31 January, when orders were received to assist the 371st Infantry in coaling the troop ship *Leviathan* and then to make preparations to board the ship for home. On 3 February, in company with the 371st Infantry, the officers and men went on board the giant ship and turned their eyes toward home.[29]

When the ship docked at Hoboken, the 372d Infantry went to docks near train facilities and then on to Camp Upton.[30] On 17 February the 372d Infantry was demobilized and disbanded, and the various National Guard companies and battalions, having reverted back to the control of their states, boarded trains and returned to their homes and communities to the applause and cheers of their families, friends, and admirers.[31]

In 1920 a monument paid for with funds donated by regimental members was erected in memory of the officers and men of the 372d Infantry killed while engaged in action from 26 September to 7 October 1918. Gen. Mariano Goybet and Col. T. C. Quillet of the French 157th Division were appointed trustees to arrange for the monument's construction and placement.[32] The monument, which sits beside the main road running south out of Monthois toward Sechault, France, is a tall obelisk standing on a square platform with replicas of artillery rounds at each corner. Below the tip of the obelisk, in relief, are the words: "157th Division." At the lower end of the shaft is a replica of a collar disk with the national symbol as worn by enlisted men of the U.S. Army; in the center of the shaft, just below a palm frond, are inscribed the words: "In Memory of the Members of the 372nd U.S. Infantry, Killed in Action September 26, 1918, to October 7, 1918."[33] Early photographs of the monument show a chain running from the tips of the artillery rounds to encircle the obelisk as an apparent safeguard, but in recent photographs the chains are not present. At some point the chains were removed, perhaps as scrap metal for use in World War II.[34]

The 370th Infantry

The 370th Infantry, the only regiment that did not serve alongside its sister regiments of the 93d Division, was relieved of duty with the French Army on 13 December and returned to operational control of the U.S. Army. On 23 December 1918 the regiment left its cantonment area at Soissons and moved to the U.S. military base at Le Mans. Just prior to the regiment's departure, Captain Patton was transferred from command of the 2d Battalion to his previous duties as regimental adjutant and Major Stokes was reinstated as commander of the battalion.[35]

On their arrival at Le Mans the men went through the usual inspections, delousing, and other functions performed in preparation for movement to a debarkation port, and on 8 January the 370th Infantry entrained for Brest and the Pontanezen Barracks. There, like the members of the other regiments of the 93d Division, the men found themselves cleaning up a camp buried in mud to bring it up to standards for the inspection by the congressional committee. They also had to endure several more delousing treatments, required because of contact with contaminated equipment and quarters in the camp.[36]

Finally, on 1 February, the 370th began loading onto the troop ship *La France IV,* which left port the next day bound for the United States. The ship arrived in New York on 9 February, and the regiment moved by train to Camp Upton, to begin preparations for demobilization. On 15 February the regiment entrained, and on the morning of 17 February arrived in Chicago, Illinois, where the citizens had prepared a gigantic welcome celebration.[37] The officers and men of the regiment detrained that morning at the station in Chicago and marched to a local coliseum to attend a gala reception. After several hours of being entertained, the regiment paraded through the downtown Loop and then later that afternoon boarded a train bound for Camp Grant, Illinois.[38] Starting on 24 February the regiment went through demobilization, and on 12 March transfer of the regiment from federal to state control was completed. The 370th Infantry, named the "Black Devils" by its division commander, General Vincendon, had returned to its state designation, the 8th Infantry Regiment, Illinois National Guard.[39]

Immediately after the regiment returned home, a movement began within the black population of Chicago to erect a monument to honor the 8th Infantry Regiment, Illinois National Guard, for its service in France as the 370th Infantry. With the help of the *Chicago Defender,* leaders in the black community began a campaign to fund the monument. The South Park Commission, which controlled the southern portion of the boulevard system of Chicago, offered strong objections, claiming a lack of available space. The community did not back down, applied some very effective political tail-twisting, and the project came into being.[40]

The impressive monument, dedicated on 11 November 1928, sits today in the Bronzeville district of Chicago at the center of the intersection of 35th Street and what was then named Grand Boulevard and is now Martin Luther King Jr. Drive. Designed by John A. Nyden of Chicago, the monument is a gray granite shaft with three inset bronze panels portraying a black soldier, a black American woman symbolizing motherhood, and a figure of Columbia holding a tablet engraved with the principal battles in which the regiment fought during its service in France.[41] The panel containing the black soldier was modeled, appropriately, after a member of the regiment, Sgt. Ozzie Levels, and like all of the panels was executed by Leonard Crunelle, the noted French-born sculptor. Crunelle later sculpted a statue, placed atop the monument in 1936, depicting a black soldier in World War I combat uniform wearing a Brodie-style steel helmet and carrying a Springfield rifle in the ready position.[42]

Taps for the 93d Division

As of February 1919 the 93d Division was no more, at least for the present; all of the regiments had either been disbanded or had reverted to state control (see appendix C for specific details).[43] And for a time it seemed that the division would fade altogether from U.S. history. A recapitulation in the official records of the U.S. Army of the forty-three American divisions that served in France reflects the interesting statistics that the 93d Division spent zero days in training in line, zero days in sector, and zero days in battle. The official record also shows zero kilometers advanced against the enemy and zero prisoners captured. Yet, in an interesting bit of contradiction, the record shows that the division lost four men who were captured by the Germans.[44]

It is difficult to imagine how the U.S. Army could have produced such a record, which essentially indicates that the division did not serve at the front. At the time the official record was compiled, the regiments of the 93d Division had one Medal of Honor recipient and one nominee whose recommendation had been lost somewhere. The division also had dozens of Distinguished Service Cross recipients, not to mention numerous French awards for gallantry in combat (see appendix B). In addition, army records indicate that the division suffered a casualty rate of 29.7 percent of its strength killed or wounded in action (see appendix A).[45]

An excuse may be forwarded that the division ceased to exist when its four regiments were sent to serve with the French Army. Yet, records that list the actions of divisions according to combat service by region in France along with notations as to the regiment serving in that region, the sector, the army and corps to which it was attached, and the time period during which it served through 11 November 1918 do list the 93d Division. Also, *93d Division, Summary of Operations in the World War*, which outlines the chronological service of the division in France, clearly shows that the U.S. Army considered the division to exist during its service with the French Army.[46]

Charles H. Williams, in his book *Negro Soldiers in World War I: The Human Side*, wrote a fitting commentary on the failure of the U.S. Army and official army historians to recognize the achievements of the officers and men of the 93d Division. In a sense, he wrote the division's epitaph:

> When, however, in Paris, on July 14, 1919—on Bastille Day, the day of freedom—the Allied generals and their armies participated in the greatest military demonstration in the history of the world, the American Negro was not there. Other nations had all the races that fought under their flags in line. Belgium had her black colonial troops; England had Indians and Africans with her own sons and her soldiers from the colonies; and France had her Senegalese, Moroccans, Algerians, Soudanese, and Madagascans: every race that came to her defence was in her victorious army on that memorable day. Only America left her Negro troops behind. The last soldiers in the Victory Parade passed down the Champs Elysées, and still the hero of the 369th or the 371st had not appeared. He alone in the day of glory was the Disowned, the Disinherited.[47]

Ironically, the French foreign legion, the outcast formation of the French Army that was forbidden to enter Metropolitan France but was temporarily forgiven its restriction so that it could come and fight on the Western Front, was allowed to march in Paris on that day. In contrast, the U.S. Army invited not one representative of the 93d Division to march with its formations in the parade. For all that was accomplished in battle by the officers and men of the four regiments of the 93d Division, they were to the U.S. Army then—and to the vast majority of the American people in the years since World War I—lost to history, the unknown souls of the Légion Étrangere Americaine, the American Foreign Legion![48]

Postscript

The U.S. government erected several monuments in France in 1937 to commemorate the battles fought by French and American troops in World War I. In the Champagne region, five kilometers north of the village of Sommepy and on the crest of Mont Blanc, stands one of the monuments. It is in the shape of a tall, square fortress tower and stands in the midst of German trenches and dugouts captured by the Marine Brigade and the Infantry Brigade of the 2d Division on 3 October 1918. On each of the exterior sides is inscribed the name of an American division that fought in the area, its insignia, the dates it served in the region, and four places where it suffered hard fighting. On one face is carved a French Adrian helmet on a rounded surface of stone in the fashion of the 93d Division shoulder patch; below is the inscription:

93d DIVISION

SEPT. 26–OCT. 6, 1918

RIPONT

SECHAULT

ARDÉUIL

TRIÈRES FARM[49]

A stone panel inside the tower is inscribed with the actions of the various units that fought in the area. The last paragraph states: "Three infantry regiments of the 93d American Division, serving with the 157th and 161st French Divisions, engaged in intermittent fighting during September and October taking part in the capture of Ripont, Sechault, and Trières Farm."[50]

Casualty and
Strength Data

Casualty Figures

Regiment	Killed in Action	Wounded in Action	Died of Wounds	Total
369th	135	679	37	851
370th	90	560	15	665
371st	108	896	31	1,035
372d	84	509	23	616
TOTAL	417	2,644	106	3,167

SOURCE: *93d Division: Summary of Operations in the World War.*

Strength of the 93d Division through the Final Offensive Operations of 1918

Regiment	31 August	30 September	31 October	30 November	Average
369th	2,781	2,328	2,529	2,528	2,541
370th	3,179	2,951	2,762	2,906	2,949
371st	2,819	2,246	2,230	2,652	2,487
372d	2,798	2,826	2,486	2,659	2,692
TOTAL AVERAGE STRENGTH					10,669

The total average division strength for the 93d Division for the above period is 10,669 officers and men, with 3,167 casualties, giving a 29.7 percent casualty rate.

Monument in France to Colored American Infantry Regiments Attached to the French Army (U.S. Congress, House, 68th Congress, 2d session, Report no. 1419, 9 February 1925, p. 1) quotes the following totals for the 93d Division, although it gives no source for them:

Battle Strength 10,000
Killed 457
Wounded 3,468
Total percentage of casualties quoted in the report: 40 percent.

Of the forty-three U.S. Army divisions that were sent to France, the 93d Division ranked twenty-third in officers and men killed and wounded based on the 29 percent casualty rate. There is no way to make accurate and justifiable comparisons with the other divisions that fought in France because of the 93d Division's provisional status, which would mean comparing a strength of about 10,000 men with the normal U.S. division strength of 28,105 men. Some divisions suffered much higher casualty rates, such as the 1st Division, with 79 percent. The 1st Division was on the line for 220 days, however, whereas the 93d Division was on the line for much less time.

Awards and Decorations

Abbreviations Used in Table

C de G	Croix de Guerre in all classes (FR)
DSC	Distinguished Service Cross (USA)
DSM	Distinguished Service Medal (USA)
It M C	Italian Military Cross
LH	Legion of Honor (FR)
MH	Congressional Medal of Honor (USA)
MM	Medaille Militaire (FR)

Awards and Decorations

Regiment	MH	DSC	DSM	C de G	MM	LH	It M C
369th	1	11	1	153	1	—	1
370th	—	23	1	71	—	—	—
371st	1	26	1	151	2	3	—
372d	—	15	—	152	1	—	—
TOTAL	2	75	3	527	3	4	1

In addition to the above awards to individuals, the 369th, Company C of the 370th, the 371st, and the 372d Infantry Regiments were awarded Croix de Guerre unit citations in various grades (*American Armies and Battlefields in Europe*). Not included in the individual awards are Purple Hearts and Certificates of the Silver Star, which were awarded later. The compilation of decorations presented by the U.S. Army and foreign armies comes from various sources and may not be exact, as different sources give different figures. The official record for U.S. awards, *American Decorations: A List of Awards of the Congressional Medal of Honor, the Distinguished Service Cross and the Distinguished Service Medal, 1862–1926,* was published by the Department of the Army in 1927, and later awards, such as to Cpl. Freddie Stowers, have been made. French awards are listed in several sources included in the Bibliography and are not to be considered complete or exact. The above figures are believed, however, to be representative of the number of U.S. and French decorations awarded to the officers and men of the 93d Division as a whole.

Officers and Men Assigned or Attached to the 93d Division Who Received American Decorations

Congressional Medal of Honor

Robb, George S., Lieutenant, Platoon Leader, 369th Infantry
Stowers, Freddie, Corporal, Squad Leader, 371st Infantry (Post.)

American Recipients of the Distinguished Service Cross

Barnes, Roberts, Sergeant, Company L, 370th Infantry
Bass, Urbane F., Lieutenant, Medical Corps, 372d Infantry (Post.)
Boston, Willie, Private, Machine Gun Company, 371st Infantry
Bryson, Samuel R., Lieutenant, Platoon Leader, 371st Infantry
Burrell, Reuben, Private, Machine Gun Company, 371st Infantry
Butler, Charles, Private, Machine Gun Company, 371st Infantry
Butler, William, Sergeant, Company L, 369th Infantry
Cooper, Thomas, Sergeant, Company K, 371st Infantry
Cope, Tobe C., Major, Battalion Commander, 371st Infantry (Post.)
Crawford, Clifford, Private, Headquarters Company, 372d Infantry
Crawford, William B., Captain, Company Commander, 370th Infantry
Cuff, Fred E., Private, Machine Gun Company, 370th Infantry (Post.)
Davis, Leroy, Private, Company L, 370th Infantry
Diggs, Junius, Private, Company G, 371st Infantry
Dovell, Chauncey E., Lieutenant, Medical Corps, 371st Infantry
Earl, Elmer, Corporal, Company K, 369th Infantry
Finch, Robert L., Lieutenant, Adjutant, 3d Battalion, 372d Infantry
Fossie, Lester, Supply Sergeant, Company M, 370th Infantry
Fuquay, James, Private, Company H, 370th Infantry
Gibson, Ralph, Sergeant, Company H, 370th Infantry
Gilmer, Robert A., Lieutenant, Platoon Leader, 371st Infantry (Post.)
Gross, George, Private, Company D, 372d Infantry
Hames, William W., Lieutenant, 37-mm Gun Section, 372d Infantry
Hammond, LeRoy H., Captain, Company Commander, 371st Infantry
Henry, Norman, Sergeant, Machine Gun Company, 370th Infantry
Holmes, Burton, Private, Company C, 371st Infantry (Post.)
Hurdle, Willie G., Private, Machine Gun Company, 370th Infantry
Irby, Spriley E., Private, Company H, 370th Infantry Regiment
Jackson, Rufus B., Lieutenant, Stokes Mortar Section, 370th Infantry
Jenkins, Matthew, Sergeant, Company F, 370th Infantry
Johnson, Arthur, Private, Headquarters Company, 370th Infantry
Johnson, Samuel M., Major, Battalion Commander, 372d Infantry
Jones, Samuel H., Private, Company L, 372d Infantry
Jones, Sandy E., Corporal, Company C, 371st Infantry
Keenan, Willis H., Lieutenant, Medical Corps, 369th Infantry

Landon, Harold, Lieutenant, Assistant Liaison Officer, 369th Infantry

Lesesne, Francis K., Captain, Company Commander, 371st Infantry

McCall, Andy, Private, Machine Gun Company, 370th Infantry (Post.)

McClelland, Lee R., Sergeant, Medical Detachment, 371st Infantry

McCowin, Elmer, Private, Company K, 369th Infantry

McLoughlin, Comerford, Lieutenant, Company Commander, 369th Infantry

Merrimon, Clifton, Corporal, Company L, 372d Infantry

Monroe, Charles T., Private, Headquarters Company, 370th Infantry

Moses, Ellison, Private, Company G, 371st Infantry

Parker, Charles W., Lieutenant, Platoon Leader, 371st Infantry

Pate, Joseph B., Major, Battalion Commander, 371st Infantry

Payne, Ira M., Sergeant, Company A, 372d Infantry

Pearson, Harry L., Private, Machine Gun Company, 370th Infantry

Pickering, Woodell A., Lieutenant Colonel, 369th Infantry

Powell, Tom, Private, Company H, 370th Infantry (Post.)

Ransom, John O., Lieutenant, Platoon Leader, 371st Infantry (Post.)

Richey, William R. Jr., Captain, Company Commander, 371st Infantry

Robison, Edward M., Captain, 372d Infantry

Sanford, William, Private, Medical Detachment, 369th Infantry

Sessions, Harry C., Lieutenant, 372d Infantry

Shepherd, Marion F., Captain, Company Commander, 371st Infantry

Shethar, Samuel, Captain, Operations Officer, 369th Infantry

Spencer, Edward L., Lieutenant, Platoon Leader, 371st Infantry

Spencer, Lorillard, Major, Battalion Commander, 369th Infantry

Stewart, Mallory, Private, Headquarters Company, 371st Infantry

Stoney, Bruce, Private, Medical Detachment, 371st Infantry

Sumner, Charles S., Captain, Company Commander, 372d Infantry

Teer, Hubert O., Lieutenant, Platoon Leader, 371st Infantry

Thompson, Emmett, Corporal, Company L, 370th Infantry

Valley, Isaac, Corporal, Company M, 370th Infantry

Van Allen, Clarence R., Private, Company L, 372d Infantry

Vinton, Thomas W., Lieutenant, Platoon Leader, 371st Infantry

Walsh, Preston F., Lieutenant, Intelligence Officer, 372d Infantry

Walton, Alonzo, Private, Machine Gun Company, 370th Infantry

Walton, Edward A., Lieutenant, Adjutant, 3d Battalion, 369th Infantry

Warfield, William J., Lieutenant, Platoon Leader, 370th Infantry

Webster, Tillman, Private, Machine Gun Company, 371st Infantry

White, Nathaniel C., Private First Class, Messenger, Company F, 370th Infantry
(Post.)

Williamson, Alfred, Private, Medical Detachment, 370th Infantry

Wilson, Harvey W., Lieutenant, Platoon Leader, 372nd Infantry

French Recipients of the Distinguished Service Cross Associated with the 93d Division

Drouhin, Robert G., Second Lieutenant of Infantry, French Army, attached to 372d Infantry

Lebre, Anton, Captain, 344th Regiment of Infantry, French Army, attached to 371st Infantry

Maxwell, Roger, First Lieutenant of Infantry, French Army, attached to 369th Infantry (Post.)

Simonet, André, Marechal des Logis, 19th Train of Military Transports, French Army, attached to 371st Infantry

Tessier, Fernand, First Lieutenant, 14th Regiment of Chasseurs, French Army, attached to 369th Infantry

Weichert, Georges, Second Lieutenant of Infantry, French Army, Attached to 372d Infantry

American Recipients of the Distinguished Service Medal

Hayward, William, Colonel, Regimental Commander, 369th Infantry

Miles, Perry L., Colonel, Regimental Commander, 371st Infantry

Roberts, Thomas A., Colonel, Regimental Commander, 370th Infantry

French Recipients of the Distinguished Service Medal

Gouraud, Henri J. E., Major General, Commanding the French Fourth Army

Goybet, Mariano F. J., Brigadier General, Commanding the French 157th Infantry Division

Note: (Post.) indicates posthumous award.

Source: American Decorations: A List of Awards of the Congressional Medal of Honor, the Distinguished Service Cross and the Distinguished Service Medal, 1862–1926.

Organization and Surviving Units

Organization and Commanders of the 93d Infantry Division

93d Infantry Division

Brig. Gen. Roy Hoffman
Maj. Mark W. Tobin, Chief of Staff

185th Infantry Brigade

Brig. Gen. Albert H. Blanding

369th Infantry Regiment

Col. William Hayward

370th Infantry Regiment

Col. Franklin R. Dennison
Col. Thomas A. Roberts

186th Infantry Brigade

Brig. Gen. George H. Harries
Col. Perry L. Miles (ad interim)

371st Infantry Regiment

Col. Perry L. Miles

372d Infantry Regiment

Col. Glendie B. Young
Col. Hershel Tupes

Note: The list of divisions that served in France and their commanders, as shown on pages 499 and 500 of *American Armies and Battlefields in Europe,* does not include the 93d Division and its commander.

Surviving Units of the 93d Division

The 369th Infantry Regiment returned to its National Guard status as the 15th New York Infantry Regiment and then went through various changes and reorganizations to become the 369th Support Battalion, New York National Guard.

The 370th Infantry Regiment returned to its status as the 8th Illinois Infantry Regiment, National Guard, and is now the 1st Battalion, 178th Infantry Regiment, Illinois National Guard.

The 371st Infantry Regiment was disbanded at demobilization.

The 372d Infantry Regiment disbanded into its original National Guard units. Headquarters and Headquarters Company, the machine-gun company, and other elements of the regiment formed to complete its structure beyond the National Guard units assigned to it were disbanded at demobilization. All of the National Guard units were returned to state control; their present status is shown below.

1. The 1st Battalion, D.C. National Guard, became the 372d Military Police Battalion, National Guard, District of Columbia.

2. The 9th Battalion, Ohio National Guard, after a long series of changes and reorganizations, became the 372d Maintenance Company, Ohio National Guard.

3. The 1st Separate Company, Maryland National Guard, went though many changes to become the 229th Support Battalion, 29th Infantry Division, Maryland National Guard.

4. The 1st Separate Company, Massachusetts National Guard, became Headquarters and Headquarters Company, 101st Engineer Battalion, Massachusetts National Guard.

5. The 1st Separate Company, Tennessee National Guard, was disbanded and never reconstituted.

6. The 1st Separate Company, Connecticut National Guard, was apparently disbanded and never reconstituted. No records were found by the historian of the Connecticut National Guard as to the disposition of the company on its return to state control.

Information courtesy of Chaplain (Lt. Col.) William Sean Lee, historian, Maryland National Guard; Capt. Randel L. Rogers, Ohio National Guard; Col. John D. Raphael, (ret.), historian, Connecticut National Guard; Maj. Les A. Melnyk, historian, National Guard Bureau, Washington, D.C.; Col. Leonid Kondratiuk, director, Military Museum and Archives, Massachusetts National Guard; and Maj. James B. McCabe, staff historian, Illinois National Guard.

Notes

Introduction: A Foreign Legion Is Born

1. Heywood, *Negro Combat Troops*, 235–36; American Battle Monuments Commission, *American Armies and Battlefields in Europe*, 526; "Cable History" [cables between General Pershing in France and Maj. Gen. John Biddle in Washington, D.C.], National Archives, Record Group 120 [hereinafter NA, RG 120], boxes 1–2, 3343–44; MacGregor and Nalty, *Blacks in the U.S. Armed Forces*, 135–44.

2. Department of the Army, *United States Army in the World War*, vol. 2; Pershing, *My Experiences in the World War*, 1:254–55, 271–73, 2:46, 98–99; Weigley, *History of the United States Army*, 377–78; Stallings, *The Doughboys*, 311; Toland, *No Man's Land*, 17, 23–26.

3 Geraghty, *March or Die*, 31–43.

4. Ibid.

5. Mason and Furr, *The American Negro with the Red Hand of France*, 16; Jamieson et al., *Complete History of the Colored Soldiers*, 11; Scott, *Scott's Official History*, 214, 228, 276–77; Sweeney, *History of the American Negro in the Great World War*, 149, 155; Isaac Fisher, "Black Devils of Illinois," in *Pullman Porter's Review*.

6. Ibid.

Chapter 1. The 93d Division's First Regiment

Epigraph. House of Representatives, *Monument in France to Colored American Infantry Regiments Attached to the French Army*, Report 1419, 68th Cong., 2d sess., 9 February 1925.

1. Scott, *Scott's Official History*, 197; Yockelson, "The United States Armed Forces and the Mexican Punitive Expedition."

2. Little, *From Harlem to the Rhine*, 111–12.

3. Ibid.

4. *National Cyclopedia*, 559–60; Little, *From Harlem to the Rhine*, ix–x.

5. Little, *From Harlem to the Rhine*, 111–12.

6. Ibid.

7. Ibid., 113, 116, 372, 373; Marshall, *The Providential Armistice*, 3; Sweeney, *History of the American Negro in the Great World War*, 135.

8. Marshall, *The Providential Armistice*, 3–4; Jamieson et al., *Complete History of the Colored Soldiers*, 38–39.

9. Marshall, *The Providential Armistice*, 12.

10. Little, *From Harlem to the Rhine*, 115–16.

11. Ibid.

12. Ibid.

13. Ibid., 116; Stallings, *The Doughboys*, 312.

14. Ibid.

15. Ibid.

16. Ibid.

17. Little, *From Harlem to the Rhine*, 119–22; Stallings, *The Doughboys*, 312.

18. Ibid.

19. Ibid.

20. Little, *From Harlem to the Rhine*, 122–23.

21. Ibid.

22. Ibid.

23. Sweeney, *History of the American Negro in the Great World War*, 135; Scott, *Scott's Official History*, 197.

24. Ibid.

25. Little, *From Harlem to the Rhine*, 9–10.

26. Ibid.

27. Scott, *Scott's Official History*, 197.

28. Little, *From Harlem to the Rhine*, 22.

29. Ibid.

30. Ibid., 23, 30–41.

31. Ibid.

32. Little, *From Harlem to the Rhine*, 33; Moss, *Company Training in the Attack, and the Defense, Including the Field Orders of Enlisted Men*, 124.

33. Little, *From Harlem to the Rhine*, 42; Williams, *Negro Soldiers*, 195–196; Scott, *Scott's Official History*, 198.

34. Ibid.

35. Little, *From Harlem to the Rhine*, 42–43, 45.

36. Ibid., 47, 124.

37. Ibid.

38. Ibid.

39. Ibid.

40. Ibid.

41. Ibid.

42. Ibid., 47, 50, 58, 71; Scott, *Scott's Official History*, 199; Letter to the Adjutant General from William Hayward, NA, RG 120, boxes 1–2, 3343–44, 4.

43. Ibid.

44. Ibid.

Chapter 2. The 15th's Trials at Spartanburg

Epigraph. Sweeney, *History of the American Negro in the Great World War*, 148.

1. Little, *From Harlem to the Rhine*, 49.
2. Ibid.
3. Ibid., 49; U.S. Army War College, *Colored Soldiers in the U.S. Army*, 3:1–3; Farwell, *Over There*, 154–55; Lanning, *The African-American Soldier*, 121–25; Muller, *The 24th Infantry*, no page numbers given, refer to section titled "1917."
4. Ibid.
5. Ibid.
6. Little, *From Harlem to the Rhine*, 48.
7. Ibid., 52–53.
8. Ibid.
9. Ibid.
10. Ibid.
11. Ibid., 58.
12. Ibid., 54–55.
13. Ibid.
14. Ibid.
15. Ibid., 57–58.
16. Ibid.
17. Ibid., 59–62.
18. Ibid.
19. Ibid.
20. Ibid.
21. Ibid.
22. Ibid.
23. Ibid.
24. Ibid., 56–57.
25. Ibid.
26. Ibid.
27. Ibid., 62–64.
28. Ibid., 64–66; Scott, *Scott's Official History*, 81; *Army Almanac*, 529.
29. Ibid.
30. Ibid.
31. Little, *From Harlem to the Rhine*, 67–69; Scott, *Scott's Official History*, 79–80.
32. Little, *From Harlem to the Rhine*, 70–75.
33. Ibid.
34. Ibid.
35. Ibid.
36. Ibid.
37. Ibid., 72, 76; Letter to the Adjutant General from William Hayward, NA, RG 120, boxes 1–2, 3343–44, 3; Scott, *Scott's Official History*, 198; Williams, *Negro Soldiers*, 197; Sweeney, *History of the American Negro in the Great World War*, 136.
38. Ibid.

Chapter 3. The "Eighth Illinois" Mobilizes

Epigraph. Photo caption in *Pullman Porter's Review.*

1. Williams, *Negro Soldiers,* 208–11; Sweeney, *History of the American Negro in the Great World War,* 153–54; Department of the Army, *Lineage and Honors,"* and Duncan, "5th Indorsement," 1–2, both furnished by Maj. James B. McCabe; Jamieson et al., *Complete History of the Colored Soldiers,* 89–93; Illinois National Guard website, accessed 12 April 2003.

2. Ibid.

3. Ibid.

4. Ibid.

5. Ibid.

6. Ibid.

7. Ibid.

8. Ibid.

9. Sweeney, *History of the American Negro in the Great World War,* 164; Illinois National Guard website, accessed 12 April 2003; Scott, *Scott's Official History,* 214.

10. "General Franklin A. Denison," *Lincoln University Herald;* "Colonel Denison and the Eighth Regiment, I.N.G.," *Lincoln University Herald;* Moebs, *Black Soldiers— Black Sailors—Black Ink,* 375, 814, 816, 817, 830, 850, 1211, 1238.

11. Sweeney, *History of the American Negro in the Great World War,* 165; Braddan, *Under Fire with the 370th Infantry,* 18; Duncan, "5th Indorsement," 2.

12. Braddan, *Under Fire with the 370th Infantry,* 17–25.

13. Ibid.

14. Scott, *Scott's Official History,* 75–76.

15. Ibid.

16. Scipio, *Last of the Black Regulars,* 46, appendix, 134; Sgt. Oscar Walker, "The Eighth Regiment in France," in *Pullman Porter's Review.*

17. Jamieson et al., *Complete History of the Colored Soldiers,* 100–101. Jamieson quotes an editorial in the *Chicago Tribune.*

18. Barbeau and Henri, *The Unknown Soldier,* 76; Braddan, *Under Fire with the 370th Infantry,* 29.

19. Ibid.

20. Braddan, *Under Fire with the 370th Infantry,* 25–26, 28, 30.

21. Ibid., 28–29; *Army Almanac,* 535.

22. Ibid.

23. Ibid.

24. Ibid.

25. Braddan, *Under Fire with the 370th Infantry,* 31.

26. *Pullman Porter's Review,* photo caption; Duncan, "5th Indorsement," 2.

27. Braddan, *Under Fire with the 370th Infantry,* 43–44; Sweeney, *American Negro in the Great World War,* 166; Williams, *Negro Soldiers,* 211.

28. Braddan, *Under Fire with the 370th Infantry,* 46; Sweeney, *American Negro in the Great World War,* 166; Williams, *Negro Soldiers,* 211.

29. Williams, *Negro Soldiers,* 211.

Chapter 4. The Draftees of the 371st Infantry

Epigraph. Sweeney, *History of the American Negro in the Great World War*, 116.

1. Ibid., 15–16; Weigley, *History of the United States Army*, 357–59; Haythornthwaite, *World War One Source Book*, 308–9; Pershing, *My Experiences in the World War*, 1:10; U.S. War Department, Annual Report, 1918, 1106–8.

2. Ibid.

3. Barbeau and Henri, *The Unknown Soldier*, 34, 36; Weigley, *History of the United States Army*, 372; Scott, *Scott's Official History*, 66–69; U.S. War Department, Annual Report, 1918, 1106–8.

4. Williams, *Negro Soldiers*, 18–19, 23; Sweeney, *History of the American Negro in the Great World War*, 73–74.

5. Barbeau and Henri, *The Unknown Soldier*, 99–100; Williams, *Negro Soldiers*, 152–55.

6. Barbeau and Henri, *The Unknown Soldier*, 33–34; Farwell, *Over There*, 150; American Battle Monuments Commission, *American Armies and Battlefields in Europe*, 515.

7. Heywood, *Negro Combat Troops*, 1; Miles, *Fallen Leaves*, 232–33; Scott, *Scott's Official History*, 231.

8. Heywood, *Negro Combat Troops*, 1; U.S. Military Academy, *Assembly*, 89–90; Officers [371st] Assigned . . . , NA, RG 120, boxes 1–2, 3343–44.

9. Heywood, *Negro Combat Troops*, 1; Miles, *Fallen Leaves*, 233, 282; Scrugham, *Nevada*, 258–60.

10. Miles, *Fallen Leaves*, 233; Kern correspondence on Col. Joseph Benjamin Pate; Officers [371st] Assigned . . . , NA, RG 120, boxes 1–2, 3343–44.

11. Miles, *Fallen Leaves*, 239; Officers [371st] Assigned . . . , NA, RG 120, boxes 1–2, 3343–44.

12. Ibid.; Heywood, *Negro Combat Troops*, 1.

13. Heywood, *Negro Combat Troops*, 2; Miles, *Fallen Leaves*, 234.

14. Miles, *Fallen Leaves*, 234–35.

15. Ibid.

16. Ibid., 233–34, 236.

17. Ibid., 235; Heywood, *Negro Combat Troops*, 2–3.

18. Miles, *Fallen Leaves*, 234; Heywood, *Negro Combat Troops*, 7.

19. Heywood, *Negro Combat Troops*, 3–4.

20. Ibid., 4–5.

21. Ibid., 4.

22. Ibid., 5, 11; Miles, *Fallen Leaves*, 236.

23. Heywood, *Negro Combat Troops*, 6–7; Miles, *Fallen Leaves*, 235.

24. Heywood, *Negro Combat Troops*, 7–8.

25. Ibid., 10.

26. Ibid., 8.

27. Ibid., 11; Miles, *Fallen Leaves*, 236.

28. Heywood, *Negro Combat Troops*, 11–12; Miles, *Fallen Leaves*, 244.

29. Heywood, *Negro Combat Troops*, 12–13; Miles, *Fallen Leaves*, 244.

30. Heywood, *Negro Combat Troops,* 13.

31. Miles, *Fallen Leaves,* 244–45.

32. Ibid., 245; Heywood, *Negro Combat Troops,* 14.

33. Miles, *Fallen Leaves,* 245; Heywood, *Negro Combat Troops,* 22.

34. Miles, *Fallen Leaves,* 250–51.

35. Tucker, *Encyclopedia of the Korean War,* 10.

36. Heywood, *Negro Combat Troops,* 23; Miles, *Fallen Leaves,* 251.

37. Ibid., 23–24.

38. Ibid.

39. Ibid.

Chapter 5. The Composite 372d Infantry

Epigraph. Mason and Furr, *The American Negro with the Red Hand of France,* 26.

1. Sweeney, *History of the American Negro in the Great World War,* 190; Williams, *Negro Soldiers,* 229–30; Scott, *Scott's Official History,* 239; Mason and Furr, *The American Negro with the Red Hand of France,* 18–19, 26; Scipio, *With the Red Hand Division,* 19; Payne, "Brief History 372d," NA, RG 120, boxes 1–2, 3343–44, 1.

2. Mason and Furr, *The American Negro with the Red Hand of France,* 26; Miles, *Fallen Leaves,* 245; Heywood, *Negro Combat Troops,* 19; Heitman, *Historical Register and Dictionary,* 2:272; U.S. War Department, Annual Report, 1918, 1205.

3. Mason and Furr, *The American Negro with the Red Hand of France,* 26; Williams, *Negro Soldiers,* 229; Scott, *Scott's Official History,* 33–24; Payne, "Brief History 372d," NA, RG 120, boxes 1–2, 3343–44, 1.

4. Mason and Furr, *The American Negro with the Red Hand of France,* 19–22, 26.

5. Williams, *Negro Soldiers,* 230; Annual Reports, Washington, D.C., National Guard, 1863–1917; Scott, *Scott's Official History,* 35–39.

6. Annual Reports, Washington, D.C., National Guard, 1863–1917; Williams, *Negro Soldiers,* 230.

7. Ibid.

8. Ibid.

9. Ibid.

10. Williams, *Negro Soldiers,* 230; Annual Reports, Ohio National Guard, 1874–1917; Ohio National Guardsman, "Battalion Organized in 1881," 8.

11. Ibid.

12. Ibid.

13. Williams, *Negro Soldiers,* 231; Annual Reports, Connecticut National Guard, 1863–1917; Connecticut Adjutant General's Office, *General Orders No. 34.*

14. Ibid.

15. Williams, *Negro Soldiers,* 230; Annual Reports, Maryland National Guard, 1879–1917.

16. Williams, *Negro Soldiers,* 231; Annual Reports, Massachusetts National Guard, 1863–1917; *Massachusetts Volunteer Militia . . . 6th Massachusetts Company.*

17. Ibid.

18. Williams, *Negro Soldiers*, 231; Annual Reports, Tennessee National Guard, 1886–1917.
19. Ibid.
20. Williams, *Negro Soldiers*, 230–32; Mason and Furr, *The American Negro with the Red Hand of France*, 27.
21. Mason and Furr, *The American Negro with the Red Hand of France*, 27.
22. Ibid., 28.
23. Ibid.
24. Ibid.
25. Ibid.
26. Ibid., 29.
27. Ibid.
28. Ibid., 29–31.

Chapter 6. The 15th New York Infantry Sails for France

Epigraph. Sweeney, *History of the American Negro in the Great World War*, 131.
1. American Battle Monuments Commission, *American Armies and Battlefields in Europe*, 515–16; Dupuy and Dupuy, *Military Heritage of America*, 358–59.
2. American Battle Monuments Commission, *American Armies and Battlefields in Europe*, 515–16.
3. Dupuy and Dupuy, *Military Heritage of America*, 361–62; Farwell, *Over There*, 71–72; Taylor, *History of World War I*, 155, 221, 225.
4. Ibid.
5. Ibid.
6. Ibid.
7. Ibid.
8. Ibid.
9. Ibid.
10. Ibid.; Gilbert, *Atlas of the First World War*, 83.
11. Farwell, *Over There*, 71–72; Dupuy and Dupuy, *Military Heritage of America*, 361–62.
12. Little, *From Harlem to the Rhine*, 76; Williams, *Negro Soldiers*, 196; Scott, *Scott's Official History*, 200.
13. Little, *From Harlem to the Rhine*, 78–79.
14. Scott, *Scott's Official History*, 198.
15. Little, *From Harlem to the Rhine*, 80; Letter to the Adjutant General from William Hayward, NA, RG 120, boxes 1–2, 3343–44, 3, 4.
16. Little, *From Harlem to the Rhine*, 81.
17. Ibid., 83; Scott, *Scott's Official History*, 198.
18. Little, *From Harlem to the Rhine*, 84; Scott, *Scott's Official History*, 198.
19. Ibid.
20. Little, *From Harlem to the Rhine*, 88–92.
21. Ibid., 92–93; Scott, *Scott's Official History*, 199.

22. Ibid.

23. Scott, *Scott's Official History*, 199.

24. Little, *From Harlem to the Rhine*, 98.

25. Ibid., 99; Scott, *Scott's Official History*, 201; Letter to the Adjutant General from William Hayward, NA, RG 120, boxes 1–2, 3343–44, 5.

26. Scott, *Scott's Official History*, 201; Letter to the Adjutant General from William Hayward, NA, RG 120, boxes 1–2, 3343–44, 5.

27. Cable no. 454, General Pershing to Major General Biddle, "Cable History," NA, RG 120, boxes 1–2, 3343–44; Williams, *Negro Soldiers*, 152–55.

28. Little, *From Harlem to the Rhine*, ix, 3, 13.

29. *National Cyclopedia*, 559–60; Farwell, *Over There*, 37, 39–41, 161.

30. "Cable History," P. 454, P. 548, A. 726, P. 592, A. 800, P. 626, A. 827, and P. 692, NA, RG 120, boxes 1–2, 3343–44; MacGregor and Nalty, *Blacks in the U.S. Armed Forces*, 135–44.

31. Pershing, *My Experiences in the World War*, 2:116–17; Bullard, *Personalities and Reminiscences of the War*, 291–92; Barbeau and Henri, *The Unknown Soldier*, 138.

32. Dupuy and Dupuy, *Military Heritage of America*, 364–65; American Battle Monuments Commission, *American Armies and Battlefields in Europe*, 17; Pershing, *My Experiences in the World War*, 2:99.

33. Letter to the Adjutant General from William Hayward, NA, RG 120, boxes 1–2, 3343–44, 5; Confidential After-Action Report of Col. William Hayward, Commanding 369th Infantry, Le Mans–Sarth, France, 7 January 1919, NA, RG 120, boxes 1–2, 3343–44, 1, paragraph 4, 1.

34. Little, *From Harlem to the Rhine*, 100–101.

35. Pershing, *My Experiences in the World War*, 2:97.

36. Cable no. 592, Pershing to Biddle, "Cable History," NA, RG 120, boxes 1–2, 3343–44; Pershing, *My Experiences in the World War*, 1:291.

37. Dupuy and Dupuy, *Military Heritage of America*, 364; Palmer, *Newton D. Baker*, 2:170–72.

38. Barbeau and Henri, *The Unknown Soldier*, 114–15.

39. Pershing, *My Experiences in the World War*, 1:255.

40. Ibid., 1:291.

41. Ibid., 1:273; Dupuy and Dupuy, *Military Heritage of America*, 359; Heywood, *Negro Combat Troops*, 36.

42. Pershing, *My Experiences in the World War*, 2:97.

43. MacGregor and Nalty, *Blacks in the U.S. Armed Forces*, 252 (letter to General Pershing from Marshal Foch, 26 August 1918).

44. Barbeau and Henri, *The Unknown Soldier*, 113.

45. Scott, *Scott's Official History*, 117–20, 125–29; Barbeau and Henri, *The Unknown Soldier*, 17–19; Haythornthwaite, *World War One Source Book*, 184–85.

46. Ibid.

47. Ibid.

48. Ibid.

49. Scott, *Scott's Official History*, 120–23; Barbeau and Henri, *The Unknown Soldier*, 18.

50. Farwell, *Over There*, 158; Carisella and Ryan, *The Black Swallow of Death;* Toland, *No Man's Land*, photograph and commentary on Eugene Bullard, 240–41.
51. David Carlisle correspondence concerning PFC John Robert Kay.
52. Barbeau and Henri, *The Unknown Soldier*, 19.
53. Little, *From Harlem to the Rhine*, 104–5.
54. Ibid., 145–46.

Chapter 7. The 15th Becomes the 369th Infantry

Epigraph. Little, *From Harlem to the Rhine*, 147.

1. Ibid., 145–46; Letter to the Adjutant General from William Hayward, NA, RG 120, boxes 1–2, 3343–44, 4; American Battle Monuments Commission, *93d Division*, 4.
2. Ibid.
3. Little, *From Harlem to the Rhine*, 146.
4. Ibid., 142, 146.
5. Laffin, *A Western Front Companion*, 143–44; Farwell, *Over There*, 16; Haythornthwaite, *World War One Source Book*, 66–69.
6. Little, *From Harlem to the Rhine*, 142.
7. Ibid., 144, 146; American Battle Monuments Commission, *93d Division*, 4.
8. Little, *From Harlem to the Rhine*, 146; Letter to the Adjutant General from William Hayward, NA, RG 120, boxes 1–2, 3343–44, 5.
9. Little, *From Harlem to the Rhine*, 144.
10. Ibid., 146, 149.
11. Ibid.
12. Ibid., 148; Mirouze, *World War I Infantry in Colour Photographs*, 58–59.
13. Ibid.
14. *Small Arms of the World*, 85–86; Laffin, *Western Front Companion*, 140; Dupuy and Dupuy, *Military Heritage of America*, 360.
15. *Small Arms of the World*, 359, 363–64; Mirouze, *World War I Infantry in Colour Photographs*, 58–59.
16. Ibid.
17. Ibid.
18. Mirouze, *World War I Infantry in Colour Photographs*, 24–25, 26–27, 30–31, 50–51, 58–59; Haythornthwaite, *The World War One Source Book*, 178, 310–11; Moss, *Origin and Significance of Military Customs*, 52, picture of "Montana peak" hat.
19. Ibid.
20. Ibid.
21. Ibid.
22. Mirouze, *World War I Infantry in Colour Photographs*, 24–25, 50–51, 58–59; MacGregor and Nalty, *Blacks in the U.S. Armed Forces*, 310.
23. Ibid.
24. Mirouze, *World War I Infantry in Colour Photographs*, 24–25, 54–55, 58–59.
25. Ibid., 24–25, 54–55, 58–59.

26. Stallings, *The Doughboys*, 314; Heywood, *Negro Combat Troops*, 134–35; Mirouze, *World War I Infantry in Colour Photographs*, 58–59, 60–61.

27. Stallings, *The Doughboys*, 313; Heywood, *Negro Combat Troops*, 33.

28. Ibid.

29. Heywood, *Negro Combat Troops*, 33; Jamieson et al., *Complete History of the Colored Soldiers*, 50; Stallings, *The Doughboys*, 313, 318.

30. Ibid.

31. Heywood, *Negro Combat Troops*, 34–35; Stallings, *The Doughboys*, 317–18.

32. Ibid.

33. Heywood, *Negro Combat Troops*, 36–37; Fuller, *Decisive Battles of the U.S.A.*, 375; Haythornthwaite, *World War One Source Book*, 309–10; Miles, *Fallen Leaves*, 260–62; Col. Hershel Tupes, Report to GHQ, AEF, France, 19 January 1919, NA, RG 120, boxes 1–2, 3343–44.

34. Ibid.

35. Ibid.

36. Hayward Report to GHQ, 7 January 1918, NA, RG 120, boxes 1–2, 3343–44, 5; Pershing, *My Experiences in the World War*, 1:131–32.

37. *Small Arms of the World*, 132–33, 377; Farwell, *Over There*, 100.

38. Ibid.

39. Ibid.

40. *Small Arms of the World*, 131, 377; Haythornthwaite, *World War One Source Book*, 66–69; Laffin, *A Western Front Companion*, 147.

41. Haythornthwaite, *World War One Source Book*, 92–93.

42. Landships, at website: http://www.landships.freeservers.com/37mm-gun.htm, accessed 5 May 2003.

43. Haythornthwaite, *World War One Source Book*, 83, 182; Laffin, *Western Front Companion*, 148.

44. Ibid.

45. Haythornthwaite, *World War One Source Book*, 18, 83, 182.

46. Ibid., 71; Scott, *Scott's Official History*, 205–6; Heywood, *Negro Combat Troops*, 47–48.

47. Ibid.

48. Ibid.

49. Little, *From Harlem to the Rhine*, 159; Letter to the Adjutant General from William Hayward, NA, RG 120, boxes 1–2, 3343–44, 5; American Battle Monuments Commission, *93d Division*, 4.

50. Ibid.

Chapter 8. The Rest of the 93d Division Ships Out

Epigraph. Braddan, *Under Fire with the 370th Infantry*, 49.

1. Ibid., 47–49; Heywood, *Negro Combat Troops*, 25–27.

2. Ibid.

3. Ibid.

4. Ibid.

5. Braddan, *Under Fire with the 370th Infantry,* 49–50; Heywood, *Negro Combat Troops,* 30.

6. Heywood, *Negro Combat Troops,* 30.

7. Walker, "The Eighth Regiment in France," in *Pullman Porter's Review.*

8. Ibid.; Braddan, *Under Fire with the 370th Infantry,* 50–51.

9. Braddan, *Under Fire with the 370th Infantry,* 51; American Battle Monuments Commission, *93d Division,* 5.

10. Ibid.

11. Heywood, *Negro Combat Troops,* 26; Miles, *Fallen Leaves,* 251.

12. Ibid.

13. Heywood, *Negro Combat Troops,* 25, 262–65; Miles, *Fallen Leaves,* 251.

14. Ibid.

15. Heywood, *Negro Combat Troops,* 31–32; Miles, *Fallen Leaves,* 253–54; American Battle Monuments Commission, *93d Division,* 5.

16. Ibid.

17. Ibid.

18. Ibid.

19. Ibid.

20. Ibid.

21. Mason and Furr, *The American Negro with the Red Hand of France,* 30–37; Scipio, *With the Red Hand Division,* 43, 45.

22. Ibid.

23. Ibid.

24. Ibid.

25. Ibid.

26. Ibid.

27. Mason and Furr, *The American Negro with the Red Hand of France,* 38, 41; Payne, "Brief History 372d," NA, RG 120, boxes 1–2, 3443–44, 1.

28. Ibid.

29. Mason and Furr, *The American Negro with the Red Hand of France,* 41–44.

30. Ibid.

31. Ibid., 44–46; Payne, "Brief History 372d," NA, RG 120, boxes 1–2, 3343–44, 1; American Battle Monuments Commission, *93d Division,* 6.

32. Ibid.

33. Ibid.

34. Ibid.

Chapter 9. The 370th Starts Combat Training

Epigraph. "The Eighth Regiment in France," in *Pullman Porter's Review.*

1. Ibid.; Jamieson et al., *Complete History of the Colored Soldiers,* 93–94; American Battle Monuments Commission, *93d Division,* 6; Sweeney, *History of the American Negro in the Great World War,* 166–67; Williams, *Negro Soldiers,* 211–12; Scott, *Scott's Official History,* 216–17; Braddan, *Under Fire with the 370th Infantry,* 58.

2. Ibid.

3. Ibid.; American Battle Monuments Commission, *93d Division*, 5.

4. Ibid.

5. Sweeney, *History of the American Negro in the Great World War*, 167; Walker, "The Eighth Regiment in France," in *Pullman Porter's Review;* American Battlefield Monuments Commission, *American Armies and Battlefields in Europe*, 164 and map, 166; Braddan, *Under Fire with the 370th Infantry*, 58.

6. Walker, "The Eighth Regiment in France," in *Pullman Porter's Review;* Laffin, *Panorama of the Western Front*, 90–91.

7. Sweeney, *History of the American Negro in the Great World War*, 167; Duncan, "5th Indorsement," 2.

8. Sweeney, *History of the American Negro in the Great World War*, 167–68; American Battlefield Monuments Commission, *93d Division*, 5.

9. Sweeney, *History of the American Negro in the Great World War*, 167–68; Jamieson et al., *Complete History of the Colored Soldiers*, 94; Duncan, "5th Indorsement," 3.

10. Braddan, *Under Fire with the 370th Infantry*, 65.

11. Ibid.

12. Ibid., 66, 71, 77; Smith, *Until the Last Trumpet Sounds*, 162.

13. Braddan, *Under Fire with the 370th Infantry*, 65–67.

14. Ibid.

15. Ibid.

16. Sweeney, *History of the American Negro in the Great World War*, 161, 168.

17. Braddan, *Under Fire with the 370th Infantry*, 73–74; MacGregor and Nalty, *Blacks in the U.S. Armed Forces*, 309 (Capt. George Marvin's report on the 370th Infantry).

18. Ibid.

19. Farwell, *Over There*, 101–3, 226–27.

20. MacGregor and Nalty, *Blacks in the U.S. Armed Forces*, 309 (Capt. George Marvin's report on the 370th Infantry).

21. Ibid.

22. Ibid.

23. Ibid.

24. Sweeney, *History of the American Negro in the Great World War*, 169, 176; Association of Graduates, U.S. Military Academy, "Register of Graduates," 319.

25. Ibid.

26. Sweeney, *History of the American Negro in the Great World War*, 167; Duncan, "5th Indorsement," 3; American Battle Monuments Commission, *93d Division*, 5.

27. Sweeney, *History of the American Negro in the Great World War*, 168; Braddan, *Under Fire with the 370th Infantry*, 71–72.

28. Ibid.

29. Williams, *Negro Soldiers*, 212; Sweeney, *History of the American Negro in the Great World War*, 168; Jamieson et al., *Complete History of the Colored Soldiers*, 94–95; Scott, *Scott's Official History*, 218.

30. American Battle Monuments Commission, *93d Division*, 5; Sweeney, *History of the American Negro in the Great World War*, 169; Braddan, *Under Fire with the 370th*

Infantry, 85; Ministère de la Guerre, *Les Armées Françaises dans la Grande Guerre*, 452–53, 457.

31. Ibid.
32. Duncan, "5th Indorsement," 3; Williams, *Negro Soldiers*, 212; American Battle Monuments Commission, *93d Division*, 5; Scott, *Scott's Official History*, 218.
33. Sweeney, *History of the American Negro in the Great World War*, 169; Braddan, *Under Fire with the 370th Infantry*, 73.
34. Sweeney, *History of the American Negro in the Great World War*, 168–69; Fisher, "Black Devils of Illinois," in *Pullman Porter's Review;* Braddan, *Under Fire with the 370th Infantry*, 85–88.
35. Ibid.
36. Ibid.
37. Ibid.

Chapter 10. The 371st Goes into the Trenches

Epigraph. Heywood, *Negro Combat Troops*, 65.

1. Ibid., 32–33; Miles, *Fallen Leaves*, 254, 259; American Battle Monuments Commission, *93d Division*, 5.
2. Miles, *Fallen Leaves*, 254–56; Heywood, *Negro Combat Troops*, 49–50.
3. Ibid.
4. Miles, *Fallen Leaves*, 257.
5. Ibid., 259, 260–61; Heywood, *Negro Combat Troops*, 33, 36–37.
6. Miles, *Fallen Leaves*, 262–63.
7. Ibid.
8. Ibid., 264; American Battle Monuments Commission, *93d Division*, 6; Heywood, *Negro Combat Troops*, 52–57.
9. Miles, *Fallen Leaves*, 267–70; Heywood, *Negro Combat Troops*, 60–61, 65, 76.
10. Ibid.
11. Ibid.
12. Ibid.
13. Ibid.
14. Fussell, *The Great War and Modern Memory*, 42, 47; Farwell, *Over There*, 113–14; Heywood, *Negro Combat Troops*, 79–82, 93; Haythornthwaite, *Photohistory of World War One*, photo of a French infantryman using a trench periscope, opposite the page entitled "World War One: 1917."
15. Ibid.
16. Ibid.
17. Heywood, *Negro Combat Troops*, 97–98, 99–100, 106–21; Miles, *Fallen Leaves*, 273–74.
18. Ibid.
19. Ibid.
20. Ibid.
21. Ibid.

22. Ibid.
23. Ibid.
24. Ibid.
25. Ibid.
26. Ibid.
27. Ibid.
28. Ibid.
29. Ibid.
30. Heywood, *Negro Combat Troops*, 138–49; Miles, *Fallen Leaves*, 274–25.
31. Ibid.
32. Ibid.
33. Ibid.
34. Ibid.
35. Ibid.
36. Ibid.
37. Ibid.
38. Ibid.
39. Ibid.
40. Ibid.
41. Miles, *Fallen Leaves*, 275–76; Heywood, *Negro Combat Troops*, 306.
42. Ibid.
43. Ibid.
44. Ibid.
45. Ibid.
46. Ibid.
47. Ibid.
48. Ibid.
49. Ibid.; Department of the Army, *American Decorations*, 195.
50. Miles, *Fallen Leaves*, 277; Heywood, *Negro Combat Troops*, 154–55.

Chapter 11. The 372d Gets Its First Taste of Combat

Epigraph. Mason and Furr, *The American Negro with the Red Hand of France*, 64.
1. Ibid., 45–47; American Battle Monuments Commission, *93d Division*, 6; Scott, *Scott's Official History*, 240; Williams, *Negro Soldiers*, 232.
2. Ibid.
3. Ibid.
4. Ibid.
5. Ibid.
6. Ibid.
7. Mason and Furr, *The American Negro with the Red Hand of France*, 48; Williams, *Negro Soldiers*, 232.
8. Mason and Furr, *The American Negro with the Red Hand of France*, 49.
9. Ibid., 50.
10. Ibid., 51.

11. Ibid., 52–53; American Battle Monuments Commission, *93d Division*, 6; Williams, *Negro Soldiers*, 232; Laffin, *Panorama of the Western Front*, 72–73.

12. Mason and Furr, *The American Negro with the Red Hand of France*, 54–57; Scipio, *With the Red Hand Division*, 61–63; Laffin, *Panorama of the Western Front*, 72–73; Tupes, Report to GHQ, NA, RG 120, boxes 1–2, 3343–44, 1.

13. Ibid.

14. Ibid.

15. Ibid.

16. Scipio, *With the Red Hand Division*, 67–69; Mason and Furr, *The American Negro with the Red Hand of France*, 67–70; Williams, *Negro Soldiers*, 232.

17. Ibid.

18. Ibid.

19. Williams, *Negro Soldiers*, 233; Scipio, *With the Red Hand Division*, 69; Laffin, *Panorama of the Western Front*. 74; Mason and Furr, *The American Negro with the Red Hand of France*, 70–73.

20. Ibid.

21. Tupes, Report to GHQ, NA, RG 120, boxes 1–2, 3343–44, 2; Williams, *Negro Soldiers*, 233; American Battle Monuments Commission, *93d Division*, 6.

22. Mason and Furr, *The American Negro with the Red Hand of France*, 74.

23. Tupes, Report to GHQ, NA, RG 120, boxes 1–2, 3343–44, 2; Williams, *Negro Soldiers*, 233.

24. Williams, *Negro Soldiers*, 233; Scipio, *With the Red Hand Division*, 71; Mason and Furr, *The American Negro with the Red Hand of France*, 75–76; Payne, "Brief History 372d," NA, RG 120, boxes 1–2, 3343–44, 1; MacGregor and Nalty, *Blacks in the U.S. Armed Forces*, 248.

25. U.S. Military Academy, "Profile of Colonel Herschel Tupes," 261–64.

26. Tupes, Report to GHQ, NA, RG 120, boxes 1–2, 3343–44, 2–3; Williams, *Negro Soldiers*, 233–34; Scipio, *With the Red Hand Division*, 71; Laffin, *Panorama of the Western Front*, 74–75, 80–81.

27. Williams, *Negro Soldiers*, 222, 233–34; Scipio, *With the Red Hand Division*, 55; Laffin, *Panorama of the Western Front*, 74–75, 80–81; Mason and Furr, *The American Negro with the Red Hand of France*, 95–97.

28. Mason and Furr, *The American Negro with the Red Hand of France*, 82–88.

29. Ibid.

30. U.S. Military Academy, "Herschel Tupes," 263–64.

31. Ibid.

32. Ibid.

33. Mason and Furr, *The American Negro with the Red Hand of France*, 95–96.

34. Ibid., 90.

35. Ibid., 93.

36. Ibid.

37. Tupes, "Employment of negros in our military establishment," NA, RG 120, boxes 1–2, 3343–44, 1–3; MacGregor and Nalty, *Blacks in the U.S. Armed Forces*, 313, 340–41.

38. Ibid.

39. Ibid.
40. Mason and Furr, *The American Negro with the Red Hand of France*, 98–100; Williams, *Negro Soldiers*, 234; Tupes, "Employment of negros in our military establishment," NA, RG 120, boxes 1–2, 3343–44, 1–3; MacGregor and Nalty, *Blacks in the U.S. Armed Forces*, 340–41.
41. Mason and Furr, *The American Negro with the Red Hand of France*, 100–101.
42. Ibid., 76, 101–2.
43. Ibid.
44. Ibid.
45. Ibid.

Chapter 12. The 93d Division's First Heroes

Epigraph. From Roberts article in summer 1918 *Saturday Evening Post*, cited in Sweeney, *History of the American Negro in the Great World War*, 148.

1. Little, *From Harlem to the Rhine*, 159, 163.
2. Ibid., 183–84.
3. Ibid.
4. Ibid.; *The Congressional Medal of Honor.*
5. Wilson, *The Black Phalanx*, 214–17.
6. Little, *From Harlem to the Rhine*, 183–84.
7. Ibid.
8. Ibid.
9. Ibid.
10. Ibid.
11. Ibid.
12. Little, *From Harlem to the Rhine*, 164–65; American Battle Monuments Commission, *93d Division*, 4; Laffin, *Panorama of the Western Front*, 70–71.
13. Ibid.
14. Little, *From Harlem to the Rhine*, 166–67.
15. Ibid.
16. Ibid., 170–71, 176–79; Haythornthwaite, *The World War One Source Book*, 76–81.
17. Ibid.
18. Ibid.
19. Little, *From Harlem to the Rhine*, 174–75.
20. Ibid.
21. Ibid.
22. Ibid., 192–93.
23. Ibid.
24. Ibid.
25. Ibid.
26. Ibid., 193–97;"Bush Germans Better Watch That 'Chocolate Front,'" *Literary Digest*, 15 June 1918, 57:43–44; Sweeney, *History of the American Negro in the Great World War*, 146–47.
27. Ibid.

28. Ibid.

29. Ibid.

30. Ibid.

31. Ibid.

32. Little, *From Harlem to the Rhine*, 197–98.

33. Ibid.

34. Ibid., 198–201; Jamieson et al., *Complete History of the Colored Soldiers*, 22–25; Sweeney, *History of the American Negro in the Great World War*, 146–48.

35. Little, *From Harlem to the Rhine*, 369.

36. Ibid.

37. American Battle Monuments Commission, *American Armies and Battlefields in Europe*, 29–31; Laffin, *A Western Front Companion*, 94; Dupuy and Dupuy, *Military Heritage of America*, 374–75.

38. Ibid.

39. Ibid.

40. Ibid.

41. Ibid.

42. Ibid.

43. Sweeney, *History of the American Negro in the Great World War*, 139.

44. Ibid.

45. Scott, *Scott's Official History*, 205.

46. Little, *From Harlem to the Rhine*, 212–13.

47. Ibid.

Chapter 13. The Elastic Defense and the 369th

Epigraph. Hayward, quoted in "Not One of the Famous 369th Was Taken Alive," *Literary Digest*, 15 March 1919.

1. Department of the Army, *United States Army in the World War*, 5:148–53; Dupuy and Dupuy, *Military Heritage of America*, 376; Little, *From Harlem to the Rhine*, 213–14; Sweeney, *History of the American Negro in the Great World War*, 140–41; Farwell, *Over There*, 177–78; American Battle Monuments Commission, *American Armies and Battlefields in Europe*, 330; "Le 38e Corps, 1918: Année Decisive," in *Biography of General Henri Gouraud*.

2. Ibid.

3. Ibid.

4. Ibid.

5. Ibid.

6. Ibid.

7. Little, *From Harlem to the Rhine*, 215, 218; American Battle Monuments Commission, *93d Division*, 4.

8. Little, *From Harlem to the Rhine,*, 215, 218. Little's claim that the 3d Battalion was located on the right of the 1st Battalion cannot be correct because Berzieux is to the left of Courtemont (facing north).

9. Little, *From Harlem to the Rhine*, 218.

10. Ibid., 219–20; Shipley, *The History of the A.E.F.*, 129.

11. Little, *From Harlem to the Rhine*, 218–21.

12. Ibid.

13. Ibid., 222, 228; Farwell, *Over There*, 242; *Biography of General Henri Gouraud.*

14. Ibid.

15. Toland, *No Man's Land*, 242; Farwell, *Over There*, 177–78; Department of the Army, *United States Army in the World War*, 5:148–53; Pitt, *1918, the Last Act*, 179; Little, *From Harlem to the Rhine*, 223.

16. Ibid.

17. American Battle Monuments Commission, *American Armies and Battlefields in Europe*, 344; Department of the Army, *United States Army in the World War*, 5:148–53; Toland, *No Man's Land*, 242; Farwell, *Over There*, 177–78; Stallings, *The Doughboys*, 121.

18. Ibid.

19. Toland, *No Man's Land*, 242–43; Stallings, *The Doughboys*, 122.

20. Sweeney, *History of the American Negro in the Great World War*, 140–41; Binding, *A Fatalist at War*, 234.

21. Ibid.; Toland, *No Man's Land*, 243.

22. "Not One of the Famous 369th Was Taken Alive," *Literary Digest*, 15 March 1919, 94; Sweeney, *History of the American Negro in the Great World War*, 140–41.

23. Ibid.

24. Ibid.

25. Ibid.

26. Binding, *A Fatalist at War*, 234–37.

27. Haythornthwaite, *World War One Source Book*, 42–43; Paschall, *The Defeat of Imperial Germany*, 159–60; Pitt, *1918*, 179–84.

28. Toland, *No Man's Land*, 246.

29. Binding, *A Fatalist at War*, 237.

30. Ibid., 235; "Not One of the Famous 369th Was Taken Alive," 95; Toland, *No Man's Land*, 245; Little, *From Harlem to the Rhine*, 225; Haythornthwaite, *World War One Source Book*, 42–43.

31. Ibid.

Chapter 14. Marshal Foch Prepares to Attack

Epigraph. Jamieson et al., *Complete History of the Colored Soldiers*, 50.

1. Little, *From Harlem to the Rhine*, 224–27; Haythornthwaite, *World War One Source Book*, 43; Farwell, *Over There*, 182.

2. Little, *From Harlem to the Rhine*, 224–27.

3. Ibid.

4. Ibid., 227.

5. Ibid, 230–31.

6. Ibid. 233–35.

7. Ibid., 236–45; American Battle Monuments Commission, *American Armies and*

Battlefields in Europe, 5; Sweeney, *History of the American Negro in the Great World War*, 141.

8. Ibid.

9. Ibid.

10. Dupuy and Dupuy, *Military Heritage of America*, 379–80; Taylor, *History of World War I*, 258; Haythornthwaite, *World War One Source Book*, 43.

11. Jamieson et al., *Complete History of the Colored Soldiers*, 39–40; Scott, *Scott's Official History*, 211–12; Department of the Army, *American Decorations*, 196; Williams, *Negro Soldiers*, 206–7.

12. Ibid.

13. Ibid.

14. Ibid.

15. Little, *From Harlem to the Rhine*, 252–56; Jamieson et al., *Complete History of the Colored Soldiers*, 67–68.

16. Ibid.

17. Ibid.

18. Ibid.

19. Jamieson et al., *Complete History of the Colored Soldiers*, 31, 50.

20. Ibid.

21. Ibid.

22. Little, *From Harlem to the Rhine*, 257–58.

23. Ibid.

24. Ibid.

25. Ibid., 259.

26. Ibid., 261–62; Williams, *Negro Soldiers*, 200–201; Hayward Report to GHQ, NA, RG 120, boxes 1–2, 3343–44, 6.

27. Ibid.

28. Ibid.

29. Ibid.

30. American Battle Monuments Commission, *93d Division*, 5; Letter to the Adjutant General from William Hayward, NA, RG 120, boxes 1–2, 3343–44, 6.

31. Ibid.

Chapter 15. The First Stages of the Fall Offensive

Epigraph. Heywood, *Negro Combat Troops*, 162.

1. Dupuy and Dupuy, *Military Heritage of America*, 383.

2. Ibid., 380–81; American Battle Monuments Commission, *American Armies and Battlefields in Europe*, 105–11; Farwell, *Over There*, 206–8.

3. Farwell, *Over There*, 218–20; Haythornthwaite, *World War One Source Book*, 44; Dupuy and Dupuy, *Military Heritage of America*, 383–85.

4. Ibid.

5. Heywood, *Negro Combat Troops*, 156; Farwell, *Over There*, 221–22; Little, *From Harlem to the Rhine*, 271; Scipio *With the Red Hand Division*, 5–76; Miles, *Fallen Leaves*, 278.

6. Ibid.

7. Ibid.

8. Ibid.

9. American Battle Monuments Commission, *93d Division*, 4–6, and *American Armies and Battlefields in Europe*, 369; Ministère de la Guerre, *Les Armées Françaises dans la Grande Guerre*, 866, 869, 878, 881, 946, 948; Miles, *Fallen Leaves*, 279.

10. Ibid.

11. Laffin, *Panorama of the Western Front*, 54–56, 68–71; Heywood, *Negro Combat Troops*, 159–60.

12. Ibid.

13. Ibid.

14. Ibid.

15. Scipio, *With the Red Hand Division*, 75.

16. Mason and Furr, *The American Negro with the Red Hand of France*, 102–11; American Battle Monuments Commission, *93d Division*, 6.

17. Ibid.

18. Heywood, *Negro Combat Troops*, 149–55; American Battle Monuments Commission, *93d Division*, 6; Miles, *Fallen Leaves*, 277–78.

19. Ibid.

20. Williams, *Negro Soldiers*, 201; Hayward Report to GHQ, 7 January 1919, NA, RG 120, boxes 1–2, 3433–44, 6; American Battle Monuments Commission, *93d Division*, 6.

21. American Battle Monuments Commission, *93d Division*, 6.

22. Heywood, *Negro Combat Troops*, 161; Mason and Furr, *The American Negro with the Red Hand of France*, 114–15.

23. Mason and Furr, *The American Negro with the Red Hand of France*, 112–15.

24. Ibid.

25. Ibid.

26. American Battle Monuments Commission, *93d Division*, 8–9.

27. Heywood, *Negro Combat Troops*, 156–57.

28. Little, *From Harlem to the Rhine*, 268–69; Scipio, *With the Red Hand Division*, 75.

29. Ibid.

30. Heywood, *Negro Combat Troops*, 160; Farwell, *Over There*, 223, 225; Mason and Furr, *The American Negro with the Red Hand of France*, 117–18.

31. Ibid.

32. Little, *From Harlem to the Rhine*, 269–70; American Battle Monuments Commission, *93d Division*, 11; Farwell, *Over There*, 220–21; Williams, *Negro Soldiers*, 201–2; Haythornthwaite, *World War One Source Book*, 44.

33. Ibid.

Chapter 16. The Attack on Bellevue Signal Ridge

Epigraph. Arlington National Cemetery website, http://www.arlingtoncemetery.net/fstowers.htm, accessed 11 October 2003.

1. American Battle Monuments Commission, *93d Division*, 11–12, and *American Armies and Battlefields in Europe*, 358, map, 359; Little, *From Harlem to the Rhine*, 270–72; Williams, *Negro Soldiers*, 201, 202.

2. Ibid.

3. Ibid.

4. Ibid.

5. Ibid.

6. Ibid.

7. Department of the Army, *American Decorations*, 200; Scott, *Scott's Official History*, 211.

8. Department of the Army, *American Decorations*, 421; Scott, *Scott's Official History*, 209–10.

9. Ibid.

10. American Battle Monuments Commission, *93d Division*, 12, and *American Armies and Battlefields in Europe*, 358, map, 359; Little, *From Harlem to the Rhine*, 273–78; Williams, *Negro Soldiers*, 202.

11. Ibid.

12. Ibid.

13. American Battle Monuments Commission, *93d Division*, 12–13, and *American Armies and Battlefields in Europe*, 358; Williams, *Negro Soldiers*, 223–24; Mason and Furr, *The American Negro with the Red Hand of France*, 120–23; Heywood, *Negro Combat Troops*, 161–62.

14. Ibid.

15. Ibid.

16. Ibid.

17. Heywood, *Negro Combat Troops*, 162–73; Miles, *Fallen Leaves*, 281; Scott, *Scott's Official History*, 235.

18. Ibid.

19. Ibid.

20. Ibid.

21. Ibid.

22. Ibid.

23. Ibid.

24. Ibid.

25. Department of the Army, Headquarters, General Orders no. 15, Award of the Medal of Honor to Cpl. Freddie Stowers; Arlington National Cemetery website: http://www.arlingtoncemetery.com/fstowers.htm, accessed 11 October 2003.

26. Ibid.

27. Department of the Army, *American Decorations*, 371.

28. Ibid., 347.

29. American Battle Monuments Commission, *93d Division*, 14–17; Little, *From Harlem to the Rhine*, 276.

30. Ibid.

31. Ibid.

32. Heywood, *Negro Combat Troops*, 170.

33. Ibid., 172–73.
34. American Battle Monuments Commission, *93d Division*, 17–20, and *American Armies and Battlefields in Europe*, 358–59.
35. Ibid.
36. Department of the Army, *American Decorations*, 321.
37. Hillman, "Remarks for Memorial Day Breakfast."
38. American Battle Monuments Commission, *93d Division*, 17–20.
39. Ibid.
40. Heywood, *Negro Combat Troops*, 173, 174, 176, 194; Miles, *Fallen Leaves*, 284; Scott, *Scott's Official History*, 232.
41. American Battle Monuments Commission, *93d Division*, 20–21, and *American Armies and Battlefields in Europe*, 359.
42. Ibid.
43. Department of the Army, *American Decorations*, 251; Heywood, *Negro Combat Troops*, 301–2; American Battle Monuments Commission, *American Armies and Battlefields in Europe*, 511, description of Medaille Militaire.
44. Ibid.
45. Heywood, *Negro Combat Troops*, 179.
46. Ibid., 179; Department of the Army, *American Decorations*, 305.
47. Heywood, *Negro Combat Troops*, 180–83.
48. Ibid.

Chapter 17. The Push beyond Bellevue Signal Ridge

Epigraph. Sweeney, *History of the American Negro in the Great World War*, 191.
1. Little, *From Harlem to the Rhine*, 290.
2. Ibid., 298–304; American Battle Monuments Commission, *93d Division*, 20–21.
3. Ibid.
4. Little, *From Harlem to the Rhine*, 286, 294, 304–5, 309; *The Congressional Medal of Honor*, 532; Schmiedeler, "George Robb, a Modest Hero"; American Battle Monuments Commission, *American Armies and Battlefields in Europe*, 360; Department of the Army, *American Decorations*, 89; George S. Robb website: http://www.snowbizz.com/HWRepublican/george_robb/georgerobb.htm, accessed 20 October 2003.
5. Ibid.
6. Ibid.
7. Ibid.
8. Ibid.
9. Ibid.
10. American Battle Monuments Commission, *93d Division*, 20–21, and *American Armies and Battlefields in Europe*, 359 and map; Little, *From Harlem to the Rhine*, 305–8.
11. Ibid.
12. Ibid.

13. Ibid.
14. Ibid.
15. Ibid.
16. Ibid.
17. Ibid.
18. American Battle Monuments Commission, *93d Division*, 21–22; Heywood, *Negro Combat Troops*, 181; C. S. Diton, Capt. Adjt. and Operations Officer, 372d U.S. Infantry, "Narrative of Action in Field of 372d U.S. Infantry in Champagne, Sept. 26–Oct. 7, 1918," 26 October 1918, and Hayward Report to GHQ, 7 January 1919, both in NA, RG 120, boxes 1–2, 3343–44, 3–5; Scott, *Scott's Official History*, 242.
19. Ibid.
20. Ibid.
21. Ibid.
22. Ibid.
23. Department of the Army, *American Decorations*, 529.
24. Greene, *Black Defenders of America, 1775–1973*. The 1st Separate Company, Maryland National Guard, actually served as Company I of the 372d Infantry, not with the 367th Infantry, 92d Division, as Greene states. Also, the 367th Infantry was not heavily engaged in the Argonne area and suffered only two wounded during that period. It thus seems unlikely that Creigler was serving with the 367th Infantry during this period, although some officers and noncommissioned officers were transferred from the 93d Division to upgrade the 92d Division.
25. American Battle Monuments Commission, *93d Division*, 22–23; Diton, "Narrative of Action in Field," and Tupes Report to GHQ, AEF, dated 19 January 1919, both in NA, RG 120, boxes 1–2, 3343–44, 4–5; Scott, *Scott's Official History*, 242–43; Mason and Furr, *The American Negro with the Red Hand of France*, 124.
26. Ibid.
27. Ibid.
28. Department of the Army, *American Decorations*, 150; Greene, *Black Defenders of America, 1775–1973*, 171.
29. Mason and Furr, *The American Negro with the Red Hand of France*, 125.
30. Department of the Army, *American Decorations*, 665.
31. Ibid.
32. Heywood, *Negro Combat Troops*, 193–94; American Battle Monuments Commission, *93d Division*, 23; *Order of Battle of the United States Land Forces in the World War*, 440.
33. Ibid.
34. Heywood, *Negro Combat Troops*, 189–92.
35. Ibid.
36. Department of the Army, *American Decorations*, 419.

Chapter 18. The 370th Attacks at Canal de l'Oise–l'Aisne

Epigraph. Sweeney, *History of the American Negro in the Great World War,* 163.

1. American Battle Monuments Commission, *93d Division,* 27; *Order of Battle of the United States Land Forces in the World War,* 441; Sweeney, *History of the American Negro in the Great World War,* 169.
2. Fisher, "Black Devils of Illinois," in *Pullman Porter's Review.*
3. American Battle Monuments Commission, *93d Division,* 27, and *American Armies and Battlefields in Europe,* 92; Sweeney, *History of the American Negro in the Great World War,* 169; Scott, *Scott's Official History,* 218.
4. Ibid.
5. Ibid.
6. Ibid.
7. Ibid.
8. Ibid.
9. Department of the Army, *American Decorations,* 628.
10. Sweeney, *History of the American Negro in the Great World War,* 157–58; Sgt. E. A. Means, "Capturing Hindenberg Cave" and "Hindenberg Cave," in *Pullman Porter's Review;* Department of the Army, *American Decorations,* 364; Sweeney, *History of the American Negro in the Great World War,* 170; Scott, *Scott's Official History,* 218.
11. Means, "Capturing Hindenberg Cave" and "Hindenberg Cave," in *Pullman Porter's Review;* Department of the Army, *American Decorations,* 364; Sweeney, *History of the American Negro in the Great World War,* 170; Scott, *Scott's Official History,* 218.
12. Ibid.
13. Ibid.
14. Ibid.
15. Ibid.
16. Ibid.
17. Sweeney, *History of the American Negro in the Great World War,* 169–70; American Battle Monuments Commission, *93d Division,* 27; *Order of Battle of the United States Land Forces in the World War,* 441.
18. Ibid.
19. Department of the Army, *American Decorations,* 456; Williams, *Negro Soldiers,* 217.
20. Duncan, "5th Indorsement," 4; Sweeney, *History of the American Negro in the Great World War,* 170; American Battle Monuments Commission, *93d Division,* 27–28.
21. Ibid.
22. American Battle Monuments Commission, *93d Division,* 27–29, and *American Armies and Battlefields in Europe,* 92; Sweeney, *History of the American Negro in the Great World War,* 171.
23. Ibid.
24. Ibid.

25. Ibid.

26. Ibid.

27. Ibid.

28. Ibid.

29. Ibid.

30. U.S. Army War College, *Colored Soldiers in the U.S. Army,* appendix 36: World War.

31. Ibid.

32. Ibid., appendix 31: World War.

33. Ibid.

34. Ibid.

35. Ibid.

36. Ibid., appendix 16: World War.

37. Ibid.

38. Barbeau and Henri, *The Unknown Soldier,* 125–27; Sweeney, *History of the American Negro in the Great World War,* 172.

39. Ibid.

40. Ibid.

41. Department of the Army, *American Decorations,* 361.

42. Ibid., 617; Williams, *Negro Soldiers,* 218.

43. American Battle Monuments Commission, *93d Division,* 29.

44. Department of the Army, *American Decorations,* 233; Sweeney, *History of the American Negro in the Great World War,* 159.

45. Department of the Army, *American Decorations,* 295.

46. Ibid.

47. Ibid., 338.

48. Ibid., 289.

49. U.S. Army War College, *Colored Soldiers in the U.S. Army,* appendix 36: World War, and appendix 31: World War.

50. Sweeney, *History of the American Negro in the Great World War,* 175–76; Department of the Army, *American Decorations,* 634; American Battle Monuments Commission, *93d Division,* 29–30.

51. Ibid.

52. Sweeney, *History of the American Negro in the Great World War,* 170–71; American Battle Monuments Commission, *93d Division,* 29–30.

53. Ibid.

Chapter 19. The 370th in Pursuit

Epigraph. Sweeney, *History of the American Negro in the Great World War,* 155.

1. American Battle Monuments Commission, *93d Division,* 27–30; Sweeney, *History of the American Negro in the Great World War,* 170–71; Scott, *Scott's Official History,* 219–21; Williams, *Negro Soldiers,* 213–14; Duncan, "5th Indorsement," 4.

2. Ibid.

3. Sweeney, *History of the American Negro in the Great World War,* 157, 171; Scott, *Scott's Official History,* 220, 479.

4. Ibid.

5. Sweeney, *History of the American Negro in the Great World War,* 171.

6. Ibid.

7. Sergt. [*sic*] Suesbury, "Hell's Half Acre," in *Pullman Porter's Review.*

8. Sweeney, *History of the American Negro in the Great World War,* 171–72; Scott, *Scott's Official History,* 221; American Battle Monuments Commission, *93d Division,* 31.

9. Ibid.

10. Ibid.

11. Duncan, "5th Indorsement," 4; Sweeney, *History of the American Negro in the Great World War,* 172; Scott, *Scott's Official History,* 222.

12. Sweeney, *History of the American Negro in the Great World War,* 172.

13. American Battle Monuments Commission, *93d Division,* 31; Scott, *Scott's Official History,* 222–23; Sweeney, *History of the American Negro in the Great World War,* 172–73.

14. Ibid.

15. Ibid.; Pvt. Tony Smith, "The Fatal Mess Call," in *Pullman Porter's Review.*

16. Sweeney , *History of the American Negro in the Great World War,* 273; Scott, *Scott's Official History,* 225; American Battle Monuments Commission, *93d Division,* 32–33, and *American Armies and Battlefields in Europe,* 514.

17. Ibid.

18. Ibid.

19. American Battle Monuments Commission, *93d Division,* 33.

20. Ibid.

21. Department of the Army, *American Decorations,* 506.

22. Ibid., 634.

23. Sweeney, *History of the American Negro in the Great World War,* 173–74.

24. Ibid.

25. Ibid.

26. Ibid.

27. Department of the Army, *American Decorations,* 303.

28. American Battle Monuments Commission, *93d Division,* 33–34; Sweeney, *History of the American Negro in the Great World War,* 174; Scott, *Scott's Official History,* 174; Duncan, "5th Indorsement," 4.

29. Ibid.

30. Ibid.

31. Ibid.

32. Ibid.

33. Duncan, "5th Indorsement," 6; Scott, *Scott's Official History,* 230; American Battle Monuments Commission, *93d Division,* 34.

Chapter 20. Final Days on the Vosges Front

Epigraph. Sweeney, *History of the American Negro in the Great World War*, 190.

1. American Battle Monuments Commission, *American Armies and Battlefields in Europe*, 419–20, and *93d Division*, 23–24; Laffin, *Panorama of the Western Front*, 114–19.
2. Ibid.
3. Heywood, *Negro Combat Troops*, 197–99, 210–11; Mason and Furr, *The American Negro with the Red Hand of France*, 130–35.
4. Ibid.
5. Ibid.
6. Ibid.
7. Ibid.
8. Ibid.
9. Ibid.
10. Ibid.
11. Heywood, *Negro Combat Troops*, 198–99; Stallings, *The Doughboys*, 313, 318.
12. Ibid.
13. Ibid.
14. Little, *From Harlem to the Rhine*, 317; *Small Arms of the World*, 130.
15. Little, *From Harlem to the Rhine*, 310–11.
16. Ibid., 310; Department of the Army, *American Decorations*, 377.
17. American Battle Monuments Commission, *93d Division*, 23; Little, *From Harlem to the Rhine*, 313.
18. Little, *From Harlem to the Rhine*, 313–16.
19. Ibid.
20. Ibid., 314.
21. Ibid.
22. Ibid., 315–16.
23. Ibid., 314; Hayward Report to GHQ, NA, RG 120, boxes 1–2, 3343–44, 11, paragraph 4, item 7.
24. Little, *From Harlem to the Rhine*, 316–19; Letter to the Adjutant General from William Hayward, NA, RG 120, boxes 1–2, 3343–44, 7–8.
25. Ibid.
26. Ibid.
27. American Battle Monuments Commission, *93d Division*, 21, 23; Heywood, *Negro Combat Troops*, 180.
28. Heywood, *Negro Combat Troops*, 186, 193.
29. Ibid., 193–94.
30. Ibid., 194.
31. Ibid., 194–95.
32. Ibid., 196–97.
33. Ibid., 197.
34. Ibid., 197–98.
35. Ibid., 211–13.

36. Ibid.
37. Ibid.
38. Ibid., 217–19.
39. American Battle Monuments Commission, *93d Division*, 23; Mason and Furr, *The American Negro with the Red Hand of France*, 124–25; Tupes Report to GHQ, NA, RG 120, boxes 1–2, 3343–44, 5–6.
40. Mason and Furr, *The American Negro with the Red Hand of France*, 126.
41. Ibid.
42. Ibid., 127.
43. Ibid., 127–28, 130–37; Tupes Report to GHQ, NA, RG 120, boxes 1–2, 3343–44, 5–6.
44. Mason and Furr, *The American Negro with the Red Hand of France*, 130–32.
45. Ibid., 132; Tupes Report to GHQ, NA, RG 120, boxes 1–2, 3343–44, 5–6.
46. Mason and Furr, *The American Negro with the Red Hand of France*, 135–36.
47. Ibid.

Chapter 21. Armistice

Epigraph. Heywood, *Negro Combat Troops*, 223.

1. Ibid., 221–23; Mason and Furr, *The American Negro with the Red Hand of France*, 136–37.
2. Ibid.
3. Ibid.
4. Heywood, *Negro Combat Troops*, 224–26; Little, *From Harlem to the Rhine*, 325–26.
5. Ibid.
6. Ibid.
7. Ibid.
8. American Battle Monuments Commission, *93d Division*, 23–24; *Order of Battle of the United States Land Forces in the World War*, 440.
9. Little, *From Harlem to the Rhine*, 326–36; Hayward Report to GHQ, NA, RG 120, boxes 1–2, 3343–44, 11; Scott, *Scott's Official History*, 230.
10. Ibid.
11. Ibid.
12. Ibid.
13. Ibid.
14. Little, *From Harlem to the Rhine*, 337–41; Hayward Report to GHQ, NA, RG 120, boxes 1–2, 3343–44, 11.
15. Ibid.
16. Ibid.
17. Ibid.
18. *Order of Battle of the United States Land Forces in the World War*, 440–41; Miles, *Fallen Leaves*, 295; Heywood, *Negro Combat Troops*, 229–30.
19. Ibid.
20. Ibid.

21. Ibid.
22. Heywood, *Negro Combat Troops*, 230–31, 274–76; Department of the Army, *American Decorations*, 228; Miles, *Fallen Leaves*, 299.
23. Ibid.
24. Heywood, *Negro Combat Troops*, 234, 242–43.
25. Ibid.
26. Ibid.
27. Ibid., 234–36; Miles, *Fallen Leaves*, 297–98; American Battle Monuments Commission, *American Armies and Battlefields in Europe*, 361, 526–27.
28. Ibid.
29. Ibid.
30. Ibid.
31. Heywood, *Negro Combat Troops*, 237–39.
32. Ibid.
33. Ibid.
34. Ibid., 57–58, 240–41; Miles, *Fallen Leaves*, 265–66.
35. Ibid.
36. Ibid.
37. Ibid.
38. Mason and Furr, *The American Negro with the Red Hand of France*, 136–37.
39. Ibid.
40. Tupes Report to GHQ, NA, RG 120, boxes 1–2, 3343–44, 6; Mason and Furr, *The American Negro with the Red Hand of France*, 138–39.
41. Ibid.
42. Mason and Furr, *The American Negro with the Red Hand of France*, 139–47.
43. Ibid.
44. Ibid.
45. Ibid., 143–47.
46. Ibid.
47. Sweeney, *History of the American Negro in the Great World War*, 174; Williams, *Negro Soldiers*, 216; Scott, *Scott's Official History*, 226; *Order of Battle of the United States Land Forces in the World War*, 442; American Battle Monuments Commission, *93d Division*, 34.
48. Ibid.
49. Ibid.
50. Ibid.

Chapter 22. Homeward Bound

Epigraph. Sweeney, *History of the American Negro in the Great World War*, 267.
1. American Battle Monuments Commission, *93d Division*, 24; Little, *From Harlem to the Rhine*, 348.
2. Little, *From Harlem to the Rhine*, 349, 351–52.
3. Ibid.

4. Ibid.
5. Ibid.
6. Ibid., 354.
7. Ibid., 355–56; *Order of Battle of the United States Land Forces in the World War,* 442.
8. Ibid.
9. Ibid.
10. Little, *From Harlem to the Rhine,* 357–62; Scott, *Scott's Official History,* 207–8.
11. Ibid.
12. Ibid.
13. Ibid.
14. Heywood, *Negro Combat Troops,* 248–49.
15. Ibid.
16. Ibid.
17. Ibid., 249–50.
18. Ibid., 250–53; *Order of Battle of the United States Land Forces in the World War,* 442.
19. Ibid.
20. Heywood, *Negro Combat Troops,* 253–56.
21. Ibid.
22. Ibid.
23. Mason and Furr, *The American Negro with the Red Hand of France,* 147–49.
24. Ibid.
25. Ibid.
26. Ibid., 150–52.
27. Ibid.
28. Ibid.
29. Ibid., 152–56; *Order of Battle of the United States Land Forces in the World War,* 442.
30. Ibid.
31. Ibid.
32. Scipio, *With the Red Hand Division,* 132–33; American Battle Monuments Commission, *American Armies and Battlefields in Europe,* 361, 526. A photograph furnished by Genevieve and Zenobio Acosta of Brussels, Belgium, shows the monument without chains.
33. Ibid.
34. Ibid.
35. Scott, *Scott's Official History,* 226–27; Williams, *Negro Soldiers,* 218; *Order of Battle of the United States Land Forces in the World War,* 442; American Battle Monuments Commission, *93d Division,* 34.
36. Ibid.
37. Williams, *Negro Soldiers,* 218–19; Scott, *Scott's Official History,* 227; Sweeney, *History of the American Negro in the Great World War,* 175; Duncan, "Fifth Indorsement," 5.

38. Ibid.

39. Ibid.

40. City of Chicago, *The Black Metropolis—Bronzeville District*, 24–25, Victory "Monument."

41. Ibid.

42. Ibid.

43. American Battle Monuments Commission, *American Armies and Battlefields in Europe*, 163, 166, 329, 336, 369, 516–17; and *93d Division*, 1, 36–37.

44. Ibid.

45. Ibid.

46. Ibid.

47. Williams, *Negro Soldiers*, 246.

48. Ibid.

49. American Battle Monuments Commission, *American Armies and Battlefields in Europe*, 349–50, 475, and website.

50. Ibid.

Bibliography

The story of the 93d Division and its four regiments as told here is not complete; this book is at best an outline of the service of the four regiments and their officers and men in World War I. I used two primary sources to achieve the most accurate representation possible of the activities, movements, and combat actions of the regiments: the four after-action reports submitted by the colonels commanding the regiments when the armistice went into effect on 11 November 1918, now in the National Archives and Records Administration in College Park, Maryland; and the *93d Division Summary of Operations in the World War* by the American Battle Monuments Commission. I found very few conflicts in dates and locations between these two sources. The movements and actions of the four regiments were followed as described in the aforementioned references on 1:100,000 (1 cm = 1 km) maps prepared by the Institut Géographique National of France. Any conflicts were resolved by accepting the data or locale that appeared the most logical.

I consulted several publications to bring alive the regiments' activities and present a better understanding of what the soldiers were experiencing at a personal level, and also to provide some background on the cause and course of the events on national and international scales.

Arthur W. Little's *From Harlem to the Rhine* is an excellent reference for following the 369th Infantry from its inception as the 15th Infantry Regiment, New York National Guard, until its return from France. Little served as a company commander and later as a battalion commander, and he was with the regiment from its formation, through its combat, and when it reverted back to National Guard status in 1919. Some dates and locations given by Little do not coincide with the official reports. Also, Little was a white officer, and although he was sincere and without bias, his characterizations of the black troops who were closest to him may appear politically incorrect by today's standards.

On the 370th, Infantry I consulted Chaplain William S. Braddan's *Under Fire with the 370th Infantry (8th I.N.G.) A.E.F.: Memoirs of the World War,* which provided useful (although not necessarily unbiased) information on the sights and scenes of the rear area of the battle zone and specific events involving individuals that Braddan observed directly. It is unfortunate that Braddan did not direct his energies toward a close account of the history and the human side of the regiment, as he was in an excellent position to do so.

Two excellent references follow the 371st Infantry from beginning to end. *Negro Combat Troops in the World War: The Story of the 371st Infantry* by Chester D. Heywood gives an intimate picture of life in the regiment, although some of the author's descriptions of the men of the regiment and their language and exploits may be offensive to modern readers. The regiment's one and only commander, Col. (later Brig. Gen.) Perry L. Miles, gives a detailed account of the actions of the 371st Infantry from the commander's perspective in his autobiography, *Fallen Leaves: Memories of an Old Soldier,* which should be studied by anyone interested in the regiment's history.

Monroe Mason and Arthur Furr's *The American Negro Soldier with the Red Hand of France* gives an intimate view of their experiences with the 372d Infantry. The writers give an excellent outline of the activities of the regiment, though many dates and places vary from official reports. Their vivid descriptions are an excellent picture of army life for the black enlisted man serving in the regiment. They provide a well-balanced description of the events concerning the poor handling of a multiracial regiment by the first regimental commander, Col. Glendie B. Young, and the feelings and actions of the enlisted men and some black officers during that ordeal. L. Albert Scipio's *With the Red Hand Division* outlines the activities of the 371st and 372d Infantry Regiments and includes some new information on the 372d Infantry given by firsthand sources. *Complete History of the Colored Soldiers* by Sgt. J. A. Jamieson et al. is one of the best personalized descriptions of the black units that served in France in World War I. Although choppy in its structure and inaccurate in casualty figures and specific dates, it nevertheless gives a strong, honest, and sometimes harsh feel for the life of the black soldier in the army and at the frontline trenches. Also see *Negro Soldiers in World War I: The Human Side* by Charles H. Williams, which offers a wealth of insight into the total experience of the black soldier and his family and community in the war. *Scott's Official History of the American Negro in the World War* by Emmett J. Scott includes appropriate excerpts drawn from other writers on the experience of the black soldier in France. *History of the American Negro in the Great World War* by journalist W. Allison Sweeney offers a broad-brush view of the participation of the black population in the war effort. These and other references used in compiling this book on the history of the regiments of the 93d Division are listed following.

Published Sources

Association of Graduates, U.S. Military Academy, "Register of Graduates and Former Cadets of the United States Military Academy." West Point, N.Y., 1990.

Barbeau, Arthur E., and Florette Henri. *The Unknown Soldier: Black American Troops in World War I.* Philadelphia: Temple University Press, 1974.

Binding, Rudolf. *A Fatalist at War.* Translated from German by Ian F. D. Morrow. Boston: Houghton Mifflin, 1929. First published in German under the title *Aus dem Kriege.*

Biography of General Henri Gouraud. Gouraud College, Morocco, North Africa. website: http://www.lyceefr.org/aaegd/gouraud1.htm, accessed 25 October 2003.

"Biography of William Hayward." In *National Cyclopedia of American Biography; Being the History of the United States,* 33:559–60. James T. White and Company.

Braddan, William S. *Under Fire with the 370th Infantry (8th I.N.G.), A.E.F.* Chicago: published by the author, no date.

Bullard, Robert L. *Personalities and Reminiscences of the War.* Garden City, N.Y.: Doubleday Page, 1925.

"Bush Germans Better Watch That 'Chocolate Front.'" *Literary Digest,* 15 June 1918, 57:43–47.

Carisella, P. J., and James W. Ryan. *The Black Swallow of Death.* Boston: Marlborough House, 1972.

"Colonel Denison and the Eighth Regiment, I.N.G." *Lincoln University Herald* 20, no. 5 (June 1916). Lincoln University, Pa.

The Congressional Medal of Honor: The Names, the Deeds. Forest Ranch, Calif.: Sharp and Dunnigan, 1984.

Dupuy, R. Ernest, and Trevor N. Dupuy. *Military Heritage of America.* New York: McGraw-Hill, 1956. Rev. ed., Fairfax, Va.: Hero Books, 1984.

Farwell, Byron. *Over There.* New York: W. W. Norton, 1999.

Fuller, J. F. C. *Decisive Battles of the U.S.A.* New York: Thomas Yoseloff, 1942.

Fussell, Paul. *The Great War and Modern Memory.* New York: Oxford University Press, 1975.

General Cullum's Biographical Register of the Officers and Graduates of the United States Military Academy. Vols. 5–9. West Point, N.Y.: Association of Graduates, U.S. Military Academy, 1900–1940.

"General Franklin A. Denison." *Lincoln University Herald* 27, no. 4 (November–December 1922). Lincoln University, Pa.

Geraghty, Tony. *March or Die: A New History of the French Foreign Legion.* New York: Facts on File Publications, 1987.

Gilbert, Martin. *Atlas of the First World War.* London: Weidenfeld and Nicholson, 1970; published in the United States by Dorset Press, 1984.

———. *The First World War, A Complete History.* New York: Henry Holt, 1994.

Greene, Robert Ewell. *Black Defenders of America, 1775–1973.* Chicago: Johnson, 1974.

Haythornthwaite, Philip J. *A Photohistory of World War One.* London: Arms and Armour Press, 1993.

———. *The World War One Source Book.* London: Cassell, 1992.

Heitman, Francis. *Historical Register and Dictionary of the United States Army, from Its Organization September 29, 1789 to March 2, 1903.* Vol. 2. Urbana: University of Illinois Press, 1965.

Heywood, Chester D. *Negro Combat Troops in the World War: The Story of the 371st Infantry.* New York: Commonwealth Press, 1928. Reprint. New York: Negro Universities Press, 1969.

Jamieson, J. A., et al. *Complete History of the Colored Soldiers.* New York: Bennett and Churchill, 1919.

Laffin, John. *A Western Front Companion, 1914–1918.* Stroud, Gloucestershire, England: Alan Sutton, 1994.

———. *Panorama of the Western Front.* Stroud, Gloucestershire, England: Alan Sutton, 1994.

Lanning, Michael Lee. *The African-American Soldier.* Secaucus, N.J.: Carol Publishing (Birch Lane Press), 1997.

Little, Arthur W. *From Harlem to the Rhine: The Story of New York's Colored Volunteers.* New York: Covici, Freide. Reprint. New York: Haskell House, 1974.

MacGregor, Morris J., and Bernard C. Nalty. *Blacks in the United States Armed Forces, Basic Documents.* Vol. 4: *Segregation Entrenched.* Wilmington, Del.: Scholarly Resources, 1977.

MacIntyre, William. *Colored Soldiers.* Macon, Ga.: Burke, 1923.

Marshall, Napoleon B. *The Providential Armistice.* Washington, D.C.: Liberty League, 1930.

Mason, Monroe, and Arthur Furr. *The American Negro with the Red Hand of France.* Boston: Cornhill, 1921.

Miles, Perry Lester. *Fallen Leaves.* Berkeley: Wuarth, 1961.

Miller, Kelly. *The World War for Human Rights.* Privately published. Washington, D.C.: Howard University. Copyright 1919, A. Jenkins and O. Keller.

Ministère de la Guerre. *Les Armées Françaises dans la Grande Guerre.* Tome 10, vols. 1 and 2. Paris: Imprimerie Nationale, 1923.

Mirouze, Laurent. *World War I Infantry in Colour Photographs.* London: Windrow and Greene, 1990, 1995.

Moebs, Thomas Truxton. *Black Soldiers—Black Sailors—Black Ink: Research Guide on African-Americans in U.S. Military History, 1525–1900.* Chesapeake Bay and London: Moebs, 1994.

Moss, James A. *Company Training in the Attack, and the Defense, Including the Field Orders of Enlisted Men.* Menasha, Wisc.: George Banta, 1917.

————. *Origin and Significance of Military Customs.* Menasha, Wisc.: George Banta, 1917.

Muller, William G. *The Twenty-fourth Infantry, Past and Present.* Privately published. Reprint. Fort Collins, Colo.: Old Army Press, 1972.

"Not One of the Famous 369th Was Taken Alive." *Literary Digest,* 15 March 1919, 60:94–96.

Palmer, Frederick. *Newton D. Baker, America at War.* New York: Dodd, Mead, 1931.

Paschall, Rod. *The Defeat of Imperial Germany, 1917–1918.* Chapel Hill, N.C.: Algonquin Books, 1989.

Pershing, John J. *My Experiences in the World War.* 2 vols. New York: Harper and Row, 1931. Reprint. Blue Ridge Summit, Pa.: TAB Books, 1989.

Pitt, Barrie. *1918, the Last Act.* New York: W. W. Norton, 1962.

Pullman Porter's Review: Heroes of 1918. Chicago: Review Publishers, 1918. Note: the various articles in this publication are referred to in the Notes by the names of the authors as no page numbers are given.

Saunders, Ernest. *Blacks in the Connecticut National Guard: A Pictorial and Chronological History, 1870 to 1919.* New Haven, Conn.: Afro-American Historical Society, 1977.

Schmiedeler, John. "George Robb, a Modest Hero, Is Dead at 84." *Salina (Kans.) Journal,* 15 May 1972. Furnished by Salina Public Library.

Scipio, L. Albert II. *Last of the Black Regulars: A History of the 24th Infantry Regiment, 1869–1951.* Silver Spring, Md.: Roman Publications, 1983.

————. *With the Red Hand Division.* Silver Spring, Md.: Roman Publications, 1985.

Scott, Emmett J. *The American Negro in the World War.* Chicago: Homewood, 1919. Reprinted as *Scott's Official History of the American Negro in the World War.* New York: Arno Press and the *New York Times,* 1969.

Scrugham, James G., ed. *Nevada: A Narrative of the Conquest of a Frontier Land.* Vol. 2. Chicago and New York: American Historical Society, 1935.

Small Arms of the World. 10th ed. Rev. by Joseph E. Smith. Harrisburg, Pa.: Stackpole, 1973.

Smith, Gene. *Until the Last Trumpet Sounds: The Life of General of the Armies John J. Pershing.* New York: John Wiley and Sons, 1998.

Stallings, Laurence. *The Doughboys: The Story of the AEF, 1917–1918.* New York: Harper and Row, 1963.

Sweeney, W. Allison. *History of the American Negro in the Great World War.* New York: Johnson Reprint Corporation, 1970.

Taylor, A. J. P. *History of World War I.* London: Octopus Books, 1974.

Thomas, Shipley. *The History of the A.E.F.* New York: Doran, 1920.

Toland, John. *No Man's Land.* New York: Ballantine Books, 1980.

"Le 38e Corps d'Armée dans la Batalle de Champagne et d'Argonne Septembre–Novembre 1918." Text of a speech made in August 1990 at Bouconville, France, to the veterans of the County of Monthois (Ardennes), France; author unknown.

Tucker, Spencer C., ed. *Encyclopedia of the Korean War: A Political, Social, and Military History.* New York: Checkmark Books, Facts on File, 2002.

Weigley, Russell F. *History of the United States Army.* New York: Macmillan, 1967.

Williams, Charles H. *Negro Soldiers in World War I: The Human Side.* Boston, 1923. Reprint. New York: AMS Press, 1970.

Wilson, Joseph T. *The Black Phalanx.* Hartford, Conn.: American Publishing Company, 1890. Reprint. New York: Arno Press and the *New York Times,* 1968.

Yockelson, Mitchell. "The United States Armed Forces and the Mexican Punitive Expedition." Parts 1 and 2. Prologue 29, nos. 3 and 4 (1997). Accessed at http://www.nara.gov/publications/prologue/mpep1.html, 13 May 2002.

Correspondence

Brambila, Mrs. Mildred, widow of Robert M. Brambila, son of Lieutenant Colonel Brambila. Materials, information, and photograph of Lieutenant Colonel Brambila. Macon, Ga., 2003.

Carlisle, David. Information on his uncle, PFC John Robert Kay, who served in a white engineer regiment during World War I. Los Angeles, Calif., dated 17 October 1994.

Hillman, Col. Rolfe L. Jr., USA (ret.). "Remarks for Memorial Day Breakfast." Alan F. Waite Post no. 299, American Legion, Yonkers, N.Y., 31 May 1987. Material furnished by Rolfe L. Hillman III, Arlington, Va., 1 March 1999.

Kern, Col. William H., USAR, great-nephew of Col. Joseph Benjamin Pate. Correspondence providing photographs and letters of Colonel Pate, Fayetteville, N.C., 25 March 1999.

Welty, Harry Robb, grandson of George S. Robb. Correspondence and website: http://www.snowbizz.com/HWRepublican/george_robb/georgerobb.htm, accessed 20 October 2003.

Government Publications

American Battle Monuments Commission. *American Armies and Battlefields in Europe.* Washington, D.C.: U.S. Government Printing Office, 1938.

————. *93d Division, Summary of Operations in the World War.* Washington, D.C.: U.S. Government Printing Office, 1944.

Annual Reports of the Adjutant General, Washington, D.C., National Guard, 1863–1917.

Annual Reports of the State Adjutant General, Connecticut National Guard, 1879–1917.

Annual Reports of the State Adjutant General, Maryland National Guard, 1879–1917.

Annual Reports of the State Adjutant General, Massachusetts National Guard, 1863–1917.

Annual Reports of the State Adjutant General, Ohio National Guard, 1874–1917.

Annual Reports of the State Adjutant General, Tennessee National Guard, 1886–1917.

The Army Almanac: A Book of Facts Concerning the Army of the United States. Washington, D.C.: U.S. Government Printing Office, 1950.

Biennial Report of the Adjutant General of the State of Tennessee, 1 January 1917 to 1 January 1919.

City of Chicago. Department of Planning and Development. *The Black Metropolis— Bronzeville District.* Christopher R. Hill, Commissioner, "Victory Monument," 28 August 1997.

Connecticut Adjutant General's Office. *General Orders No. 34.* Hartford, 16 July 1917.

Duncan, Col. Otis B., 8th Infantry Regiment, Illinois National Guard, Commanding the Regiment, 29 September 1924. "5th Indorsement." Furnished by Maj. James B. McCabe, staff historian, Illinois National Guard. [Note: This document appears to be in response to a memo from the Adjutant General, Illinois National Guard, concerning a request for the shoulder patch for the 93d Division to be adopted for the 8th Illinois Infantry Regiment.]

"Freddie Stowers, Corporal, United States Army." Arlington National Cemetery website: http://www.arlingtoncemetery.com/fstowers.htm, accessed 11 October 2003.

History of the 178th Infantry Regiment, Illinois National Guard. Illinois National Guard website: http://www.il.ngb.army.mil/b-1-178thhistory.htm, accessed 12 April 2003.

House of Representatives. *Monument in France to Colored American Infantry Regiments Attached to the French Army.* Report no. 1419, 68th Congress, 2d session, 9 February

1925. Washington, D.C.: U.S. Government Printing Office, 1925.

Massachusetts Volunteer Militia, Roll of Members, Officers and Enlisted Men of Company L, 6th Massachusetts Infantry Regiment, 30 November 1915. Furnished and certified by Massachusetts National Guard, Military Archives and Museum, Worcester, Mass.

Ninety-third Division G3 Reports for the 369th, 370th, 371st, and 372d Infantry Regiments. National Archives, Record Group 120, boxes 3343–44, 2W1/27/4/D.

Ninety-third Division Historical Files, 369th, 370th, and 371st Infantry Regiments. National Archives, Record Group 120, boxes 1–2, 2W1/12/2/C. [Note: The records of the 372d Infantry Regiment in this section have been reported as missing from the files of the National Archives.]

Ohio National Guardsman. "Battalion Organized in 1881" [History of the 2d Battalion, 372d Infantry], January 1937. Columbus, Ohio.

Order of Battle of the United States Land Forces in the World War, American Expeditionary Forces: Division. Vol. 2. Washington, D.C.: U.S. Army, Center of Military History, 1988.

Profile of Colonel Herschel Tupes, Cadet No. 3702, West Point Class of 1896. U.S. Military Academy Annual Report, 10 June 1939.

Tupes, Col. Herschel, I.G.D., War Department. Letter to Col. Allen J. Greer, General Staff, War Department, Washington, D.C., 26 March 1919. "Employment of negros in our military establishment," 1–3. From the files of the U.S. Army Military History Institute, Carlisle Barracks, Carlisle, Pa.

United States Army War College. *Colored Soldiers in the U.S. Army.* Washington, D.C.: U.S. Government Printing Office, 1942.

United States Department of the Army. *Lineage and Honors, 178th Infantry (Eighth Illinois).* 6 December 1982. Furnished by Maj. James B. McCabe, staff historian, Illinois National Guard, 1301 North MacArthur Blvd., Springfield, Il. 62702.

United States Department of the Army. Adjutant General's Office. *American Decorations: A List of Awards of the Congressional Medal of Honor, the Distinguished Service Cross and the Distinguished Service Medal, 1862–1926.* Washington, D.C.: U.S. Government Printing Office, 1927.

United States Department of the Army. Headquarters. General Orders No. 15. Award of the Medal of Honor, Corporal Freddie Stowers, 1872491, 371st Infantry Regiment. Washington, D.C., 31 May 1991.

United States Department of the Army. Historical Branch. *Brief Histories of Divisions, U.S. Army, 1917–1918.* War Plans Division, General Staff, June 1921.

———. *United States Army in the World War, Military Operations of the American Expeditionary Forces, 1917–1919.* Vols. 2 and 5. Washington, D.C.: U.S. Government Printing Office, 1948.

United States Department of War. *Annual Report, 1918.* Washington, D.C.: U.S. Government Printing Office, 1919.

———. *Annual Report, 1919.* Washington, D.C.: U.S. Government Printing Office, 1920.

Index

About the Author

Frank E. Roberts retired from the U.S. Army Corps of Engineers in 1986 as a lieutenant colonel. He had served in the enlisted ranks for seven years and then as a commissioned officer for twenty-five years on both active and reserve status. His civilian career includes management and engineering positions in industry, most recently as president and chief executive officer of an electronics instrument manufacturing firm in Austin and partner in a professional recruitment consulting firm in Rockwall, Texas. Presently he is teaching industrial technology at a middle school in Mesquite, Texas.

Roberts earned a bachelor of business administration degree from the University of Texas at Austin in 1971 and a bachelor of science degree from the University of North Texas at Denton in 1986. He is the author of several articles published in military journals. This is his first book.

The Naval Institute Press is the book-publishing arm of the U.S. Naval Institute, a private, nonprofit, membership society for sea service professionals and others who share an interest in naval and maritime affairs. Established in 1873 at the U.S. Naval Academy in Annapolis, Maryland, where its offices remain today, the Naval Institute has members worldwide.

Members of the Naval Institute support the education programs of the society and receive the influential monthly magazine Proceedings and discounts on fine nautical prints and on ship and aircraft photos. They also have access to the transcripts of the Institute's Oral History Program and get discounted admission to any of the Institute-sponsored seminars offered around the country.

The Naval Institute also publishes *Naval History* magazine. This colorful bimonthly is filled with entertaining and thought-provoking articles, first-person reminiscences, and dramatic art and photography. Members receive a discount on *Naval History* subscriptions.

The Naval Institute's book-publishing program, begun in 1898 with basic guides to naval practices, has broadened its scope to include books of more general interest. Now the Naval Institute Press publishes about one hundred titles each year, ranging from how-to books on boating and navigation to battle histories, biographies, ship and aircraft guides, and novels. Institute members receive significant discounts on the Press's more than eight hundred books in print.

Full-time students are eligible for special half-price membership rates. Life memberships are also available.

For a free catalog describing Naval Institute Press books currently available, and for further information about subscribing to *Naval History* magazine or about joining the U.S. Naval Institute, please write to:

Membership Department
U.S. Naval Institute
291 Wood Road
Annapolis, MD 21402-5034
Telephone: (800) 233-8764
Fax: (410) 269-7940
Web address: www.navalinstitute.org